THE EQ LEADER

THE EQ LEADER

INSTILLING PASSION, CREATING SHARED GOALS, AND BUILDING MEANINGFUL ORGANIZATIONS THROUGH EMOTIONAL INTELLIGENCE

STEVEN J. STEIN

WILEY

Cover image: © chemc/iStockphoto
Cover design: Wiley

Published by John Wiley & Sons, Inc., Hoboken, New Jersey.
Published simultaneously in Canada.

For general information about our other products and services, please contact our Customer Care Department within the United States at (800) 762-2974, outside the United States at (317) 572-3993 or fax (317) 572-4002.

Wiley publishes in a variety of print and electronic formats and by print-on-demand. Some material included with standard print versions of this book may not be included in e-books or in print-on-demand. If this book refers to media such as a CD or DVD that is not included in the version you purchased, you may download this material at http://booksupport.wiley.com. For more information about Wiley products, visit www.wiley.com.

Library of Congress Cataloging-in-Publication Data:

Names: Stein, Steven (Steven J.), author.
Title: The EQ leader : instilling passion, creating shared goals, and building meaningful organizations through emotional intelligence / Steven J. Stein.
Description: Hoboken, New Jersey : John Wiley & Sons, Inc., [2017] | Includes bibliographical references and index.
Identifiers: LCCN 2017007229 (print) | LCCN 2017016246 (ebook) | ISBN 9781119349006 (cloth) | ISBN 9781119349013 (epdf) | ISBN 9781119349037 (epub)
Subjects: LCSH: Leadership. | Emotional intelligence.
Classification: LCC HD57.7 (ebook) | LCC HD57.7 .S7268 2017 (print) | DDC 658.4/092—dc23
LC record available at https://lccn.loc.gov/2017007229

Printed in the United States of America

SKY10084484_091224

To Micah and Gemma,
my grandchildren.
I hope we can advance the state of the art of leadership
to the benefit of your world.

Contents

Chapter 1

Leadership

What Do We Really Know about Leadership?

If the highest aim of a captain were to preserve his ship, he would keep it in port forever.

—THOMAS AQUINAS

What do we really know about leadership? There's been a lot of talk about leadership lately. Judging from the vast number of books, articles, blogs, TED Talks, and more, you would think we have a treasure trove of information about the subject. A quick search on Amazon.com returned 192,136 books dedicated to leadership. In addition, there are hundreds of theses, thousands of articles in journals as well as thousands more research papers on the web. They have been written by a variety of professionals that not only include psychologists but also management theorists, historians, politicians and political scientists, theologians, philosophers, journalists, and other social commentators. Their contributions include scientific analyses, scholarly biographies, and popular accounts of leaders' lives. Knowing how to most effectively lead others can be pretty confusing with that amount of knowledge swirling around. In fact, it's hard to imagine that anyone could think of themselves as an expert in leadership in today's world when there's so much information available.

The Leadership Explosion

How do you deal with so many books on a single subject? Well I have to admit there's no way I was going to go through that many publications. But as I started doing my research, I found that most books fell into one of three categories.

Leader's View

The first group of books are written (or cowritten) by successful leaders. These include biographies of Bill Gates,[1] Steve Jobs,[2] Rudi Giuliani,[3] Jack Welch,[4] Carly Fiorina,[5] Michael Dell,[6] Richard Branson,[7] and many others. These books can be very enlightening and educational, and the insights gained by the experiences of these successful people can guide others along certain pathways.

However, the downside I find is that the views presented tend to be idiosyncratic to those leaders. It's how the individual leader sees the world, which, unfortunately, doesn't always match events as they actually happened.

Having interviewed direct reports of some notable leaders, I can assure you that there are often discrepancies between a leader's reality and that of their direct reports. Anyone who has been involved in 360-degree evaluations of leaders, in which performance reports are taken from subordinates, peers, supervisors, and clients, will also know that the leader can see herself or himself somewhat differently than those around her or him. Therefore, although we can learn from each leader's perspective, these perspectives should not be misinterpreted as universal truths.

Observer's View

The next set of books I would classify as the *observer's view*. The observer is usually a consultant, a professor, a business writer, a business coach, or some variation of these. These people have had a lot of experience with one or more leaders (although they tend not to be leaders of organizations themselves). They bring a lot of insight out of their experiences working with leaders, theorizing about leaders, or studying leaders. Examples include books by John Maxwell,[8] David Cottrell,[9] Michael Useem,[10] Peter Northouse,[11] Simon Sinek,[12] and others.

The caution with some of these books is that they may come out of preconceived theories with minimal empirical evidence, limited range of leadership settings, use of platitudes, and selective use of examples. There are often useful lessons from these books, but the recommendations are not always practical or easy to apply.

Researcher's View

The third group of books I call the *researcher's view*. These books tend to come from people with perhaps a few preconceived notions of what makes a good leader, and they approach the subject by evaluating data that encompasses both successful and unsuccessful leadership. Basically, these books use evidence-based procedures in interesting and enlightening ways to evaluate what truly differentiates successful and unsuccessful leaders. Examples include Kouzes and Posner[13] and Jim Collins.[14]

Jim Collins, for example, in his book *Good to Great*[15] started his work by practically discounting the importance of leadership and focusing on the structures, rules, and processes of large iconic companies that had been around for many years. By contrasting successful and unsuccessful companies, matched within the same industry, he came to the conclusion, which was contradictory to his expectations, that leadership does make a difference, in fact, a rather large one. He has championed the *Level 5 Leadership* in which humility and "fire in the belly" play a dominant role. As he states it:

> The best CEOs in our research display tremendous ambition for their company combined with the stoic will to do whatever it takes, no matter how brutal (within the bounds of the company's core values), to make the company great. Yet at the same time they display a remarkable humility about themselves, ascribing much of their own success to luck, discipline and preparation rather than personal genius.[16]

In this book, I hope to borrow largely from the researcher's tradition. While I start out with the preconceived notion that emotional intelligence does make a difference in leadership, it has taken more than 20 years for me to reach the clarity of this position. When I started researching emotional intelligence and its importance in the workplace in the early 1990s, my focus was largely on individual performance and the enhancement of performance through emotional intelligence. I was interested in how emotional intelligence could help people better achieve their desired level of success—both at work and at home. Much of this work appears in the book I coauthored with Howard Book, *The EQ Edge: Emotional Intelligence and Your Success*.[17] Then I went on to explore how organizations, as a collective whole, could be emotionally intelligent.[18]

Over the years, the pull toward my study of leadership increased. It was an area I consciously avoided at first, maybe because of what I didn't want to find out about mistakes in my own leadership. But as more articles, books, blogs, and talks came out about emotional intelligence and leadership, I eventually felt I had to join the conversation. Part of the motivation was some of the misconceptions out there about the connection. There were spurious reports of overly high estimates—85 percent or so—of effective leadership due to emotional intelligence and very few of the claims were based on good evidence. At the same time, at Multi-Health Systems (MHS), where we have been testing people's emotional intelligence since the early 1990s, we've built up a database of approximately 2 million people. Many thousands of these were currently leaders, emergent leaders, or identified as high potential future leaders. Not only do we have lots of data, but it's global. We've tested the emotional intelligence of people from all parts of the world; as a result, we are compelled to share our findings on how emotional intelligence influences leadership.

So while I've been committed to the importance of emotional intelligence in human performance for many years, I didn't start with any preconceived notions of how emotional intelligence might impact leadership. In fact, early on in this endeavor, I had radio and TV interviews in which commentators told me why they believed emotional intelligence was a detriment to good leadership. I was told that being "nice" would get you eaten for breakfast in some companies. Of course, I'd have to explain that emotional intelligence was not about being nice. We'll get to the definition in Chapter 3.

Leadership: What's the Status?

What does it take to be a successful leader in today's organizations? Everyone has his or her own image of who a great leader is or what a leader should be. To complicate matters even further, experts have developed hundreds of theories about leadership. We probably know more about leadership today than we have at any other time in our history. Yet, we continue to read about the poor state of leadership in organizations around the world.

In a recent report, the Deloitte Global Human Capital Survey (2014)[19] questioned more than 2,532 leaders in 94 countries and found that the biggest workforce "readiness gap" was leadership. Over 38 percent of respondents rated this issue as "urgent" for their organizations (86 percent rated it as either important or urgent)—more than 50 percent higher than the next identified gap—retention and engagement. Interesting, these two issues are quite closely tied together.

The biggest leadership needs reported include developing new leaders faster, globalizing leadership programs, and building deeper bench strength for succession planning. As you will see in the following case study, finding great leaders is not always solved by promoting from within.

Promoting Leaders from Within

Demetri never felt so anxious before. It was worse than his first day at work at the exclusive menswear store. He had been the top salesperson for four years in a row and had fought hard to be promoted to sales manager. He had all the best customers on his roster. Out of the entire sales force, he was the best at establishing profitable relationships. Now that he was rewarded with a promotion and pay raise he felt the pressure to perform at a much higher level than before.

Worry set in. First, he was unsure about how his coworkers would react to him in his new role. He knew at least one of them, Carlos, also applied for the manager position. Would Carlos be upset, perhaps even jealous? Then he worried about the effect his promotion would have on the team. They were a tight team, not just celebrating each other's successes, but socializing together. How would they now respond to him? How should he treat them? Could he keep the relationships the same? Treat them all as his buddies still? Never did Demetri think a promotion, something he worked so hard for, would create so many mixed emotions. Unfortunately, there was no preparation provided for him or the team he was now supposed to lead.

This scenario has been repeated so many times across many industries. People with good technical or sales skills are placed into management positions. The thinking seems to be—if they can sell, do great accounting, make the most widgets, design the best buildings, build the best software, well, then they can probably lead and help others do just as well as they did on the front line.

Unfortunately, leadership doesn't work quite that way. The skills and competencies that help you sell things, build things, analyze things, fix things, and so on, have little to do with being a good leader. Many people I've spoken with shake their heads when they hear about companies such as GE, Google, Microsoft, FedEx, and American Express that spend so much money on leadership training. They're even more surprised when I talk about it in terms of succession planning, but, the fact is, without a willingness to invest in selecting and training leaders, companies are likely to suffer the adverse effects of poor leadership.

When I speak with fellow CEOs they usually can recount a situation where they promoted someone on the basis of technical or industry skills and knowledge. While these skills are important for frontline job performance, leadership, whether supervisory or upper management, requires a different or additional skill set. What are these skills precisely? How do we develop them? These questions will be the theme of this book. I'll be presenting a combination of real stories, modified examples, research studies, personal anecdotes, new data that we've compiled at MHS and some very public examples to illustrate these points. Our emotional intelligence testing over the past 20 years includes over 2 million working people worldwide, and we'll use these sources to inform our leadership discussion.

Yesterday's Leaders

Whenever I give leadership presentations, I generally ask audiences to name an iconic business leader from 100 years ago. Anywhere in the world, whether I'm in Beijing, Buenos Aires, Helsinki, St. Lucia, Sydney, Bangkok, Dubai, Vancouver, or New York City, the name Henry Ford always comes up. While there are a number of reasons that Ford stands out, not the least of which is his innovations in the production of the automobile, he is mostly associated with a particular quote. It seems everyone everywhere remembers at least part of what he said, *"to hell with the customer, who can have any color (car they want) as long as it's black."*

What is it about this quote, or attitude that stands out? Well most strong leaders have at least one *signature* characteristic they carry with them, perhaps as a legacy. For Henry Ford, it was most likely *steadfastness*. Leaders at that time were seen as captains of the ship. When the CEO made a decision, it was up to everyone in the organization to defend that decision. Not sticking with it was almost akin to treason. And the captain would go down with the ship, protecting his point of view.

This kind of leader is ego driven. The decisions this person makes are more about himself than about what is best for the company. This leader fears *looking* bad as much as he fears *doing* bad. In those days, changing your mind (or altering the course of the ship) was perceived as an unbearable weakness. It was the kiss of death upon which the leader would lose respect and no longer be able to face his workers. In parts of Asia, the concept of "saving face" is still a big issue.

While this type of leadership may appear strong to some, it usually comes with negative consequences. According to Lee Iacocca, who wrote the seminal article on Henry Ford for *Time* magazine, "The problem was that for too long they [Ford] worked on only one model. Although people told him to diversify, Henry Ford developed tunnel vision. He basically started saying 'to hell with the customer,' who can have any color as long as it's black. He didn't bring out a new design until the Model A in '27, and by then GM was gaining."[20]

Tunnel vision at that time gave Ford's biggest competitor, General Motors, the break it needed to take significant market share. It was Ford's son who stepped in and finally insisted on bringing out new models (such as the Model A) and new colors that were needed for the continued survival of the company.

Ego-driven leaders tend to be driven by the past in that they look to past experiences for confirmation of their decisions, which facilitates steadfastness. What worked before should continue to work today and tomorrow. This supports their need for consistency—steadfastness. However, this can come at the cost of missing out on new opportunities, whether its technologies, changing economies, new strategies, or changes in customer focus.

Today's Leaders

Fast forward to iconic leaders of the late twentieth century. Who stands out in your mind? There are probably a number of names that you can generate, but one that always makes that list is Bill Gates. It was the development of software operating systems that enabled the personal computer to take off and basically change the world as we knew it. Of course, it was Bill Gates and his company Microsoft that made it all happen. Gates has long been seen as enthusiastic about new technologies and the potential they have to change our lives. But not too many people remember that in the early days of the Internet, Gates was decidedly pessimistic and slow off the mark.

I was one of about 2,000 people that attended what was seen at the time as a pivotal talk he gave in a large convention center ballroom back in the early 1990s. Gates spoke about how Microsoft had invested several million dollars exploring the potential of the Internet. His conclusion was that the best commercial use of the World Wide Web would be for video-on-demand, which was already available via cable and satellite. Unfortunately, he estimated that it would take another 20 years to make it practical and commercially viable. To quote Gates, "Bandwidth is a big issue. Unfortunately, it's not like microprocessors where every year you're going to see exponential improvements. *But to make this happen will take something like 20 years* [italics added]. And the main reason is that to get these high-speed connections to be pervasive, particularly getting them into homes around the world, will take a long time."[21]

Microsoft chose to take a pass on the Internet.

Or did they?

It was only a short time after that when a fresh college graduate from the University of Illinois named Marc Andreessen teamed up with an industry veteran named Jim Clark. They created a small start-up called Netscape in Clark's kitchen. Their mission was to simplify and speed up access to the Internet. As soon as their little company went public, it changed the landscape of initial public offerings. It also changed the world. In one blow, Microsoft lagged behind in new, cutting-edge technology.

And Microsoft, in the public's mind, meant Bill Gates, who in numerous forums had staked out a steadfast position that now looked untenable. He was captain at Microsoft, and old-style captains of industry have traditionally gone down with their sinking vessels. At best, they'd find ways to shore up and continue to defend their positions because the worst thing a leader could do would be to publicly change his or her tune. Being inconsistent was worse than being wrong; it would be considered a weakness and waffling under pressure.

So how did Gates handle that situation? After all, at the time he already was one of the richest humans on the planet. Would he stick with his position and take a pass on the Internet? Or would he risk publicly changing his mind? Would he base his decision on what others would think of him? Was he concerned about his ego? Come on, do you really think Bill Gates would be concerned about what other people thought of him in a situation like this?

Gates turned a multibillion-dollar organization around immediately and went flat out after the Internet. Microsoft Explorer was developed and eventually became the world's most widely used web browser. As documented in *Time* magazine, "The World Wide Web emerged in 1994, making browsers necessary, and Netscape was founded that same year. Sun Microsystems developed Java, the Internet programming language. Gates hung back. It wasn't until 1996 that Microsoft finally, according to Gates himself, 'embraced the Internet wholeheartedly.' "[22]

Why did he behave that way? Because Gates, like many of today's successful leaders, was and remains more concerned with success than with what people might think of him. He is driven by the future and opportunities, not by the past or his ego. Learning from the past is valuable, but preserving it can waste energy. Worrying about looking good, being consistent, or keeping the status quo were yesterday's virtues, but today's kiss of death. Successful leaders put their egos behind their missions, move forward with the times, and aren't afraid to alter their positions as necessary.

Tomorrow's Leaders

Having tested so many leaders, both young and old, I have been able to see the trends and where leadership seems to be headed. There is a new signature characteristic that I believe will be essential for tomorrow's leaders. I see it getting more and more important as we look at today's leadership successes and failures. However, I'm not ready to divulge this characteristic yet. Read on and you will discover it.

Good Leader, Bad Leader

Often when doing presentations on leadership I assign the audience an exercise. With participants working in small groups, each team is assigned one of two tasks. Each group is asked to write on a poster either the leadership characteristics *most* valued by their organization or the leadership characteristics *least* valued by their organization. On one of the posters, I found this list of descriptors:

Explosive

High ego

Always being right

Results driven

Ability to minimize ethical issues

Rigidity

No emotional control

Having serious "attitude"

I stopped to chat with the gentleman leading the group with these items on the board. When I started to ask how these behaviors were discouraged in his organization, he quickly corrected me and explained that these were the valued characteristics at the organization he and several others in the group had worked in. He then explained to me he had worked at Enron and that these were the characteristics valued by the senior team during the two years before it imploded.

We went through the list to see how these factors could be applied to leading an organization. Being explosive was a way of getting other people's attention. It also scared potential detractors and showed them you were serious. Most people would rather not confront someone in that state. Having a high ego is another tactic that implies you are right. After all, if you are so sure of yourself, well, why would anyone argue with that?

Always being right is a show of strength. If you are known around the organization as always being on the right side of an issue, then more people are likely to come onboard with you next time around. It reduces the amount of opposition you're likely to face and will help you win arguments more often than not. Being results driven is not an uncommon corporate position. The problem comes when nothing else matters. Treating people badly, taking shortcuts in processes, making promises you can't keep to customers, all these things are secondary to driving results.

The ability to minimize ethical issues is my favorite, especially when I'm presenting to lawyers and compliance officers. It sometimes gets referred to as ethical overrides. That is, you reward people for finding ways around codes of ethics, sometimes referred to as *loopholes*. So if I can justify why I needed corporate money for that private jet rental, luxury hotel, great meals, side trip with my family, and so on, everything is okay. I guess at Enron this only worked for a period of time, or until they got caught.

Being rigid is another way of telling people "it's my way or the highway," something that seems to go over well in Texas, which conveniently is the home of Enron. Similarly, not having, or not displaying, emotional control is a fairly effective way to signal to others that one is not to be crossed/questioned. So is having strong attitude, which was described to me as being bold and assertive, in such a way that people knew not to question the leader's authority. This was described to me as a Texas attitude, which goes along with "don't mess with me."

In looking at these traits it seems like they can be boiled down to being steadfast (high ego, always being right, results driven, rigidity, serious attitude) and being above questioning/criticism (no emotional control, ability to minimize serious issues, explosive).

It's hard to believe (at least for me) that companies can still operate this way in this day and age. Nevertheless, I've come across variations of this in my travels. Needless to say, some of these procedures can get you short-term results, but, as we've seen in this example, they don't seem to be viable long-term strategies. When I first started this work, it would often take a lot of convincing for some leaders to buy into the idea that managing emotions, for example, not using random anger to motivate, could be good for business. In the following chapters, we'll explore the case for emotionally intelligent leadership and what you can do to get there.

EQ Leader: Things to Think About

1. What were some of the best books you've read on leadership?
2. What did you like about them?
3. Are you familiar with a situation in which someone got promoted to a leadership position and was not well prepared for it?
4. Can you think of a "signature characteristic" that defines your current or a previous boss?

(continued)

(*continued*)

5. What would be the "ideal" signature strength of a leader you'd like to work for?
6. How would you want to be different from bosses you've had to work for?
7. What would be your signature characteristic as a leader?
8. Think about your own adaptability and willingness to change direction on important issues.
9. What do you think the signature strength of tomorrow's leaders will be?

EQ Leader: Actions You Can Take

1. Ask some of the people you work with for one-word descriptions of your boss.
2. Ask these same people what they would do differently if they were the leader.
3. Ask your coworkers about what they like best about their favorite leaders.
4. If you are a leader, ask some trusted subordinates how they would describe your leadership style.
5. Ask your subordinates what gets them most excited about their job. Then think about what role you play, as a leader, in cultivating their excitement.

Chapter 2

What Have We Learned about Leadership?

Effective leadership is not about making speeches or being liked; leadership is defined by results, not attributes.

—PETER DRUCKER

The scientific study of leadership is about 100 years old. There are hundreds of studies that have looked at such things as personality, leadership style, cognitive intelligence (IQ), as well as leadership potential and performance. There have been a number of major reviews of the psychological and business/managerial literature summarizing much of what we know about leadership. One such review by Robert Kaiser and his colleagues nicely summarizes much about what we know from the academic literature.[1] For example, they point out the overwhelming evidence that leadership styles are associated with certain effects—"considerate leaders enhance the job satisfaction of subordinates, structured leaders have higher performing teams, and transformational leaders inspire greater commitment."

In addition, certain styles of leadership have been found to be better in order to get specific results. For example, the best way to lead when you have a high degree of control over a situation is with a task-oriented approach. On the other hand, when you don't have as much control over the situation a people-oriented approach can be better. In other words, in situations with low control, you would need to spend more time dealing with the people and their needs before getting them focused on the task you want done.

Defining Leadership

There are many different definitions of leadership that have been documented in the scientific literature as well as in popular writings. And many of them are very good. However, for the purpose of this book, I will define leadership as:

> Behaviors used in any situation where you influence the thoughts, behaviors, or feelings of one or more people.

I see leadership not only based on skills, abilities, and actions, but as situational as well. Today, I am the leader and CEO of a company that employs about 160 people. This role carries a lot of responsibilities, weight, and prestige. However, once I get home, my responsibilities differ greatly. For example, my wife will order me to take out the garbage. She'll then give me several other tasks to do that include going through the mail, washing the dishes, and so on. Unlike being the queen or king, most leaders today are not 24/7 leaders. I participate in a number of groups for CEOs, and the size of their organizations can vary from 5 people to 500. I know very few, if any, leaders today who rule their kingdoms night and day.

The next important aspect for me is the concept of *influence*. For most of today's leaders, it's all about influence. We no longer live in a command and control society, whether in the workplace or at home. You can give orders, but that doesn't mean you will get the obedience of yesterday. Also, many people work in cross-functional teams where there is no designated leader per se. In order to be successful in leading others where you have no or limited authority over them you will have to be able to influence their behavior.

Today's leaders don't just guide behavior. If you truly want to be successful, you have to change minds and hearts. As the saying goes, "You can lead a horse to water, but you can't make him drink." People today want to be inspired into action. You have to make them want to do what needs to be done.

Finally, how many followers does it take for a leader to be a leader? This almost sounds like the old light bulb joke. Well, in this definition you're a leader even if you only have one follower. You can be a leader if you can convince your partner to do their chores, get your child to do her homework, convince a friend to see the movie you want to see, or even convince your manager to let you take charge of the project. Many of the skills used to influence one person can, when used appropriately, be used to influence dozens, or even hundreds of people. One politician I know, started her career at a local level, convincing enough people, one at a time, to support the installation of a crosswalk at a busy intersection. From there, she went on to win a local election. After that she was elected at a regional (provincial) level. She eventually went on to be a cabinet minister with a major government portfolio, overseeing hundreds of millions of dollars. She was able to leverage her interpersonal skills from one-on-one to one-to-many.

Measuring Leadership

One of the breakthroughs in our understanding of leadership in an academic sense came in a review paper by psychologist Robert Lord and his colleagues at the University of Akron back in 1986.[2] While looking at the (then) controversial area in organizational psychology around the usefulness of personality traits in leadership, he found an important distinction. Most organizational psychologists at the time had written off the importance of personality in leadership. This was based on a few poorly designed studies that focused on the importance of IQ in leadership by mainly looking at leader performance, and mostly in academic settings. Of course, you don't need to be an organizational psychologist to realize that personality plays a big part in leadership—if not in leadership performance, at least in leadership selection. For example, it would be hard to imagine a political election in which the personality of the candidates doesn't come into play.

Although it may seem intuitive, this was a big realization. How we select leaders is completely different from how we evaluate their performance. So Kaiser and his group reformulated our understanding of leadership using this distinction and classified studies into two groups: one group of studies that focused on how a leader is seen by others and another group that focused on the effectiveness of the groups that were being led. Basically, this differentiated the groups into leaders who were "looking good" versus those who were "doing good." Just think about how we select leaders, whether it's CEOs or politicians.

We generally go by how they present themselves. Another way to look at it is that the first group of studies focused on the individual leader and the second group looked at how the team, group, or organization was functioning.

Political Leaders

It's interesting how this plays out in the world of politics. Stephen Harper was a Canadian prime minister known for being very effective at getting things done. He was elected prime minister for two terms. He had a strong record of accomplishments but was seen as an introvert. He had come to lead the party through his work in the backroom, as opposed to the more traditional glad-handing politicians are known for. For his first two terms as prime minister, he had run against candidates who were seen as even less personable or likable than he.

He ran again, attempting a third term, against a young, charismatic drama teacher named Justin Trudeau, son of the late former Prime Minister Pierre Trudeau. At a dinner meeting during the election, I sat at a table with one of his senior cabinet ministers. We got into a discussion about the decreased likability of Harper and the effect his lack of personal appeal (compared to his rival) may have on the upcoming election. She tried to assure me that this wasn't a personality contest. Voters would decide on the candidate's record and would not be swayed by personality. Besides, she told me, Trudeau had no record of accomplishments. As you may know, Harper lost the election by a huge margin to the former drama teacher, who, as she said, had very little record to speak of. Harper's loss may seem like an anomaly, but, as I will illustrate, choosing leaders based on personality, not achievement, is fairly common.

Understanding the Ideal Political Candidate

Of course, the presidential race between Hillary Clinton and Donald Trump presented an ideal laboratory and a historical opportunity for those of us interested in leadership and how leaders are chosen. At MHS, we decided to take advantage of this opportunity, and we conducted two surveys at the beginning of September 2016, before the election. In order to get a better handle of what the emotional intelligence of an ideal leader (in this case, president) would look like, we surveyed 1,000 American voters. The sample

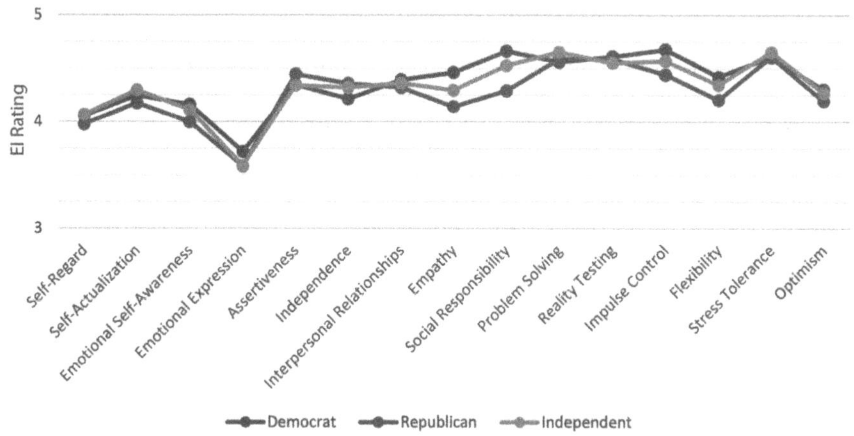

Figure 2.1 Ideal President EQ Profile by Party Affiliation (© MHS, 2016)

selected was one-third Democrats, one-third Republicans, and one-third Independents. Their ideal president, by political affiliation, can be seen in Figure 2.1.[3]

As seen in Figure 2.1, the results were fairly similar across the political divide, which is interesting as this was one of the most divisive elections in recent history. There were some differences: whereas self-declared Democrats prefer, in order of preference, a president who is highest in Impulse Control, Social Responsibility, and Reality Testing. Republicans prefer a president who is strongest in Stress Tolerance, Problem Solving, and Reality Testing. Independents want to see a president highest in Stress Tolerance, Problem Solving, and Impulse Control (see Table 2.1).

All three groups seem to be in agreement that the least important of the emotional skills for a president are Emotional Expression, Self-Regard, and Emotional Self-Awareness.

What are the biggest differences between Republicans and Democrats? The biggest difference was in Social Responsibility, with Democrats rating that higher than Republicans. The Independents were close to the Democrats on this. So to win over Independents, the candidates had to show at some level they care about their communities and the world around them. Just caring about your own and nobody else may not win the hearts and minds of Independents.

Table 2.1
Top Three Qualities of an Ideal President by Party Affiliation

	Party Affiliation	
Top-Rated Qualities	**Democrats**	**Republicans**
First	Impulse Control	Stress Tolerance
Second	Social Responsibility	Problem Solving
Third	Reality Testing	Reality Testing

Perhaps Hillary Clinton was seen as too self-motivated to win over Independents. Or perhaps Donald Trump's message of bringing back jobs and repealing Obamacare (due to its escalating costs to subscribers) was demonstrative of Social Responsibility.

The next biggest difference was in Empathy, with Democrats rating Empathy as a more important trait in a president compared to how Republicans rated it. Independents fell right between the two. Democrats want a president who can read the thoughts and feelings of others. This seems less important to Republicans. This is a skill that Bill Clinton is widely regarded as excelling in. A turning point here may have been Hillary Clinton's declaring Trump supporters as "deplorable" and "irredeemable." Many Independents may have found it unacceptable to write off nearly 50 percent of the electorate.

Finally, the groups differed on Impulse Control. Democrats wanted a president higher in Impulse Control; that is, more able to manage what they say and their behavior. They prefer a president who is more thoughtful and doesn't shoot from the hip. Independents fall somewhere between the two, but slightly closer to Democrats. This factor is less important for Republicans, which may explain why many Republicans are not bothered by Trump's penchant for impulsive use of Twitter.

Comparing Trump and Clinton to the Ideal

We then surveyed a new group of about 1,000 voters, once again almost equally divided among party affiliation. They were sampled with one of two alternate surveys, with 500 voters completing each survey. In one survey,

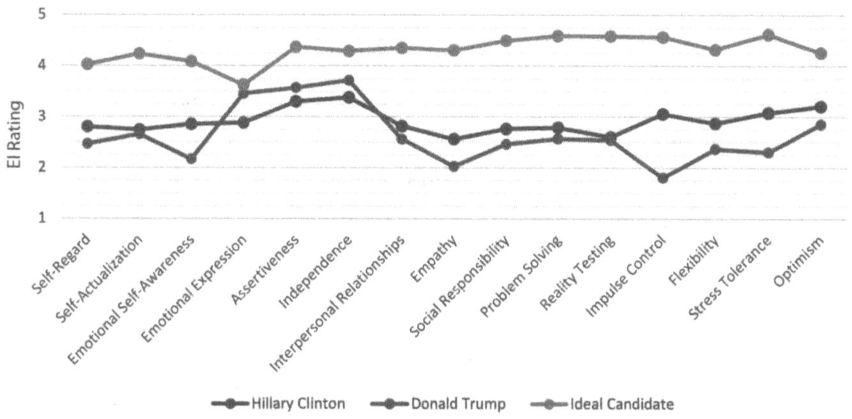

Figure 2.2 Emotional Intelligence Ratings of Hillary Clinton and Donald Trump Compared to Ideal President

Clinton's emotional intelligence was rated first; in the other survey, Trump's was rated.

As seen in Figure 2.2, neither candidate reaches the ideal president in terms of their emotional intelligence scores. They each have their peaks and valleys, though both Clinton and Trump score highest in Independence and Assertiveness.

The biggest differences between the two are Clinton scoring higher in Impulse Control, Stress Tolerance, and Emotional Self-Awareness, while Trump scores higher in Emotional Expression and Assertiveness, and slightly higher in Independence. It could be that, contrary to what voters say they want, emotional expression and assertiveness are more attractive characteristics of political leaders. While I don't have the evidence here to support it, I would venture to speculate, based on my experience in screening hundreds of candidates for reality TV shows and following up on characteristics of successful contestants, that the combination of high emotional expression and assertiveness, and low impulse control may have been a contributing factor to Trump's victory. Just as Bill Clinton is a natural when it comes to demonstrating empathy, Donald Trump uses his well-honed skills to his advantage. His emotional expression (at times including mocking opponents), assertiveness (clearly expressing his likes and dislikes), and low impulse control (often drifting away from carefully scripted speeches) were a sharp contrast to Hillary Clinton's more often than not standard stump speeches. It helps explain, as one radio interviewer pointed out to me, how Trump filled stadiums with more than 20,000 people. In our president's study, we used other peoples' ratings to look at leadership, something that is becoming more common in leadership research and in organizations.

How Researchers Have Looked at Leadership

Kaiser and his colleagues further extended Lord's work on leadership into four different ways that researchers have looked at leaders. They have examined: (1) what causes leaders to stand out, (2) how the approval of leaders is determined, (3) what constitutes an effective leader, and (4) the performance/outcomes of teams.

Standing Out

The first, sometimes referred to as emergent leadership, has to do with standing out. The focus here has been on people who stand out in one way or another, that is, they are seen by others to be leader like. That can include everything from being tall, having a deep voice, being extraverted, having charisma, or any of a number of characteristics that "stand out." If you ever worked on a team that was put together to work on a project without a designated leader, you have some understanding of this. Eventually, someone will be seen as the group leader, even if informally. Without a leader, any team will have a difficult time functioning.

If there is one place that "standing out" is seen as important, it has been in the corporate world. Unfortunately, selecting leaders who stand out may be a contributing factor to our problems in corporate leadership, as well as staff engagement, today. In an entertaining book Leonard Sayles,[4] almost like a fly on the wall, has documented the steps one takes in climbing the corporate ladder in today's organizations. The sad truth is that it almost reads like the book used in the old Broadway show *How to Succeed in Business Without Really Trying*.

Based on Sayles's observations in a number of organizations, starting from an entry position and getting promoted generally requires following a few rules. First, you want to avoid confrontation. People seen as argumentative or challenging the status quo are not seen as management material. Second, withholding suggestions for improvement in the organization will make you seem more agreeable. By favoring the status quo and resisting change, you are seen as supporting what management has put in place. Third, do not ask your boss to champion "unpopular" positions. Even if these positions could save the company thousands of dollars, you're better off keeping your head down. Fourth, and very importantly, always agree with your boss. If your boss sees you as disagreeable you are unlikely to get promoted. Fifth, spend your time on presentation skills and looking good. Dressing right, being well spoken, and wowing an audience—either in a boardroom or staff meeting—will get you noticed. And, of course, getting noticed as a smooth talker is what this type of leadership is about. Sixth, you have to be seen as having a strong desire to advance your career and look better than your peers. So it's important to drop hints to people with power that you could add a lot to the organization once you have the right position in the organization. Of course it helps to let them know how some of your coworkers may be slacking off, or just not up to snuff, in your humble opinion. And finally, always be working on your next advancement. Spend most of your time and energy, not on the tasks assigned to you per se, but on the activities and behaviors that are important to get that next promotion.

Unfortunately, as you can probably guess, being overly career focused does not lead to team or organizational success. One of the best examples of being overly focused on career has been documented by the former army officer and psychologist Norman Dixon.[5] He researched the British military during the eighteenth and nineteenth centuries. What he found was astounding. Basically, the British officers' preoccupation with status and promotion caused the death of tens of thousands of soldiers and the loss of dozens of strategic positions. It was all about "looking good" instead of "doing good." His observations from the military can easily be applied to many organizational settings even today.

The skills one uses in career success are usually unrelated to, and sometimes the opposite of, the skills a leader needs to achieve team success. For example, to manage your career you should focus on socializing or networking with others, politicking (paying attention to who is important and who isn't and how to get closer to those with power), and networking with outsiders. Basically, you should be building your reputation both inside and outside the organization so when it comes time for a promotion, or when someone you've networked with outside the organization hears of a new opportunity, you immediately come to mind as a likely candidate.

On the other hand, in order to be an effective team leader and get things done, a different set of skills come into play. These include communicating clearly and delivering the right messages to subordinates or team members. Getting things done means that everyone on your team needs to know exactly what is expected of them. You also need to know how to motivate others to work for a common cause. As a team leader you may have to know how to discipline team members who are performing poorly. As conflicts arise within the team you will have to know how to resolve these conflicts. Conflict resolution is a key component of leading an effective team.

In order for you to lead a team it's also important to know how to staff the team. When adding new members or replacing old ones you need to know what skills are required and how to select for them. Finally, as a team leader it's important to know the training needs of your subordinates. People tend to grow in their jobs and will need to pick up new information and skills to keep current.

Approval Ratings

The second way leaders have been measured in the research literature has been based on approval ratings. While standing out has been common in corporate environments, approval is likely most common in the political arena. We generally cast votes on politicians based on how we feel about them. While many people vote by political party, and some vote for policies, the deciding factor in most elections has likely more to do with how you feel about the candidate (either good or bad). Even when looking at research in the corporate environment, Kaiser's review reported that most studies focused on people's feelings about the leader, as opposed to the results or outcomes attributed to that leader. Sometimes we see this in 360 ratings that subordinates complete on their supervisors.

Leader Effectiveness

Next, there have been studies that have focused on leader effectiveness. When looking at the effectiveness of a leader, we can look at two different kinds of studies. The first group looks at the effectiveness of leaders in influencing team members, or the process of how the team functioned, for example, were they engaged? The second group of effectiveness studies focuses on the outcomes achieved by the team or organization.

In the first group of effectiveness studies, how the team plays is mainly about process and engagement. I sometimes compare this to the kind of outcome you look at with religious leaders. It's like measuring the effectiveness of a minister, priest, or rabbi by how many seats are filled in the pews each week, or how involved people are in the activities of the organization. The leader's effect on the team is the focus here. Are they present, are they engaged? I can almost hear them saying, "Amen." When measuring this kind of influence that leaders have researchers would look at things like the group dynamics, climate, and culture as measurable factors.

One of the ways researchers have studied this type of leader effectiveness has been through what is called transformational/transactional leadership measures. Bass and Avolio[6] developed the concept of transformational leadership to examine the ways in which leaders are influencing their teams or groups. Basically, they look at a leader's ability to inspire and enhance the performance of their followers. When successful, the leader gets workers to set aside their own self-interest pursuits and work toward a collective purpose. The leader achieves this through her use of vision, appealing group goals, high standards, intellectual stimulation, role modeling, and relationships.

Team Performance

The final group of studies looked at leader effectiveness through the actual outcomes or the performance of the team or organization led by that person. There are a number of different examples of outcomes for an organization. These can be financial (gross earnings, profitability), productivity (number of widgets produced, projects completed), customer retention or satisfaction, human resource measures (absenteeism, engagement), and innovations (successful new products created, money/time saving processes implemented).

Outcome measures are most common in the sports world. Sports leaders—coaches or managers—are often judged by the outcomes of the teams they have worked with. Coaches of winning teams tend to be more sought after than those with less stellar outcomes.

So a lot of what we know about leadership from the academic world comes out of one of these four ways of evaluating leadership. We can look at who stands out, or appears leader like. This is most often seen in how we reward and promote corporate leaders. We can look at the approval or how people feel about a leader. This is often what we see in who wins political elections. We can look at how engaged people are with the leader. This is often how we might look at religious leaders. Finally, we can look at what outcomes have been achieved by the team. This is most often how leaders are judged in the world of sports. In my own study of leadership, I have found you can best understand a leader by the effect they have on others and by their accomplishments. By engaging others, giving them purpose, getting things done, and making the world a better place, you can be a successful leader.

EQ Leader: Things to Think About

1. How do you define leadership and who are some of the leaders that have influenced your life?
2. How much of your time do you see yourself in a leader role?
3. How do you tend to judge the leaders around you?
4. How would you like to be judged as a leader?
5. When you lead others what are some of the outcomes you strive for?

EQ Leader: Taking Action

1. Write down some of the things about yourself that might make you stand out as a leader.
2. What are some of the qualities that people might see in you that would make them feel good about having you as a leader?
3. How do you get other people excited about something you would like them to do?
4. What are some actual tasks or activities that you were able to get someone else to complete?
5. Set some goals for how you would like to be seen as a leader. Include what you would like to accomplish.

Chapter 3

Leadership

Why Emotional Intelligence?

No doubt emotional intelligence is more rare than book smarts, but my experience says it is actually more important in the making of a leader. You just can't ignore it.

—JACK WELCH

One day I was giving a presentation to a large group of leaders in education. I asked them all to think back to the time they graduated from high school. "Do you remember your high school valedictorian?" I asked. As usual when I ask this question the majority of hands in the room go up.

"How many of you know where that person is now?" Once again, as usual, about half the hands in the room go up.

And then the closer, "how many of these people have lived up to your expectations of what they would become in life?" At this point, I usually get a small scattering of hands that go up. Occasionally, someone talks about the student who went on to be a professor at Harvard or MIT.

More often than not, I get a scattering of stories about the nonachiever at school—Fred, the nerdy guy who went on to make millions in a start-up, or Jill the loner, who ended up singing in a rock band and getting rich and famous. Who would have known?

But this one time an older gentleman came up to me and said, "not only do I remember who was valedictorian at my high school, but I still see him quite regularly."

"Really?" I asked.

"Yes," he pointed out. "You see, George and I were classmates since third grade. He was a genius. He excelled in math and sciences. There wasn't a math problem he couldn't solve. We were friends all the way through high school. And he was the school valedictorian—just brilliant. Me? I wasn't so good. I just made it through each year. But I was the go-to guy. I knew where the parties were and where to go to have fun. I gotta say, I was one of the more popular guys at school."

"So what happened to George?" I asked.

"Well, we both went on to be teachers. We remained friends. Eventually, I got promoted to principal. After a while longer, I became a superintendent for the district."

"And George?" I asked again.

"Well, George is still a teacher at the school we started out at. I still see him about once a month. Last time we met he said he was looking forward to retirement. George worked under me for all these years—most of our working lives. So I guess you could say that our expectations for him career-wise were a lot greater than teaching at the same school all these years. And I never thought that I, the C+ student, would ever be his boss. Crazy world, huh?"

For years we've relied on and many employers still believe that cognitive intelligence, or IQ, is a good predictor of leadership abilities. While it's quite likely, on average, that leaders may have higher IQs than followers, IQ is not a very good predictor of leadership ability. In fact, there are now studies that have found that high IQ leaders may be less effective than others with lower IQ scores. But before we get to that, let's look at how we became so reliant on IQ as a predictor of successful leadership.

The Evolution of Intelligences

It's now been more than 100 years that psychologists have been testing IQ, or cognitive intelligence. Interestingly, after all these years, and hundreds of research studies, we still don't have an agreed-upon definition of cognitive intelligence. How is it that IQ and its related ability and achievement tests have dominated our society—through schools, college entrance tests, professional school admissions, and many workplaces?

Well it all started back in 1905 when the French psychologist Alfred Binet, together with his colleague, psychiatrist Theodore Simon, developed the first formal intelligence test.[1]

Binet had been asked by the Parisian school commission to come up with a way children could be categorized according to ability. The aim was somewhat less than benign: to weed out the "feeble-minded" (i.e., those who would not benefit from a publicly funded system). Binet had long believed that intelligence was an interlocking process that involved judgment, problem solving, and reasoning. Now he could put his theories into practice. He and Simon completed and published an IQ test—administered, at first, to children—that enabled him to obtain performance standards for different age groups. These formed the basis of what became known as "mental ages." The results of the test would give the mental age of a person in relation to average levels of growth and intellectual development.

In 1910, the Binet-Simon test migrated to the United States, where the educator and psychologist Henry Goddard[2] founded his own school for the "feeble-minded" in New Jersey. Later the test was modified and standardized for a wider American population by Lewis Terman at Stanford University, and it began to be administered to both children and adults, and became known as the Stanford-Binet test.[3]

At this time, the ability to measure cognitive intelligence assumed new importance. Not only could it identify and sidetrack the "feeble-minded" who could only marginally benefit from education, but it could pick out those who scored high and could be expected to put their learning to best effect. IQ soon took on a life of its own. It was generally viewed as a major factor not only in school but in the workplace and in personal relationships.

Subsequently, there has been a lot of controversy around the concept of IQ, both at schools and in workplaces. There have been debates around the influence of genetics and the environment (i.e., nature vs. nurture). More controversies arose over cultural and racial differences. Nevertheless, IQ or cognitive intelligence has been a powerful force in the selection of students for university, graduate and professional programs, and for many workplaces.

What Is IQ?

IQ testing has evolved somewhat since the days of Binet and Simon. Let's look at what cognitive ability tests actually measure today. They evaluate your ability to concentrate and plan, to organize material, to use words to understand, assimilate, and interpret facts. In essence, IQ is a measure of your personal information bank—your memory, vocabulary, mathematical skills, and visual-motor coordination. Some of these skills are clearly relevant in the workplace.

We've had a hundred years of research on cognitive intelligence testing and its ability to predict outcomes. Where do we stand on the ability of IQ to predict work success? Richard Wagner, in a major review of the topic, examining reviews of reviews and covering hundreds of studies with thousands of subjects, came to some interesting conclusions. His review of reviews (or meta-analysis) found that overall, proponents of IQ testing interpret the research estimating that it accounts for 25 percent of the variance in predicting job performance. In other words, 25 percent of an individual's job performance is attributable to their IQ. However, looking more realistically at the studies, and taking out some of the inflationary estimates, Wagner concludes the number is closer to 4 to 9 percent of the variance.[4] Even if 25 percent of job performance was accounted for by IQ, that leaves 75 percent unaccounted for. The left-out factors could include experience, education, technical skills, and others.

In another review by Robert Sternberg when he was at Yale University, the IQ was estimated to account for only 4 percent of the variance in job performance.[5] That means about 96 percent of work performance was due to variables other than cognitive intelligence. Sternberg goes on to stress the virtues of practical intelligence, or common sense, in predicting job success. In my own experience, emotional intelligence can account for a substantial amount of variation in job performance.

What Is Emotional Intelligence?

While emotional intelligence is a relatively new concept, the skills we talk about have been around as long as humans have lived together in groups. The set of skills that make up emotional intelligence have evolved along with humankind. The need to cope, to adapt, and to get along with others was crucial to the survival of the early hunter-gatherer societies. The human brain reflects this undeniable fact. Sophisticated mapping techniques have confirmed that many thought processes pass through the brain's emotion centers as they take the physiological journey that converts information into individual action or response.

On the one hand, then, emotion is as old as time. In the 1870s, Charles Darwin published the first modern book on the role of emotional expression in survival and adaptation.[6] Darwin's book was titled *The Expression of Emotions in Man and Animals*. As already mentioned, there has been a great deal of controversy over our measures of cognitive intelligence being fair among races and cultures. In fact, there are prohibitions on this type of testing in some jurisdictions. When it comes to understanding emotions, however, Darwin went beyond cultures and examined the transferability of emotional expressions among species. I often ask audiences in my presentations if they have pets. Of the many that do, I ask how many pet owners recognize when their pet is happy, sad, excited, or scared. Without hesitation they all nod and smile. Well, if we can read emotions across species, then there should be fairly clear rules that work across cultures and race. And our research demonstrates this to be true. Of course sometimes it takes a lot of effort and expense for researchers to discover things that many people already know from their own experience.

Why is this important? Darwin documented the importance of emotions as a signaling system. The angry look on the wolf's face serves as a signal that the hunter ignores at his peril. The flight-or-fight response kicks in when reading the anger on the wolf's face. This ability to read these emotions, according to Darwin, led to humans' survival. The lower, more primitive areas of the brain mediate this response. These are the same parts that control your emotional responses today. The sections of the brain are called the *limbic system* and the *hippocampus*.

These emotional parts of the brain influenced the way humans' higher, more advanced areas—called the *neocortex*—function. When you make complex decisions (such as when you interact with people, solve problems, and so on), the lower parts of the brain are still active; they play a role in how effectively you carry out various tasks. Emotions affect your decisions and your reactions to events (even seemingly insignificant ones) and people.

Having good emotional intelligence involves optimal functioning of your higher and lower brain functions. The lower parts of the brain that helped humans survive as hunters by helping them keep vigilant to dangers and opportunities are just as important today in ensuring people react appropriately to everyday stressors and possibilities they encounter. By moderating your reaction to challenging people and situations—reading them correctly—you learn to moderate your flight-or-fight response into more socially acceptable responses. Being smart combines knowing what to do as well as how to do it best.

Some of the supporting research for this comes from neuroscientist Antonio Damasio. He studied patients with specific brain damage and who had lost the ability to emote and feel. He found that patients with damage to the emotional parts of the brain had difficulty making even simple decisions. He concluded, "Far from interfering with rationality, the absence of emotion and feeling can break down rationality and make wise decision-making almost impossible. Most effective decisions are assisted by emotion."[7]

Another, more recent, study looked at higher-functioning problem solving and the role of emotions. Publishing in the *Harvard Business Review*, Roderick Gilkey, Ricardo Caceda, and Clinton Kilts looked at the brain functioning of business people trying to solve strategic business problems.[8] They were given the high level types of problems leaders would need to solve, generally using a rational-logical approach. While they were working on the problems their brain activity was measured with fMRI imaging procedures. Their solutions to the problem were rated by an independent group of experts. When they matched the results of the experts rating the strategic solutions to the brainwaves from the fMRI, they found that the best strategic thinkers showed more activity in parts of the brain linked with emotion and intuition. It may be that their nervous systems may even suppress rational thought to free those areas up during problem solving.

Psychologists have proposed a number of definitions of emotional intelligence, but they all tend to center around the idea behind why some people who are so smart in some ways (book sense) can be rather dumb in other ways (lack street smarts). A person can have book smarts, but not street smarts because of a lack of emotional awareness and control, part of which encompasses emotional intelligence.

For example, you can probably think of a politician who was brilliant, inspirational, and ready to change the world. Then, seemingly out of nowhere came a sexual scandal or charges of taking bribes. The politician couldn't manage his or her sexual appetite or greed well enough (or long enough) to realize a successful political career.

This was actually the inspiration for the first published article that initiated the concept of emotional intelligence as we recognize it today. Peter Salovey, a psychologist at Yale University at the time (currently president of Yale) and a researcher on emotions, was friends with his colleague John (Jack) Mayer, a psychologist at the University of New Hampshire and personality researcher. These two friends were also collaborators in research projects related to emotions, intelligence, and personality.[9]

At the time, both Peter and Jack had hopes for a young presidential candidate named Gary Hart. They saw him as young, fresh, and intelligent—a sure winner. Then, something unbelievable happened. During the primaries, a reporter confronted Gary Hart and suggested, based on some rumors, that he was having an extramarital affair. He famously responded by denying the allegation and then daring all the reporters around him that day to "follow me around. I don't care. I'm serious. If anybody wants to put a tail on me, go ahead. They'll be very bored."

Within 24 hours, the *Miami Herald* broke the story of his now-famous affair with Donna Rice with their photo together onboard the yacht named *Monkey Business*.[10]

Meanwhile Peter and Jack, hearing the news while painting Jack's house one afternoon, were trying to understand how someone so intelligent could do and say something so lacking in intelligence under the circumstances. The *New York Times* described Hart as "a brilliant and serious man, perhaps the most visionary political mind of his generation, an old-school statesman of the kind Washington had lost its capacity to produce."[11] Could it be he was very intelligent in one area (political policy) and not so intelligent in another area (managing his emotions)?

They then came up with the idea that people must have some other kind of intelligence, which they called an emotional intelligence, quite separate from the cognitive intelligence (or IQ) that everyone knows about. They reasoned that they could probably find some way to measure this intelligence in the same way that widely used intelligence tests measure IQ.

Peter and Jack further developed the concept and then wrote a scientific paper titled "Emotional Intelligence," which they published in a relatively obscure scientific journal.[12]

One day while Peter was giving a talk on this new concept, *New York Times* science reporter and psychologist Daniel Goleman was in the audience. Finding the title of the talk very appealing Goleman asked Peter if he could use the title for a new book he was working on, related to emotions. Peter, the consummate gentleman, saw no harm in it. Goleman's book *Emotional Intelligence: Why It Can Matter More Than IQ* went on to be a bestseller, racking up more than 5 million copies sold, a record in the field of psychology.[13]

Subsequently, Peter and Jack teamed up with psychologist David Caruso and developed an ability or performance test of emotional intelligence known as the MSCEIT® (Mayer-Salovey-Caruso Emotional Intelligence Test).[14] Our team at MHS has worked closely with these authors in developing and validating this test. In fact, I took many of the photos used in the original version. The MSCEIT has become the most researched and widely used performance test of emotional intelligence in the world.

The definition used by Mayer and Salovey for emotional intelligence is:

> The ability to perceive emotions, to access and generate emotions so as to assist thought, to understand emotions and emotional knowledge, and to regulate emotions as to promote emotional and intellectual growth.

The MSCEIT model consists of the following branches:

Perceiving emotions: involves your ability to successfully read other people's emotions. It also includes your ability to express emotions accurately to others in order to be an effective communicator.

Facilitating thought: or using emotions, involves using emotions to generate and feel emotions in order to communicate feelings, and to use emotions in cognitive processes. What we feel has a big influence on how we think. Also, emotions can help us focus our attention and guide us as we solve problems.

Understanding emotions: helps us use our emotions to predict the future. Knowing our emotions helps us navigate through life. It helps to understand why we feel sad, angry, or giddy. For example, feeling angry may be because of bad traffic in the morning and taking that anger out on your coworkers is not going to help you at work. Understanding where your anger comes from makes it easier to deal with it.

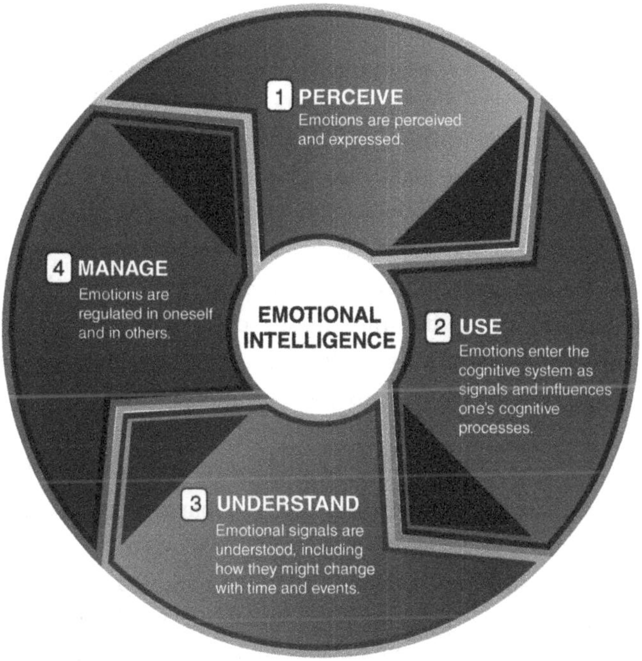

Figure 3.1 The MSCEIT Model of Emotional Intelligence

Source: Reprinted with permission of Multi-Health Systems (2005).

Managing emotions: this is where you can really put your emotions to your advantage. By managing the way you feel, you can: get along better with others, solve problems more easily, make sounder judgments, and manage your behavior more effectively.

The MSCEIT model is represented by the diagram shown in Figure 3.1.

How Does the MSCEIT Relate to Leadership?

Leadership is an area where there are a growing number of studies looking for the links to emotional intelligence. In Australia, David Rosete at the University of Wollongong carried out a study that helps shed some light in this area.[15] His research looked at the degree to which emotional intelligence predicts leadership performance over and above traditional personality and reasoning or cognitive intelligence (IQ) measures.

He tested 117 executives from a large Australian public service organization for personality, IQ, and also used the MSCEIT. As well, he got ratings of leadership effectiveness from the managers' annual feedback discussions with their supervisors. These ratings basically boiled down to two main areas: (1) *What* had been achieved and (2) *how* it had been achieved. The first part of the ratings focused on deliverable and measurable outcomes. The second focused on the way in which leaders behaved to get these results.

David found that personality factors were not related to the managers' performance ratings. He did find, however, that the MSCEIT showed some interesting relationships with performance. The MSCEIT overall score was significantly related to the "what" and the "how" of getting things done.

While it may not seem like much, of all the measures used the MSCEIT was the best predictor of "what" was achieved, accounting for 5 percent of the variance above and beyond personality and IQ. In terms of the "how" measure, the personality measure was not significant. The ability to accurately perceive emotions accounted for 18 percent of the variance in "how" ratings, further, the entire MSCEIT accounts for 22 percent of the variance in "how" ratings. Somewhat contrary to popular belief, the IQ score did not influence the ratings of "how" the job was done. These findings confirm that there is a role for the emotional intelligence ability among leaders.

An important aspect of leadership involves the ability to motivate others. Developing an effective vision statement is an important part of that process. A study was carried out looking at the relative effects of personality and emotional intelligence on vision statements produced by 137 women and men by Stéphane Côté, Peter Lopes, and Peter Salovey. Greater levels of emotional intelligence, as measured by the MSCEIT, were associated with higher-quality vision statements, above and beyond one's personality.[16]

What's the importance of a leader's emotional intelligence to those people lower down in the organization? In a study carried out at the University of New South Wales in Australia looking at two small groups of managers (13 each from public and private organizations) along with 108 people reporting to them, S. Giles found a significant relationship between the employee's commitment to the organization and the managers' emotional intelligence. In other words, employees were more committed to their organization if their manager had higher levels of emotional intelligence. A manager's ability to manage and understand their emotions bore the largest influence on employee commitment.[17]

There are many studies looking at the relative importance of IQ, EQ, and other factors in leadership success. I will present one more study in this area. It was carried out by W. Lee Turner at Northcentral University, School of Business and Technology Management.[18]

Turner started his review by pointing out the trend in the U.S. government sector of using "outdated methods to identify leadership potential." He reports that IQ measures have been used in that sector for the past 60 years.

He looked at the relationship between emotional intelligence, IQ, and leader performance. Fifty-two first- through third-line government managers in Hanford, California, took the MSCEIT and the Wonderlic IQ test, a measure of cognitive ability. To measure the leaders' performance two outputs were examined. The first was their schedule performance index—amount of value you invest in a project, and the second was cost performance index—the value of work completed compared to the actual cost of the project.

What he found was a significant positive correlation between emotional intelligence and schedule performance. As well, there was a significant negative correlation between intelligence quotient and schedule performance. In other words, the higher your emotional intelligence and the lower your IQ, the better you were at achieving a good schedule performance. In terms of cost performance there was a positive correlation with emotional intelligence and no significant correlation with intelligence quotient. So, in this study emotional intelligence was a better predictor of leader performance than IQ. It is important to note that this study looked at the actual results of a working population (as opposed to students); therefore, we can be confident that the results are generalizable to other working populations.

The Self-Report of Emotional Intelligence

Meanwhile, back in 1985, another psychologist named Reuven Bar-On completed his doctoral dissertation developing a test that would measure a person's emotional quotient, or EQ, just like intelligence tests measured the IQ or intelligence quotient. He had been in the military and had used traditional psychological testing with soldiers. He noticed that traditional tests—IQ, personality—did not seem to predict who performed well on missions and who didn't. Some people, with high IQs, would not hold up well in the field, while others, with average IQs would be stellar performers. For his doctoral dissertation he researched and created a tool that would attempt to measure emotional strengths that would be more predictive of performance and resilience. He defined emotional intelligence as "an array of non-cognitive capabilities, competencies, and skills that influence one's ability to succeed in coping with environmental demands and pressures."[19] The tool was called the Emotional Quotient Inventory or EQ-i®.

The team at MHS has worked with this assessment and revised it based on ongoing research. The current version, referred to as the EQ-i 2.0® has been used in many work settings around the world. Approximately 2 million people have been tested with the EQ-i and EQ-i 2.0, worldwide.[20]

The model, as shown in Figure 3.2, is divided into five general areas and 15 specific scales. The Self-Perception module deals with your ability to know and manage yourself. It encompasses Emotional Self-Awareness—the ability to recognize how you're feeling and why you're feeling that way, and the impact your emotions have on the thoughts and actions of yourself and others; Self-Regard—the ability to recognize your strengths and weaknesses and to feel good about yourself despite your weaknesses; and Self-Actualization—the ability to persistently try to improve yourself and pursue meaningful goals that lead to a richer life.

The Self-Expression module deals with the way you face the world. It includes Emotional Expression—the ability to express your feelings both in words and nonverbally; Assertiveness—the ability to clearly express your thoughts and beliefs, stand your ground, and defend a position in a constructive way; and Independence—the ability to be self-directed and self-controlled, to stand on your own two feet.

The Interpersonal module concerns your "people skills"—your ability to interact and get along with others. It is composed of three scales. Interpersonal Relationship refers to the ability to forge and maintain relationships that are mutually beneficial and marked by give-and-take in the sense of trust and compassion. Empathy is the ability to recognize, understand, and appreciate what others may be feeling and thinking. It is the ability to view the world through another person's eyes. Social Responsibility is the ability to be a cooperative and contributing member of your social group and to society at large.

Figure 3.2 Emotional Quotient Inventory 2.0 (EQ-i 2.0)

Source: Reprinted with permission of Multi-Health Systems (2011, based on the Bar-On EQ-i model by Reuven Bar-On, 1997).

The Decision-Making module involves your ability to use your emotions in the best way to help you solve problems and make optimal choices. Its three scales are Impulse Control—the ability to resist or delay a temptation to act rashly; Reality Testing—the ability to see things as they actually are, rather than the way you wish or fear they might be; and Problem-Solving—the ability to find solutions to problems where emotions are involved using the right emotion at an optimum value.

The Stress Management module concerns your ability to be flexible, tolerate stress, and have a positive outlook. Its three scales are Flexibility—the ability to adjust your feelings, thoughts, and actions to changing, challenging, or unfamiliar conditions; Stress Tolerance—the ability to remain calm and focused, to constructively withstand adverse events and conflicting emotions without caving in; and Optimism—the ability to maintain a realistically positive attitude, particularly in the face of adversity.

There is also an independent indicator of your Happiness. Happiness is the ability to feel satisfied with life, to enjoy yourself and others, and to experience zest and enthusiasm in a range of activities.

Other Models

The MSCEIT and EQ-i were the original two models of emotional intelligence. There have since been many additional models, most of which are variations of these. If you want a simplified explanation of emotional intelligence, virtually all of the different models share these three components:

1. The ability to **identify** emotional information in oneself and in others.
2. The ability to **manage** emotional information in oneself and in others.
3. The ability to **focus** emotional energy on required behaviors to get things done.

Can Self-Reporting Emotional Intelligence Be Valid?

There continues to be questions among some about what self-report emotional intelligence may contribute over and above IQ and personality to leadership performance. First, let's clear up some misperceptions about self-report tests. There are high quality self-report tools that take years to develop because they go through rigorous testing standards developed by the American Psychological Association.[21] They require the gathering of well-representative normative samples of the populations that will be tested, extensive reliability testing, validity testing, and more. There are other legal and ethical standards around the use of psychological testing in the workplace.[22] Of course, if you search the Internet, you can find several EQ tests that were developed on the back of an envelope and have questionable accuracy.

Some people question the very nature of self-report testing of emotional intelligence. They say if someone lacks self-awareness, for example, how can they respond to items about their level of awareness? Also, if you ask people if they are emotionally intelligent, won't 95 percent of them just answer yes? After all, studies with IQ have found that 87 percent (in this case, Stanford MBA students) rated themselves as more intelligent than the mean when asked to self-rate their intelligence.[23] Of course, 87 percent of people can't be in the top half if, by definition, 50 percent are above and 50 percent below the mean. We will look at the reliability of self-report emotional intelligence in Chapter 15.

Psychology has a long history of developing psychometrically sound, self-report tests. As previously mentioned, Binet measured IQ with the first standardized IQ test. But the first test for psychopathology, the MMPI, was developed in 1939 by Starke Hathaway and Charles McKinley.[24] It remains, to this day, the most widely used and researched standardized test of personality and psychopathology. The test was designed to measure disorders such as depression, anxiety, and schizophrenia. How, you might ask, can a schizophrenic person rate themselves on a self-report test? Wouldn't they just say, "No, I'm not schizophrenic"? Well it's been working successfully for more than 70 years and there doesn't seem to be much controversy around it.

The answer is quite simple. You don't just ask a person if they are emotionally intelligent in the same way as you don't just ask a person if they are schizophrenic. The key is to develop a number of indirect and non-obvious or subtle items that reflect the way that schizophrenic people (or high EQ people) answer items differently from the general population. Is that an easy task? No, but that's what separates the high-value tests, like the MMPI and EQ-i 2.0, from the rest.

Self-Report Emotional Intelligence, IQ, Personality, and Work Performance

While there is still much controversy in the academic literature over what actually constitutes emotional intelligence, or how it is defined, there seems to be growing agreement on the predictive ability of the various models of emotional intelligence. For example, in a recent review covering all the available research that related job performance to IQ, personality, and emotional intelligence, Dana Joseph and colleagues[25] point out that "recent empirical reviews have claimed a surprisingly strong relationship between job performance and self-reported emotional intelligence (also commonly called trait EI or mixed EI by the academics), suggesting self-reported/mixed EI is one of the best-known predictors of job performance. Results further suggest mixed EI can robustly predict job performance beyond cognitive ability and Big Five personality traits."[26]

In their review, which covered hundreds of studies, emotional intelligence accounted for around 22 percent of the variance of job performance while cognitive intelligence accounted for about 19 percent of the variance of job performance. While the difference may not seem like a lot, in practice the effects could be significant.

Leaving aside the academics, what do employers around the world have to say about emotional intelligence? There have been some interesting surveys reported recently on the importance of emotionally intelligent people in the workplace. According to the World Economic Forum's *Future of Jobs Report*,[27] the awareness that emotional intelligence is an important job skill, in some cases even surpassing technical ability, has been growing in recent years. The report states, "Overall, social skills—such as persuasion, emotional intelligence and teaching others—will be in higher demand across industries than narrow technical skills, such as programming or equipment operation and control."

In a 2011 Career Builder Survey[28] of more than 2,600 hiring managers and human resource professionals, 71 percent stated they valued emotional intelligence in an employee over IQ; 75 percent said they were more likely to promote a highly emotionally intelligent worker over a worker with just high IQ; and 59 percent claimed they'd pass up a candidate with a high IQ but low emotional intelligence.

The importance of emotional intelligence in the workplace is increasingly becoming recognized by employers everywhere worldwide.

EQ Leader: Things to Think About

1. Think of some of the bosses you've worked for, either in your current workplace or in the past. Did they get to their position mainly because of their technical ability, general intelligence, or people skills?

2. What combination of the four skills/abilities—technical, IQ, personality, emotional—would you think would make a good fit for a leader in your industry?
3. Of the different emotional abilities and skills described in this chapter, which ones do you think are most important for leaders?
4. Which of the abilities or skills described would *you* say were your strongest emotional skills?
5. If you asked a *family member*, which of the emotional skills would *they* say were your strongest?
6. If you asked a *coworker*, which of the emotional skills would *they* say was your strongest?
7. If you could pick three of the emotional skills defined in this chapter to develop, which would they be?
8. How would you start developing these skills?

Chapter 4

Emotional Contagion

If your actions inspire others to dream more, learn more, do more and become more, you are a leader.

—JOHN QUINCY ADAMS

Barry is a friend of mine. Like me he runs a successful business employing around 160 people. When we get together, he's a cheerful, fun-loving guy. His company develops software for the manufacturing industry. They build software and have been marketing it mostly throughout North America. Also like me he's been doing it for more than 30 years. However, he seems to complain often about the turnover rate at his company. Programmers are getting harder to find, he reports, and more expensive to train. Turnover also causes delays in getting out new versions of the software and repairing software bugs. In addition, they are being held back in making a major push to release their software in the cloud and have faced a number of delays mainly due to staffing.

Barry also tells me his revenues have stalled for the past five years. Up until that time, the company enjoyed double-digit growth each year. Part of the reason for the stall has been the shrinking market for enterprise software and anticipation of cloud versions. Barry invited me to come and look at what was going on in his organization.

One of the first things I noticed when I walked into the building was the general mood of the organization. Everyone I passed by had their head down into their screens. It was quieter than a library. Not only that, but as we walk by the workstations people's heads seem to go down even deeper, into their computer screen. They don't even look up to acknowledge our presence.

When people walk into our offices at MHS, they're bound to hear laughter from somewhere in the building and see people congregating around workstations. They may even see people playing foosball in the Starbucks-like cafeteria (named the Greenbean by staff). At MHS, when visitors come through the building you are greeted with at least a smile, and more often with a "hello."

When I point this out to Barry, he looks at me like I'm from Mars. "What do you mean?" he says, "This is a workplace, people are here to do their jobs. I need productivity. They're not here to party."

"Don't you think their mood affects their work?" I ask.

"Okay, now you're trying to pull that psychology stuff on me. They can go to the bar after work to feel good. This is where they come to work. That's what I pay them for."

I could see this wasn't going to be an easy discussion with a quick answer. But it became clearer to me that I had to be able to better articulate the role of emotions at work. Workplace culture is something that I've cultivated for years. We started our company as a family business in a basement. We always believed that MHS was family oriented, in terms of how we treated people. While the majority of people thrive in this environment, I have to admit, at times this can be challenging. Not everybody reciprocates, as there are people who will abuse privileges by wasting time at work or slacking off, or not working to their fullest potential. But these risks are minor compared to the productivity you can get if you select the right people and create an empowering culture. That is, people who really care about the work they do. As well, you learn to build in checks and balances on people's productivity.

Not only have our results (in terms of revenue, profits, and number of employees) shown tremendous and consistent growth, but we've won a number of awards from independent judges who have come and examined our organization. For example, we were awarded the Profit 100 Fastest Growing Companies in Canada (three years in a row), Best Managed Companies in Canada, Ernst & Young Entrepreneur of the Year (Province of Ontario, Health Category), and Canada's 10 Most Admired Corporate

Cultures (Waterstone). I strongly believe that culture accounts for a major part of our success. As part of building a great culture we select people not only for their specific job skills and talent, but also for their culture fit. To help with that, we test every serious MHS job applicant for emotional intelligence—whether it's customer service, programming, business development, shipping and warehouse, graphic design, research and development, or web design. We use the EQ-i 2.0.

Spreading Emotions @work

Workplaces have a mood. I almost always get a sense of an organization by the mood when I walk around their premises. The mood generated in an organization comes from the top. The leaders set the organization's tone. It can be formal, friendly, austere, whimsical, creative, fun, serious, anxious, relaxed, or any of a number of emotional tones.

Research has shown that emotions spread at work. When working in a group, you can "catch" other people's feelings. These can be either positive or negative emotions. Think about the last time you were in a workgroup celebrating the success of a major sale. Or perhaps when you did that post mortem on the big sale you didn't get. The formal, scientific term for this is "emotional contagion." It usually manifests itself in face-to-face contact with others. More likely than not, you experienced similar emotions to those around you.

First, let's look at some laboratory research on this effect. Sigal Barsade[1] has published a number of studies documenting the emotional contagion effect. In one study she divided business students into small groups. They had to role-play a situation in which they played a department head advocating for an employee's merit-based increase. All the other students in the group were part of a "salary committee," whose job it was to balance the limited funds available. As well, each participant had to take a turn negotiating for their own candidate's increase. This was all to be executed while maximizing the overall benefit to the company.

Each of the groups had an actor (confederate) secretly placed in it. The actor was trained to embed one of four different emotions into the group: (1) cheerful enthusiasm, (2) serene warmth, (3) hostile irritability, or (4) depressed sluggishness. Barsade found that the emotions shown by the actor had a significant effect on the group's mood. Groups in which the confederate had "spread" positive emotion experienced an increase in positive mood. But the emotional contagion did not stop with a spread of feelings. She reported, "These groups also displayed more cooperation, less interpersonal conflict and felt they'd performed better on their task than groups in which negative emotions were spread by the confederate. And, groups in which people felt positive emotions had actually made decisions that allocated the available money more equitably."[2]

In the same way that my friend Barry had no idea that his employees' moods may affect their work, the subjects in Barsade's study did not attribute any of their decisions to mood. In fact, when her subjects were asked why they allocated the funds the way they did, they attributed it to their negotiating acumen, or the qualities of the "candidate" they had been assigned. None of them reported that their behavior or decisions had anything to do with the confederate's or their own emotions.

Emotional Temperature

While I've always believed, and this is true at MHS, that there is an emotional component to an organization's culture, there is now empirical support for this idea in the business literature. Some of that work has been summarized by Sigal Barsade and Olivia O'Neil in a *Harvard Business Review* article.[3] They write about two types of culture every organization has. The first is a *cognitive* culture, "the shared *intellectual* values, norms, artifacts, and assumptions" that guide the organization's survival. The second is the *emotional* culture, "*affective* values, norms, artifacts, and assumptions" that determine which emotions people feel at work as well as which emotions are suppressed. Other than the obvious differences between these two, they are also transmitted differently. The cognitive culture is spread verbally and through language, whereas the emotional culture spreads through nonverbal cues such as body language and facial expressions. Taking the emotional temperature of an organization gives you an indication of the kinds of feelings people are having (and perhaps spreading) at work.

Barsade and O'Neill go on to cite research studies that found that emotional culture influences employee satisfaction, burnout, teamwork, and even hard measures such as financial performance and absenteeism. They summarize these findings:

> Positive emotions are consistently associated with better performance, quality, and customer service—this holds true across roles and industries and at various organizational levels. On the flip side (with certain short-term exceptions), negative emotions such as group anger, sadness, fear, and the like usually lead to negative outcomes, including poor performance and high turnover.[4]

Another interesting thing about the emotional culture is that it is developed via day-to-day interactions. It's not all about the big annual company gala (although that helps). Rather, it's mostly determined by the small interactions that happen every day. Think of each day at work as a series of positive and negative exchanges in feelings that chalk up on a ledger board. The goal is to come out of each day with a net positive credit rating. While it would not be possible to go through a workweek without stress, the idea here is that you could still feel good about how you handled those daily hassles, whether or not you've completely overcome them.

A Tale of Two Leaders

How might a leader's emotions play out in an even bigger way, in the real world, such as in the performance of a large organization? It's not really possible to set up a study that controls for this scientifically, but we can look at two well-known, high profile leaders and examine how their emotional signals may have affected their organizations' performance. Let's look at Steve Jobs and Carly Fiorina.

Steve Jobs showed significant changes in his behavior throughout his career. He was clearly a fairly complex character, and I don't want to go into his psychological profile. I want to focus on Steve Jobs II. This is after he left Apple, created and sold NeXT, and left Pixar to rejoin Apple. When Jobs returned to Apple he had a tremendous effect on the culture there. The company was struggling and in poor financial shape.

In terms of how he spent his time at Apple, based on a feature about him in a *Fortune* magazine article (where he was named CEO of the decade), it was reported that he focused his time on what he was best at: creating products, recruiting, marketing, and, of course, being the public face of the company.[5] Jobs said, "I get to spend my time on the forward-looking stuff. My top executives take half the other work off my plate. They love it, and I love it." This was a huge change from the way he first ran Apple. Previously known for his micromanaging and personal emotional tirades, after his experience at Pixar he learned to stay out of the day-to-day work of creative people.[6]

But even more important, what did people at Apple think and feel about him? What was the emotional temperature at Apple? We hear so much about the troubled and difficult aspects of his personality, but one honest gauge of how he was perceived by the people working at Apple was provided by the website Glassdoor where employees anonymously rate their leaders. Amazingly his approval rating by employees was 97 percent, exceedingly high, and slightly higher than the CEOs of Facebook (Mark Zuckerberg) and Google (Eric Schmidt).[7]

It seems almost legendary that Jobs bullied and was difficult with subordinates. Some of this was reinforced by Walter Isaacson's biography of Jobs. Many people reacted negatively to what seemed to be significant bullying and lying to subordinates. Isaacson subsequently wrote an article in the *Harvard Business Review* clarifying this perception of Jobs's behavior.[8]

In it he stated, "But those who worked with him admitted that the trait, infuriating as it might be, led them to perform extraordinary feats . . . 'It was a self-fulfilling distortion,' recalls Debi Coleman, a member of the original Mac team who won an award one year for being the employee who best stood up to Jobs. 'You did the impossible because you didn't realize it was impossible.' "

He went on to explain, "Jobs was famously impatient, petulant, and tough with the people around him. But his treatment of people, though not laudable, emanated from his passion for perfection and his desire to work with only the best." Admitting that he tended to go overboard with rudeness, "Was all his stormy and abusive behavior necessary? Probably not. There were other ways he could have motivated his team. 'Steve's contributions could have been made without so many stories about him terrorizing folks,' Apple's cofounder, Wozniak, said. 'I like being more patient and not having so many conflicts. I think a company can be a good family.' But then he added something that is undeniably true: 'If the Macintosh project had been run my way, things probably would have been a mess.' "

But then the most important part of this behavior that most people miss: "It's important to appreciate that Jobs' rudeness and roughness were accompanied by an ability to be inspirational. He infused Apple employees with an abiding passion to create ground-breaking products and a belief that they could accomplish what seemed impossible. And we have to judge him by the outcome. Jobs had a close-knit family, and so it was at Apple: His top players tended to stick around longer and be more loyal than those at other companies, including ones led by bosses who were kinder and gentler. CEOs who study Jobs and decide to emulate his roughness without understanding his ability to generate loyalty make a dangerous mistake."[9]

An important point here is that, emotional intelligence, is not about always being nice. Rather it's about the ability to use the right emotion at the right time to get the right result. It requires the ability to read the other person, know how far you can push their buttons, and knowing when to back off and when to persist. If it is done with good intentions, even though unpleasant at the time, the payoff can be rewarding. One of Apple's top performers, Debi Coleman, was asked about how she felt as a target of Jobs's behavior. "He would shout at a meeting," Coleman recalls, "yet I consider myself the absolute luckiest person in the world to have worked with him."

One more thing: Jobs promoted face-to-face meetings, the most important vehicle for emotional contagion to be spread. Isaacson reported, "Jobs was a strong believer in face-to-face meetings. 'There's a temptation in our networked age to think that ideas can be developed by e-mail and iChat,' he told me. 'That's crazy. Creativity comes from spontaneous meetings, from random discussions. You run into someone, you ask what they're doing, you say 'Wow,' and soon you're cooking up all sorts of ideas.'"

What about Apple's performance? Well there's a reason *Fortune* named Jobs CEO of the decade. As reported in *Forbes* magazine in 2013: "Apple is the most valuable brand in the world for a third straight time at $104.3 billion, up 20 percent over last year. It is worth nearly twice as much as any other brand on the planet by our count."[10]

Now let's look at Carly Fiorina. In 1998, her picture was on the cover of *Fortune* magazine for being named The Most Powerful Woman in American Business.[11] She was brought in to shake up Hewlett-Packard, the iconic tech company whose stock and culture was stalled. One of her opening moves was to merge HP with competitor Compaq. Fiorina was described as having a "job focused" leadership style. For example, she expected subordinates to carry out their one-year plan in three months. Her management style was described as Authority-Compliance leadership, and she was known to have worked people hard, paying no attention to their needs. She was also known for under-delegating and overcontrolling subordinates.[12]

Fortune magazine published its first-ever "100 Best Companies to Work For" in 1998. The rankings were based on five values related to trust developed by the Great Places to Work Institute. The five values included the organization's credibility, respect, fairness, pride, and camaraderie. HP was rated in 10th place for both the first and second year of the ratings. But by the fourth rating they dropped off the list completely. They were gone for the next nine years. After Fiorina had settled in and made her presence known, the *Washington Post* described Hewlett-Packard as a company with "undermined and frayed" values, and one in which employee trust had been severely, if not irretrievably damaged.[13]

In a detailed analysis of the management of HP during Fiorina's taking charge, Kimberly Elsbach and her colleagues found that HP's fall from the rankings was not due, primarily, to diminishing employee trust, but to an increase in employee distrust.[14] In particular, they attributed this state of affairs to HP's leader at the time, "Thus, an important implication of the current study is that *expressions of satisfaction with employees may be important to building organizational trust.* Further, given the positive performance of HP when initial signals of dissatisfaction were introduced by Carly Fiorina, such signals may have been especially distressing and 'untrustworthy' to employees."

Further, they documented the creation of distrust, "behaviors and language that signal values of disrespect, dissatisfaction, and unfair treatment with regard to employees are likely to not just lower trust, but actually produce distrust."[15]

Peter Burrows and Michael Malone further documented employee dissatisfaction under Fiorina. They reported on a survey of 8,000 employees that revealed widespread unhappiness about poor communication and poorly implemented decisions. This was a complete reversal of earlier surveys, which found that HP had some of the highest employee satisfaction scores in corporate America. Some workers booed the CEO at company meetings. Quite the opposite of the famous Steve Jobs employee briefings.[16]

InfoWorld reported the tech industry's 25 all-time flops, with number 6 being Carly Fiorina, where they "call her the anti-Steve Jobs. During her 1999–2005 tenure as CEO of Hewlett-Packard, Carly Fiorina proved that she could reverse decades of geek goodwill and alienate customers like no one else."[17]

Finally, Jeffrey Sonnenfeld gave his well-publicized opinion piece during Fiorina's run for leadership of the Republican Party: "I have studied her business record, challenged her leadership abilities and have come to agree with the assessment that she was one of the worst technology CEOs in history. I stand by that evaluation."[18]

He summed up her record, "In the five years that Fiorina was at Hewlett-Packard, the company lost over half its value. It's true that many tech companies had trouble during this period of the Internet bubble collapse, some falling in value as much as 27 percent; but HP under Fiorina fell 55 percent. During those years, stocks in companies like Apple and Dell rose. Google went public, and Facebook was launched. The S&P 500 yardstick on major U.S. firms showed only a 7 percent drop. Plenty good was happening in U.S. industry and in technology."[19]

The board dismissed her in 2005, and HP's stock price rose by 7 percent immediately afterward. Meanwhile, Fiorina fell to earth with the aid of a $40 million golden parachute.

Now I'm sure it could be argued that factors other than the cultures these leaders created were responsible for their company's performance. You could look at their decision-making ability, personality, intelligence, or any number of factors. But in both cases if you review what most of the biographers, pundits, and analysts say, you will find most of the discussion focuses on how they influenced employees—for better or worse.

What Does the Research Say about Emotional Contagion?

There have been dozens of studies looking at leaders' emotional intelligence and its relationship with employee satisfaction. This is another way of understanding a leader's influence at work. Employee/job satisfaction has been one of the most-studied areas by organizational psychologists. Research has found that job satisfaction directly effects job performance, organizational citizenship behavior (employees going above and beyond the call of duty in their job), counterproductive work behavior (behaviors that harm the organization, workers, or customers), physical and psychological health outcomes, and withdrawal cognitions and behaviors (thinking about and/or actually leaving the company).

Leaders have a significant influence on the mood and feelings of employees. Leaders who are high in emotional intelligence are capable of creating enthusiasm among employees. Many psychologists agree that this is a major function of a leader. There are different ways in which managers and leaders influence team member's moods.

One way they do this is by understanding how to respond to different emotional workplace events that occur. They also influence others by role-modeling good responses to various situations. Some leaders create shared emotional experiences that bond group members together.

Before getting any more specific about how leaders influence their people through emotions, let's look at the research demonstrating that leaders' emotional intelligence is directly related to employee moods—specifically satisfaction at work. Researchers Chao Miao, Ronald H. Humphrey, and Shanshan Qian carried out a recent review of all the studies available that looked at the relationship between a leader's emotional intelligence and employee's work satisfaction.[20] In all, they located 20 workplace samples that included 4,665 people. Their most important finding is that a leader's emotional intelligence has a positive effect above and beyond both personality and cognitive intelligence in influencing employee's happiness at work.

They found that personality and cognitive intelligence, together, accounted for 50.1 percent of their subordinate's job satisfaction. Self-reported emotional intelligence (such as the EQ-i 2.0) accounted for 49.9 percent of subordinates' job satisfaction. The amazing thing is that the personality and IQ measures included six different factors, which meant administering multiple tests to people to get at these factors. The emotional intelligence (self-report) results were based on a single test, such as the EQ-i 2.0. Thus, the EQ-i 2.0 is a parsimonious solution for those looking to predict employee satisfaction.

In addition, these authors looked at the importance of leaders' emotional intelligence and their subordinates' own emotional intelligence in relation to their subordinate's job happiness. You would expect that emotionally intelligent people would be happier at work. In fact, this study found that an employee's emotional intelligence accounted for 52 percent of their work happiness. But, among the same people, their leader's emotional intelligence accounted for 48 percent of their employee's job satisfaction. In other words, the leader's emotional intelligence was almost as important as the worker's own emotional intelligence in determining happiness at work.

How Does a Leader's Emotional Intelligence Affect Others?

We already know that being emotionally intelligent means that you are aware of your own and others emotions, you can manage your own and others emotions, and you can use emotions to make decisions, deal with stress, and so on. But how exactly does that make you a good leader? How does your emotional intelligence actually influence others?

Jennifer George outlined the steps that may help explain how this works.[21] She laid out five key elements that successful emotionally intelligent leaders do.

First, they develop collective goals and objectives. They can sense where each person is at and helps them work toward a shared objective. They know what appeals to the other person and can frame the shared goal as a win-win situation.

Second, they instill in others the importance of work activities. They can do this by giving meaning to the tasks that have to be done. No job is too small. Everything we do counts toward the big picture.

Third, they generate and maintain enthusiasm, confidence, optimism, cooperation, and trust. They use their own emotions to infect passion in others. If you see how passionate I am, then you too will get excited about the mission we're on. High emotionally intelligent people can keep that fire burning and keep the passion alive day in and day out. They build confidence by believing in people's ability, or like Steve Jobs by pushing them to their best work. These leaders are also optimistic. Even when the going gets tough and it looks like things are going badly, tomorrow is another day and we'll come up with a new solution to the problem. Cooperation and trust are built by showing that you care. Sometimes it means digging in and working together. It means delivering on your word—walking the walk.

Fourth, encouraging flexibility in decision making. Instead of telling people how to do the job you want done, you let them know what outcome you are looking for and let them get there the best way they can. Encouraging flexibility in others requires you to be flexible as well. By focusing on clear outcomes and setting general parameters on getting there (like don't break these rules) you allow people to be more creative in their solutions.

Finally, it includes establishing and maintaining a meaningful identity for an organization. This would fit into the generally accepted practice of setting a mission, vision, and values for the organization. One of the challenges of this, I have found, has been for the leaders to articulate this mission and vision so clearly that it has been embraced and executed throughout the organization. Great missions and visions can also be clearly seen and understood by people outside the organization—clients, suppliers, partners, and so on. By applying the passion and communication skills as outlined above, emotionally intelligent leaders can infuse people with just the right messages to make it happen.

We'll delve more deeply into the skills required to enable these competencies to thrive over the next several chapters.

EQ Leader: Things to Think About

1. How would you describe the mood in your current workplace?
2. How do you think the mood affects people's work?
3. What would you do, if anything, to change the mood?
4. Think about the most passionate people in your workplace. Does their work performance differ from other people's?
5. What kind of emotions does the leader at your work place spread? If you are the leader, what emotions do you think you spread?
6. How well do people at your workplace know the mission and vision of the organization?
7. What could you do to infuse people with your organization's mission and vision?
8. Can you state your organization's vision in less than 25 words? How about in 10 words or less?

PART I

The Building Blocks of Emotional Intelligence

Basic emotional skills are the building blocks of emotionally intelligent competencies.

—STEVEN STEIN

Self-Perception and Leadership

Emotional Self-Awareness
The ability to be aware of and understand one's feelings and their impact

Self-Regard
The ability to accept and respect one's strengths and weaknesses

Self-Actualization
The ability to improve oneself and pursue meaningful objectives

Chapter 5

Self-Perception

Know Thyself

The place to start managing is not in the plant. You start with managing yourself by finding out your own strengths . . . and making sure you set the right example.

—PETER DRUCKER

Your visions will become clear only when you can look into your own heart. Who looks outside, dreams; who looks inside, awakes.

—C.G. JUNG

Joanne was getting ready to make an important town hall presentation at her company. She was the CEO of a medium-sized engineering firm and after five years of great performance she had to report to her staff that their revenues were down this year for the first time. Everyone's bonus would be affected. She never had to deliver bad news of this magnitude to her employees before. She was typically uncomfortable with public speaking, even while delivering good news, but this was her worst nightmare.

She spent the past week preparing—looking for ways to spin the news. How could she present the results so that it looked like a temporary blip? How could she lessen the blow? How will her staff react to the loss of bonuses? She knew many of them were counting on the extra money. Annual bonuses were now seen as a given, almost a ritual at the company.

When the big day of the town hall came, she put on her best business suit, made herself up, practiced her best power pose, and prepared everything she needed to face her employees and deliver the news. She greeted people as they came into the large meeting room, finding it a bit difficult to smile and make small talk.

As the staff gathered in and filled the seats she suddenly began to feel queasy in her stomach. It started small, but gradually grew, making her uncomfortable and distracting her thoughts. Could it have been a reaction to the seafood she ate the night before? Was it from skipping breakfast in the morning? Were her nerves starting to get frayed in anticipation of her presentation? The more she tried to ignore the feeling the worse it got. She was completely confused by what she was feeling, but she had to forge ahead.

Unfortunately, her presentation came across as distracted, lacking in focus and confidence. She was so self-focused she neglected to read her audience's reactions. It came across as somewhat uncaring, overly engrossed in the numbers and what went wrong, and lacked emphasis on how disappointing it must be to everyone, or what the next steps were. Some empathy would have shown that she shares in their frustration. Or she could have given some indication that there was a way forward, a better future ahead. As well, she did not pay enough attention to the questions that came her way afterward and seemed to stumble over the answers. Her thoughts were thrown off by her jittery feelings inside.

Some people excel at reading their own emotions. They can distinguish between physical symptoms and thought-provoked reactions to stress. They can focus on the symptoms—jittery stomach, throbbing headache, sweaty palms, racing heartbeats, and they can understand the thoughts that are leading to the emotions that are leading to the physical reactions. By identifying emotions and managing their thinking, they can take more control over their reactions. They can exercise control through distractions, such as meditation, breathing exercises, or mindfulness, or by questioning the assumptions leading to the trouble-making thoughts, or even by redefining the situation. On the other hand, if it's actual physical complaints, perhaps the right medication can ease the pain.

We tend to underestimate how important our emotions can be in not only getting through our day, but in getting to where we want to go in life. We refer to knowing your feelings in the moment as Emotional Self-Awareness. I find that people who are successful in life tend to be not only good at recognizing exactly how they feel about other people, things, and situations, but they tend to know themselves as well. That is, they know their strengths and weaknesses and how to best deal with them. Knowing your strengths and weaknesses, and having the right amount of confidence is referred to as Self-Regard. Truly successful leaders also have a sense of how they are doing in terms of their life plan. They know, in their gut, that they are doing the kind of work they love to do, living the life they chose, and pursuing learning experiences that reinforce their work-life choices. They also, along the way, contribute to other people's success. We refer to this as Self-Actualization.

Emotional Self-Awareness: Know Your Feelings

Let's start at the micro-level—by focusing on the basic feelings we experience. We will then work our way up to the macro level, or larger picture of knowing ourselves. People who can better self-identify their emotional states tend to have a more advanced emotional vocabulary. Not only do they know the words that differentiate one emotion from another—such as anger versus frustration or anxiety versus fear versus anticipation—but they tend to experience emotions on multiple levels. Emotions can be experienced through our senses—visually (think of a beach scene), auditory (imagine the music from *Jaws*), sensory (imagine the feeling of a slithery eel), or smell (imagine a perfume you enjoy). Each of these experiences can be tied to specific emotions, and some people are skilled at quickly associating their experience with an appropriate emotion.

These people that can better self-identify their emotions know what various emotions look like (body language, facial expression), and feel like in bodily sensations (butterflies in stomach, sweating, trembling hands). Further, they can also attribute sounds (loud, quiet, grinding, soothing) tastes (salty or sweet) and smells (pine scented or rancid) to emotional experiences. Emotions have many unique memory tags for all of us. For example, we can likely all remember the joy of the first time we tasted our mother's French toast, or the disgust the first time we tried drinking ginger beer. However, the detail with which these sensations remain is influenced by our self-awareness.

Interestingly, there is evidence that these memory tags could be localized to specific areas of the brain. In 1934, Canadian neurosurgeon Wilder Penfield pioneered the use of local anesthetics in brain surgery.[1] He specialized in treating epileptic patients surgically while still conscious. He is most famously remembered by the quote, "Dr. Penfield. I smell burnt toast," from Mrs. Gold, one of his patients undergoing brain surgery.

His technique, referred to as the Montreal procedure, involved destroying nerve cells in the part of the brain where the seizure originated. He could locate the part of the brain by asking patients what they experienced as he probed and stimulated various points in the brain. In Mrs. Gold's case, she smelled burned toast just prior to her seizures. When his probe stimulated a specific part in her temporal lobe, she recalled the burned-toast memory. While not all patients have experienced specific emotions tied to an identified spot in the brain, there seems to be enough evidence that we retain or "tag" many of our emotional experiences.

Taking a completely different approach to looking at the connection between emotion and memory, there are several researchers looking at the connection between music and nostalgia. Apparently, music provides us with one of the strongest links to reviving memories of the past. Fredrick Barrett and his colleagues at the University of California, Davis, completed a study in which subjects listened to music from when they were young after completing several mood and personality surveys.[2] While some people were more nostalgia prone than others, they found that listening to meaningful music from the past increased people's joy *and* sadness, while listening to less relevant music from the past resulted in irritation.

We all have feelings stored away in our brains that are associated with events, people, and circumstances. These emotions range from joy and happiness to fear, disgust, and anger. Some of us are better able to recall these emotions and reexperience them. Others spend their lives suppressing many past emotional experiences.

By gaining awareness and analyzing your feelings and thoughts you will then be better able to take control of your emotions and modify them as needed. For example, knowing that your frustration comes from thinking you can't change the circumstances, such as the financial results at work, you may try channeling the frustration into a more motivating emotion, such as a bit of excitement or challenge. That may lead you toward looking at ways you may, in fact, be able to come up with creative solutions, such as enlisting employees into looking for ways to save money/reduce spending, and looking at new opportunities for customers or products and services. You might want to meet with some of your more senior staff to help you look for solutions, or perhaps set up a special committee involving employees in helping find solutions. Remember, your emotions can be a call to action, as opposed to a reason to withdraw.

Changing Your Perception of Stress

Being aware of your stress is the first step in managing it. Often we first become aware of our physical cues: our heart rate increases, we get butterflies in our stomach, our skin may become flushed, our muscles tense, we start to sweat, and our voice suddenly gets louder. You can try and control your feelings, even fight them, but that doesn't tend to work. In fact, the symptoms may get worse once we get anxious about our lack of control over the anxiety symptoms.

Another way to deal with these situations is to change your perception—your thoughts or interpretation about what is happening. How you interpret the symptoms, for example, can affect how you deal with anxiety. Instead of Joanne focusing on her speedy heart rate and sweaty palms and instantly connecting it to her fear of public speaking, and then worrying about all the things that can go wrong, she could have restructured her thoughts. She could feel her symptoms and then reinterpret them as part of the excitement of a new challenge. She could then try to revisualize her presentation as a great leadership encounter that she can conquer.

Looking at her experience as a challenge rather than a threat can make a big difference. For example, Joanne could focus on viewing this as a new learning trial. She could see it as an opportunity to try some new approaches in her presentation, such as new slides, new format, more interaction with employees, new kinds of information to present, more requests for feedback and suggestions.

By restructuring the experience, you can change the "fear" response to one of excitement. Those butterflies in the stomach, or a faster heartbeat could be reinterpreted as cues for a new, exciting adventure, similar to the excitement an athlete feels before a big game. The same physiological response, but a different mind-set, can lead to completely different results.

Research has documented the benefits of this approach. Andreas Keller and his colleagues published a report that examined surveys of nearly 186 million U.S. adults who participated in the 1998 National Health Interview, which was linked to the National Death Index.[3] In the survey data, 55 percent of participants reported experiencing moderate to high levels of stress during the previous year. Almost 34 percent (33.7 percent) indicated that this stress had negatively impacted their health to some extent during that time.

The researchers found that both higher perceived stress and the belief that stress negatively influences health were independently associated with worse physical and mental health outcomes. Those who reported higher stress and beliefs that stress negatively influenced their health had a 43 percent increased risk for premature death. In other words, people who interpret their stress as not having a negative impact on their lives have a better chance of living longer. The study supports the idea of reappraising the stressors that are in your life. It supports using interventions such as cognitive restructuring and problem solving techniques to manage stress.

The authors conclude, "Stress appraisal plays an important role in determining health outcomes. These findings also suggest that perceived stress and beliefs about the impact of stress on health might work synergistically to increase risk for premature mortality."[4]

So, whether you have taken the EQ-i 2.0 to gauge your emotional self-awareness, this is an area that always has room for improvement. If you find that recognizing and understanding your emotions are a challenge for you, you might want to consider exercises such as mindfulness or meditation. These kinds of exercises teach you to slow down and focus on the experience of your emotions.

Looking at Self-Awareness and Self-Regard

There have been some recent challenges to our common notion of self-awareness. Psychologist Robert Hogan framed it as Freud versus Socrates,[5] the idea being that most of us think of self-awareness as introspection, similar to the ideas Freud pioneered in his work on psychoanalysis. By introspection we get at how we see ourselves, which can often be different from how we really are (or at least as we are seen by others). However, our self-perception may be somewhat flawed by the unrealistic view we have of ourselves. Hogan refers to this as our identity, which may be self-fulfilling or self-sabotaging.

On the other hand, how others see us is referred to as our reputation. This may be closer to Socrates's version of self-awareness. Rather than simply introspecting on ourselves, as Socrates said, "To know thyself" goes beyond self-reflection. In the Greek concept, self-knowledge means being aware of your personal performance limits and understanding your strengths and shortcomings. And that kind of self-knowledge comes from experience, not introspection. That experience goes beyond your own self-reflection and considers evidence from others as well as your successes and failures in navigating the world.

This helps explain why some people's self-report on 360 assessment measures (360s are where your self-rating is compared to other people's ratings of you, such as subordinates, peers, supervisors, and so on) fail to match the report that others make on them. Now it may be that some of your thoughts and beliefs cannot be observed by others and therefore are not available for them to accurately evaluate. However, most 360 assessments try to compensate for this by being based on observable behaviors. In any event, people at work are often rewarded (or punished) because of how their performance at work is seen by others, most often their superiors. Their self-perception can be important, but your fate is often based on the judgment of others.

The ideal self-awareness, or self-perception, would be one that considers the way you see yourself along with objective data (your performance in life) and the views of others who know you well. In our EQ-i 2.0 model we refer to this form of self-understanding as Self-Regard.

How Does Self-Regard Relate to Leadership?

Clearly, some people are much more aware of their behaviors, and how they are perceived, than others. When it comes to leaders, how does their degree of self-regard affect their leadership abilities? An interesting study by Virginia K. Bratton and her colleagues at Montana State University looked at this issue.[6] They looked at 146 managers and supervisors and 1,314 of their subordinates at a North American manufacturing unit of a large international technology company. They asked these managers to rate their own management style and effectiveness in terms of how transformational they believed they were as leaders.

Transformational leadership is regarded as one of the most effective management styles in today's leadership research literature. Specifically, transformational leadership has four components. These include individualized consideration, intellectual stimulation, inspirational motivation, and idealized influence. These are factors that have been shown in many studies to be important for successful leadership in today's world.

What are these leadership factors? Individualized consideration involves demonstrating genuine concern for the needs and feelings of each employee. Intellectual stimulation measures a leader's ability to challenge followers to be more creative and innovative in their work. Inspirational motivation is the ability to motivate and inspire people to perform at work. Idealized influence looks at how well a leader serves as a model for subordinates, basically, "walking the walk."

In Bratton's study, not only did leaders rate their own ability in these skills, but they were also rated by their followers. One of the big questions in research using self-report tools in general and specifically in emotional intelligence, such as the EQ-i 2.0, is whether leaders tend to overestimate their own abilities. While the EQ-i 2.0 self-report version was built with special scales embedded to detect most types of faking or embellishment, there have been few research studies evaluating whether there is an overabundance of leaders who overrate themselves in the workplace. Bratton and her colleagues found that they could place leaders into one of four buckets based on the comparison of their self- and follower-ratings of transformational leadership.

First, there were two buckets with those leaders who accurately rated themselves. In these cases, both the leader and their followers agreed that the leader was either a good leader or a poor leader. They found that 31 leaders agreed with their subordinates that they were good leaders on the dimensions measured. There were 23 leaders who agreed with their followers that they were poor leaders.

Secondly, there were those leaders who saw themselves differently from the way their subordinates experienced them. There were 48 leaders who underestimated their ability as a leader when compared to their followers' ratings. That is, their followers saw them as better leaders than they saw themselves.

Then there were 44 managers who fit into the box that self-report measurement critics often refer to, the overreporters. These are people who overestimate their leadership abilities when compared to the way their followers rate them. They represent approximately 33 percent of leaders, not quite the 99 percent that the critics of self-report measures like to claim. We will see in Chapter 15 that this pattern also applies to self-report emotional intelligence.

What can we learn about each of these groups of leaders? One of the strongest relationships they found was with the leaders who underestimated their leadership abilities. These leaders had the highest ratings of transformational leadership from their followers. They also had the strongest relationship between their emotional intelligence scores and their follower ratings. It's possible that these leaders have lower self-ratings because they are more modest, or humble as leaders. This type of leader can be effective in many ways. But there can also be drawbacks in being too humble, as we will see.

Managers who agreed with their followers (both good and bad leaders) also had positive relationships between their emotional intelligence scores and their follower's ratings, but not quite as strong as the humble leaders. The overestimators, however, showed a negative relationship between emotional intelligence and their follower's ratings. That is, the higher they rated their emotional intelligence, the lower their subordinates rated their leadership skills. Their tendency to overrate themselves may be part of numerous behaviors that tend to put them in a more negative light. These may also be the type of managers who try "looking good" instead of "doing good" and play up to their superiors. Sometimes this is referred to as "managing up." These are the 33 percent of leaders that we most likely need to watch for as they can be harmful in organizations.

Managers who agreed with their followers about their leadership skills (good or bad) were highest in the interpersonal skills component of emotional intelligence. The "good" managers were high in self-perception (referred to as Intrapersonal in the older version EQ-i) and decision making (referred to as Adaptability in the old version of the EQ-i). In other words, part of being a good manager means being self-aware and adaptable.

The managers who agree with their subordinates that they are poor leaders score higher in self-awareness, but lower in most other emotional intelligence scales. This may, in fact, be healthy, and contrary to what many might have predicted. These managers are aware of their poor management ability, or social skills, but they just may not know what to do about it. We see this profile in managers who are new and not yet sure of their management abilities, and in managers who have not been trained in managing others. Some of these people may have been promoted for the wrong reasons—they had strong technical skills—programming, sales, finance, or legal but have not been prepared, or may not know how, to manage other people.

Self-Regard and Toxic Leadership

Another group of researchers looked at self-regard and leadership but used a different methodology and population. This work was undertaken by Jonathan Bryson of the International Coaches Federation together with the U.S. Army.[7] Looking more specifically at interpersonal competencies of leaders and self-awareness, the study used a series of focus groups where soldiers were interviewed about their experiences with various leaders.

A large group of officers and noncommissioned officers (NCOs) from three army installations were questioned about their fellow soldiers and leaders. As in the previous study, leaders were divided into four different groups. There were two groups with good agreement between leader and follower (i.e., they agreed with followers on their leadership ability) and two with poor agreement (i.e., they did not match their followers in how they rated their leadership effectiveness).

The groups were described as:

1. *Underestimators*—"I don't think I have great interpersonal skills," but behaviorally demonstrates good interpersonal skills to followers.
2. *Overestimators*—"I think I have great interpersonal skills," but their behaviors don't show it based on follower's experience.
3. *Self-aware ineffective*—"I don't think I have great interpersonal skills," and their behaviors show it to followers.
4. *Self-aware effective*—"I think I have great interpersonal skills," and their behaviors show it to followers.

Based on their work, each of these four leadership groups come with their own pros and cons. The most effective leaders in this case were found to be the ones who were both accurately self-aware and seen as effective by subordinates.

Let's start by looking at the two groups that have lower agreement with their followers.

First, the positive attributes of leaders who are *underestimators* are that they tend to be team players, they provide subordinates' opportunities to shine, they delegate well to subordinates, and they give credit to subordinates where due. On the other hand, they tend to make poor decisions, they avoid dealing with conflict, allowing situations to deteriorate, and they don't ask for help when needed.

The *overestimators* have few positive traits as leaders. In fact, one of the best things about them is that they act as examples of what *not* to do for their subordinates. However, they can motivate followers and they are often eager to take charge of new situations. The negative characteristics of this group are that they lack flexibility in decision making, take credit for the work of others, and shuffle blame to others when things go wrong.

Then there are the two groups of leaders with accurate agreement with their followers. Those who are *self-aware and effective* interpersonally are good at developing subordinates. They are effective communicators and they foster trust and cohesion. On the negative side, they can appear over confident and over optimistic. They may have unrealistic expectations of others. These expectations of others have some resemblance to the stories reported about Steve Jobs and his subordinates. He was known for pushing subordinates beyond what they thought they were realistically capable of.

The *self-aware ineffective* leaders were identified as having some positive traits as well. For example, they tend to make others look good through their bad behavior. Once again, they provide followers with an example of what *not* to do. They also can create a negative cohesion among subordinates—in other words, an us-versus-them kind of mentality. On the negative side, they tend to take on too much work, likely due to their overconfidence. They don't seem to be able to keep their emotions in check, and they are likely to avoid uncomfortable situations.

Does Leader Self-Perception Relate to Subordinates' Performance?

While it seems that there are many advantages to having leaders high in self-regard, the real question is whether it relates to organizational performance. In a study carried out by Prajya Vidyarthi and her colleagues[8] this was the primary question. They looked at 86 managers and 350 of their employees working on assembly lines in a large multinational manufacturing organization in India. All the managers rated their own levels of emotional self-awareness. Their emotional self-awareness was then compared to the productivity ratings of their direct reports. Each employee had been rated on the quality of their actual performance at work. What they found was that the leaders' emotional self-awareness was directly related to and accounted for 24.3 percent of the workers' variance in job performance. In other words, employees with leaders who had greater emotional self-awareness were more productive. Self-aware leaders do make a difference. The study even suggests using emotional intelligence, and specifically self-awareness, as one of the selection criteria for leaders.

Discovering Your Self-Regard

There are various ways to learn more about your own self-regard. An easy way is through an emotional intelligence assessment, either self-report or 360. One of the exercises I use when working with leaders who have taken the EQ-i 2.0 is to have them estimate their scores on each of the 15 subscales of the inventory before they get back their scored reports. In my experience, most leaders believe they know their strengths and weaknesses well. However, it's one thing to look at your relative strengths and challenges, but there's an additional dimension to looking at how you compare to a large sample of other leaders. Leaders can see how they stack up against others because their EQ-i 2.0 scores are based on our large sample of normative data. Once they review their reports they quickly discover whether they tend to be over-, under-, or precise estimators of their emotional skills in the different areas. For many leaders, this is their first insight into how they see themselves in comparison to other leaders who have self-assessed.

This self-perception discovery is even more dramatic when you add 360 assessment results. That is, when subordinates, peers, supervisors, and others have also rated the leader on the very same 15 factors. When the Leadership EQ360 is used, I also ask leaders to estimate how their subordinates, peers, and others may have rated them in each of the 15 areas. I especially ask them to focus on what they see as their top three strengths and their top three challenges. This is a powerful eye-opener for most leaders. Very few leaders,

I find, accurately rate themselves. Even fewer know how they are perceived by the people they regularly interact with.

I will be presenting data on thousands of Leadership EQ360s and the patterns we find by gender, geographic region, and industry in a later chapter. What do we know about leaders who accurately rate themselves and those who correctly match what others think of them? We will further discuss these findings.

What Do We Know about People Who Score High in Self-Regard?

Leaders high in self-regard are confident leaders. They feel good about themselves and where they are in life. They tend to be in tune with their emotions. That means they can recognize what they're feeling emotionally and can predict how they might feel in certain situations. Further, they can detect nuances in their emotions. Understanding these differences can be helpful when making both large and small decisions. As we will learn in a later chapter, whether you know it or not, all your decisions are affected by your emotions.

On the other hand, leaders who score low in self-perception are not in touch with their feelings. They tend to lack inner strength and confidence. They often feel insecure and will sometimes come across to others as erratic or not in control. Instead of using emotions as a guide to making choices and managing stress, their emotions either elude them or are likely to confuse them. They often have difficulty understanding the emotional landscape and this hinders their ability to be effective as a leader.

Emotional Self-Regard: What to Do about It

Leaders who are emotionally self-aware have many advantages. First, they know how to accurately label and describe their emotions. They understand even slight nuances between emotions. And, an important aspect for leaders, they are conscious of the impact their emotions have on their performance and on others. Leaders strong in this area know how to use emotions to gather information.

Mary, a senior director I worked with, was always encouraging her subordinates to come to her with solutions to problems, not just the problems themselves. She trusted most of her staff in their ability to solve problems. However, whenever Graham came to her with a problem he felt he was solving, Mary could feel her stomach muscles tighten, her breathing slow down, and her mind starting to race with distracting thoughts. One day Jill, when Graham was away, asked Mary why she was always so short-tempered with Graham when he was trying to help her.

Mary was quite shocked to hear that. She saw herself as a listening person who treated everyone equally and fairly. She felt she was more patient with Graham than with many others, although she often disagreed with his solutions. She tried to prove to Jill how she let him try certain solutions even when she disagreed with them.

"That's true," replied Jill, "but then you pounce on him letting him know you knew all along it was the wrong way to go."

Mary never thought of it that way, but now she could make a conscious effort to deal with her impatient behavior by paying more attention to her feelings. Mary learned to pay more attention to her feelings when dealing with Graham. As soon as she felt herself getting tense, she reminded herself to let go, relax, and hear him out. That way she began to focus more on what he was saying and where he was coming from.

I then helped her learn to act more like a coach. Instead of interjecting with what could go wrong, she waited until he made his point, and then she would ask him questions that would ensure he thought through all the possible outcomes of his suggestions. Over time he came to her with better, more thought out solutions. Knowing that he would be asked good, solid questions, rather than be pounced on, also increased his motivation to do a better job.

By using her feelings as a signal, just like a traffic light, she could work more effectively with Graham. Before long her behavior changes became apparent to other staff members as well. Rather than having to witness Mary's predictable hammer coming down on Graham, and the embarrassment of him trying to save face, the whole atmosphere had changed. People became more comfortable and more willing to share their suggested solutions to problems.

Sometimes it doesn't take a major organizational change to get improvements in staff engagement and performance. The leader's behavior, and changes in their behavior, can lead to significant improvements throughout the organization.

Know Thyself—Self-Actualization

The third level of self-perception zooms out to a more comprehensive view of who we are and where we are going in life. Self-actualized people know they are in the right place, or at least going in the right direction in life. They are comfortable with who they are and are doing the things in life that matter to them the most. As well, they have a positive influence on others. Few people are fortunate enough to be fully self-actualized. That is, they are actively learning, developing, and contributing to others in areas they are passionate about. There are small steps you can take to develop this area. For example, you can pay attention to your life's passion and spend more time developing it, whether it's music, photography, yoga, martial arts, tennis, cooking, painting, gardening, skiing, or whatever.

Carlos had just celebrated his first year as the manager of the sales division of a large distribution company. It took him seven years of success as a front-line salesperson, steadily building accounts and territories. He had always aspired to be a manager as that is how he gauged success. However, something wasn't sitting right with him. He was restless in his management position. He didn't feel satisfied.

Carlos was wise enough to request a coach to work with him. The coach, getting to know Carlos better, had administered an EQ-i 2.0 to him after their first meeting. One of Carlos' lowest areas was his self-actualizing score. The coach was quite surprised after just hearing about how long Carlos had coveted the leadership position in sales. This led to an in-depth discussion about where Carlos saw himself in life. It became clear that the manager position was something that Carlos wanted for the prestige, status, and his own ego. However, the job itself gave him no satisfaction. After a year, in fact, it started feeling tedious.

He resented having to deal with all the sales reps' issues and complaints, especially when they were below their agreed-upon targets. After all, it wasn't that long ago that he was a sales rep. He could manage his territories and quotas. What's wrong with this group, who were once his peers? Now he must have serious discussions with them about performance issues. He then has to justify to his boss why the sales results aren't where they expected them to be.

Managing his former peers, some of whom also applied for the manager position and were somewhat resentful, putting together budgets, attending management meetings, writing reports, and a series of other administrative tasks were not what he wanted to spend his time doing. He missed schmoozing with customers, being on the road, visiting with prospects, and the excitement of closing the big sale. Nobody prepared Carlos for, nor did he think about, what the manager position would be like.

Being a sales rep and being a manager of sales reps are completely different functions. Somehow Carlos remembers being much happier as a sales rep than as a manager of other sales reps; unfortunately, it took Carlos a prolonged and costly journey to learn this. This is a lesson that is quite common and can cost an organization significant time and money and in this case caused Carlos to reset his career path.

Gauging Self-Actualization

Assessing your self-actualization can help determine if you are on the right path for you. If you have taken the EQ-i 2.0 you will already have a good idea if you are satisfied with your life plan. If this is an area you need to develop, there are several steps you can take to get on track. People who achieve high self-actualization understand their basic values, beliefs, and preferences. It's as though they have a life mission and work each day to fulfill that mission.

You probably already have a gut feeling about your life satisfaction level. How you feel about your work, relationships, family, social life, level of fitness, contribution to others, leisure time, hobbies, learning and development, involvement in your community, and your religious or spiritual life, all contribute to your self-actualization. Think about each of these areas. Consider how you would rate your satisfaction, from 1 to 5, in each of these life areas:

	Unhappy				Very Happy
	1	2	3	4	5
Work/school					
Intimate relationships					
Close friends					
Casual relationships					
Family					
Social life					
Fitness					

	Unhappy				Very Happy
	1	2	3	4	5
Contribution to others					
Leisure time					
Travel/vacation					
Hobbies					
Learning and development					
Community involvement					
Religious/spiritual life					

Now that you've reflected on these aspects of your life, what should you do? First, you should celebrate your successes. Focus on the areas you feel happiest with. Think about what it is that makes you happy in these areas. Think about how long you have been happy in each of these areas, and how you have maintained this level of satisfaction over time.

Then look at the least happy areas of your life. What have been the challenges for you in these areas? Are there goals you could set for yourself in each of these areas? What has prevented you from reaching these goals in the past? What changes would you have to make in your life to achieve these goals?

Some of the most self-actualized people I have met have been well rounded in their lives. While their work was important to them, and they tend to be in leadership roles, their work does not consume their lives. They have an internal GPS that seems to guide them from one activity in their life to another. They are focused and goal oriented but not obsessed. They also are passionate about the things they choose to do. If you strive to increase your happiness levels in the areas above that are most important to you, you will become more self-actualized in your life and, most likely, a much better leader.

EQ Leader: Things to Think About

1. How well do you know your own emotions and how do they guide your behavior?
2. Are there ways you can get to know your emotions better—meditation, mindfulness?

(*continued*)

(*continued*)

3. How confident are you in your abilities at work?
4. Do you come off to people at work as overconfident?
5. Do your find your (lack of) confidence hinders you from getting ahead?
6. Do people at work think of you as humble?
7. Are there things in life you feel you are missing?
8. If so, what? And what's stopping you from getting there?
9. What would be your ideal job?
10. What about that ideal job appeals to you (e.g., freedom, money, doing cool things, travel, meeting people)?
11. How could you get more of that in your current position?

PART II

Self-Expression and Leadership

Self-Expression and Leadership

Emotional Expression
The ability to express one's feelings verbally and nonverbally

Assertiveness
The ability to express feelings, beliefs, and thoughts in a nondestructive way

Independence
The ability to be self-directed and free of emotional dependency on others

Chapter 6

Self-Expression

Communication through Words and Action

The challenge of leadership is to be strong, but not rude; be kind, but not weak; be bold, but not bully; be thoughtful, but not lazy; be humble, but not timid; be proud, but not arrogant; have humor, but without folly.

—JIM ROHN

Great leaders are almost always great simplifiers, who can cut through argument, debate, and doubt to offer a solution everybody can understand.

—GENERAL COLIN POWELL

Communication was never one of David's strong points. As the company CEO, he knew exactly what message he wanted to give and where he wanted his team to go, but he often struggled in getting their buy-in to his ideas. He wanted to develop a new line of products, but his executive team felt it would be costly, have a high risk of return on investment, and be disruptive to the organization's ongoing projects.

"This doesn't really fit in our strategic plan," said Ari, the CFO.

"I know that," David replied, somewhat annoyed, "but I think we need to do this."

Jill, the marketing manager added, "But we haven't budgeted the costs of a launch and additional trade show attendance."

"We can find the money," he fired back, getting more frustrated.

Phil, the production manager pointed out, "We will have to stop work on some of our products already in the pipeline to push those through. You sure you want to delay the releases that are already scheduled? That might hurt our revenue projections."

"I know that. Yes, I think it's worth it. Let's just move ahead," retorted David, now verging on anger.

Whether David's decision was right or wrong we can't really say at this point. However, it's clear that he has not done a great job of convincing his team of the new direction. His presentation style, his apparent lack of control over his emotions, all contribute to both his own and his team's frustration. At this point, they stop challenging him over fear that his anger will explode. They decide to go along even though they believe there is a high likelihood of failure and disruption to ongoing activities.

The good news is that his team feels comfortable challenging his proposal, even though they eventually gave in. In some companies I've visited this scenario would play out quite differently. The senior team would immediately acquiesce, believing the plan would fail, yet they would reluctantly move forward. In some cases, they would passive-aggressively sabotage it—just because they felt left out of the decisions that went into it or disliked the way it was presented to them.

How could David have communicated his plan differently? For one thing, he could have started out exploring the rationale for his idea in a way that involves the team. It might go something like this.

"You know how we've talked about all the disruptive technologies that have hurt businesses similar to ours?" David began.

"Oh yes," said Jill. "Like the online build-to-order system that Harrison's put out last year."

"Yes," Phil added, "and how that completely knocked Delta out of the market, in less than a year."

"Exactly. Well, I've been thinking about some of our products lately and it seems to me that we might be at risk in a similar way," said David. "Just think about how the same kind of disruption could knock us out of the market."

Ari jumped in, "Well I've been wondering about a few of the projects we have in the pipeline and whether they will survive in the digital world."

As the discussion continued, and everyone was on the same page, David began to lay the groundwork for a new product in an uncharted direction for the team to consider, something out of their comfort zone. Once everyone was in the right frame of mind, and looking for solutions to an agreed-upon threat, it was easier for David to make the case of trying something new. It may not have evolved exactly as David had envisioned it; however, with all the active discussion and contributions from the team, the new product development morphed into something a bit smaller, with less risk, but still able to test the marketplace. As well, and most importantly, he now had the buy-in of his senior team.

Good leaders can communicate well. That doesn't mean they need to be great public speakers; rather, they are just effective at making meaningful connections with others. There are three emotionally intelligent aspects of effective communication or self-expression. The first is emotional expression—the ability to use the right emotion in the right proportion at the right time. Expressing emotions well helps you be seen as more authentic and honest in your approach. The second is assertiveness—expressing the way you think, feel, and believe in a cooperative way. Assertiveness is a skill that requires balance—too much and you might get what you want, but sacrifice the relationship; too little and you preserve the relationship but might not get what you want. And finally, independence—your ability to "walk the talk." This includes demonstrating you mean what you say. Your actions are often a tell-tale sign of your true beliefs. Your ability to act independently says a lot about who you are.

Your Emotional Expression

One of the historical starting points or origins of emotional intelligence as a field of study can be traced back to the work of Charles Darwin.[1] Known for his work in evolution, Darwin also wrote a groundbreaking book on emotions 13 years after his publication on evolution. The book, titled *The Expression of Emotions in Man and Animals*, contained hundreds of photographs of emotional expressions in humans and animals. The central thesis of the book was that the expression of emotions—happiness, sadness, anger, disgust—was not only universal across cultures but also among many animals, as well as people. Much of this should not be surprising to those of you who own pets. Knowing when your pet is happy or sad, for example, is probably pretty obvious to a pet owner.

But Darwin's book was very controversial in its time and remained in dispute for many years. The anthropologist Margaret Mead was one of those who was very outspoken against Darwin's theories. The anthropologists, in general, argued that we were born as blank slates, and it was our culture that determined our emotional and social behaviors. Darwin had argued that there are common emotions that were innate in both man and animals. Only recently has the evidence accumulated enough for Darwin's views to be more widely accepted.

Before the anthropologists rejected his work, however, he had a great deal of opposition from the religious community, who were also opposed to his theory of evolution. In fact, one of the ways he tried to sell his views on emotion was to carefully claim that there were "human traits in animals" and not say that humans had "animal traits." So, the science of emotions was upended twice, first by religious belief, and second by academic dogma.

Another important aspect of Darwin's thesis had to do with the evolutionary purpose of emotions. He described them as a signaling system that alerted others (of the same species) as a form of communication. One example would be the expression of fear and its purpose of warning others of impending danger. Sheep, for example, have been found to recognize various emotions in other sheep and can interpret emotions of others to know when a predator is approaching the flock.[2] Other emotions, such as the expression of sadness, for example, would communicate the need for comfort, and so on.

While we no longer live in the woods in packs, the same signaling system is equally important in today's leadership environments. Subordinates regularly search their leader's demeanor for various emotional signs. Signals can indicate approval, disapproval, continuing on a safe path, changing direction, appreciation, disdain, surprise, excitement, "I told you so," and many other emotional messages. Many leaders do not verbalize these signals well, which can force followers to often rely on the leader's nonverbal messaging, whether intentional or not, for clarity. Even in cases where messages are delivered verbally—"the results this quarter have been great"—facial expressions, such as a frown, or tone of voice, posture, and other nonverbal cues can give a different story. Which are you more likely to believe?

The importance of emotional expression in leaders is not often emphasized in leadership training programs; yet, it can have important repercussions. It's not hard to picture the effects of emotional expression in leaders when we think of George Patton rallying up his troops, Martin Luther King Jr. giving inspiration to civil rights activists, or even Bill Clinton expressing shame over his infidelity. Several research studies have systematically examined the effects of leaders' emotional expression.

There's already a lot of evidence that leaders can express positive emotions such as enthusiasm (an active positive emotion) and satisfaction (a passive positive emotion) to motivate followers. But what are the effects of a leader's negative emotions on followers? In one study looking at this, Kristi Lewis of the California School of Professional Psychology,[3] set up a situation in which a CEO delivered a message using a specific negative tone. She looked at the effect of sadness (a passive negative emotion) and anger (an active negative emotion) on followers. Specifically, she looked at what effect these emotions would have on the feelings of followers, and, perhaps even more importantly, what impact it would have on their ratings of leader effectiveness.

In the study, 368 subjects watched one of six videos with a male or female CEO of a company delivering a presentation. Controlling for various effects (such as gender and emotion, by design), each video showed the leader presenting the company's poor financial results for the year. The CEO then requested each employee to work harder in order to improve the company's performance. The words used were basically the same in each of the presentations. However, the videos varied in that the CEO was either male or female, and the tone used by the CEO was either neutral, sad, or angry.

The leader's emotional tone, or affective expression, had a direct influence on how the observers felt and in how they rated the effectiveness of the CEO. The participants had a lower arousal level (they felt less enthusiastic, more fatigued) when they experienced the message with a sad tone. On the other hand, they felt more aroused (more nervous, less relaxed) after being exposed to the angry leader.

One reason suggested for lower emotional levels after a sad message delivery was that a sad delivery indicates that there is little that can be done to improve the situation. It implies the company performance decline is stable and cannot be fixed. On the other hand, when a leader displays anger, anger may be more of a call to action. There's still a chance to turn things around. The financial decline may be due to outside forces and we need to unite and fight these external threats.

When it came to leader effectiveness, however, the story was somewhat different. The leader using a neutral tone was rated as significantly more competent than the sad or angry CEO. There was an interesting gender effect. Male leaders received lower effectiveness ratings when expressing sadness compared to neutrality, while female leaders received lower ratings when expressing either sadness or anger. In other words, for female CEOs they were rated most effectively if they expressed a neutral tone. The main difference here being that it may be more acceptable for male leaders than female leaders to express anger.

A related area of importance for leaders is the use of negative emotions in times of crisis. After all, it's usually in times of crisis that a leader either shines or fails. Consider the contrasting examples of James Burke, the CEO of Johnson & Johnson during the Tylenol tampering crisis in the fall of 1982 and Tony Hayward, the CEO of BP during the oil spill in the Gulf of Mexico in April of 2010.

In the Burke example, seven people died near the city of Chicago due to cyanide poisoning that was linked to Tylenol capsules. It turns out that someone had tampered with the bottles and inserted the poison. It had nothing to do directly with Johnson & Johnson. Without a contingency plan to deal with emergencies like this, Burke instinctively made a number of public appearances at the time. He immediately got on TV and condemned the poisonings. He spoke emotionally about the situation and had tears in his eyes. He also took action, recalling all the Tylenol bottles in the market and then introducing a safety barrier that would be added to all new bottles of Tylenol. Burke's immediate action not only preserved Johnson & Johnson's reputation, it saved the Tylenol brand from demise. In this case, the emotions expressed were pertinent to the situation.

Compare that to Hayward, who was slow to react when the accidental oil spill occurred on *Deepwater Horizon*. His first response was reported to be, "What the hell did we do to deserve this?"[4] In May, weeks after he knew about the spill, he falsely reported that it was relatively tiny, knowing that wasn't the case. Later on, when questioned by reporters, he gave his half-hearted apology, "We're sorry for the massive disruption it's caused to their lives. . . . There's no one who wants this thing over more than I do," followed by the now famous line, "I would like my life back." This showed little concern for the people and environmental damages caused. Hayward was subsequently dismissed from BP and the episode ended up costing billions of dollars, as well as significant reputational damage.

The role of sadness and anger in CEO delivered messages about a crisis was looked at in a study by Juan Madera and Brent Smith at the University of Houston and Rice University.[5] In their research 322 employees from various organizations and occupations (accountants, teachers, nurses, etc.) were presented a message from a company CEO related to the recall of a failed product that was reportedly linked to cancer.

The leader expressed a specific negative emotional tone, either anger, sadness, or both anger and sadness and either accepted responsibility for the situation or did not accept responsibility. Basically, they found that emotional expression was important in how the leader was evaluated. Leaders who responded to the crisis expressing anger and sadness or sadness alone were seen as more effective leaders than those who expressed anger alone. The leader's emotional response also affected the followers' emotions. This was especially true when the leader expressed anger, in which case there was a negative impact on the feelings of the followers. This in turn resulted in negative ratings of the effectiveness of the leader.

In this case, sadness signaled empathy and concern and was seen as appropriate in the situation. Anger was only acceptable if the leader also demonstrated sadness, indicating concern about the situation. A leader who accepted responsibility for the crises was seen more favorably than one who did not. In this study, only a male leader was used.

What Emotions Motivate Your Staff?

One of the most frequent questions I get from leaders is about how to motivate their people. What are the right emotions to use to get people inspired? While there are many factors important in motivating people at work, including pay, benefits, work environment, interesting work, amount of work, control over how to do the work, flexible time at work, learning environment, constructive feedback, purposeful work, supportive leadership and more, let's start with the basics. The emotional tone you set at work is an important step in creating an optimal work environment.

Extensive research has been carried out on the emotions that are most likely to lead to optimum performance. Researchers have looked at the productivity associated with various emotional states.[6] By projecting the right emotions into your workplace and avoiding the wrong ones, you can increase the chances of improving the performance in your workplace.

In terms of emotions, people who are motivated by hope and pride do significantly better than people who are driven by anger, shame, boredom, anxiety, and hopelessness. The important message here is that your emotions influence your ability to achieve your goals and help your workforce reach theirs. Emotions have a significant mediating effect on success. For example, there is a relation between emotions expressed by a leader and the amount of effort a follower is willing to contribute through their work. Also, the better your ability to know which emotions you need, and how to summon them when needed, the more likely you will succeed in your work.

Emotions Not to Use

Anger: "I've been waiting two weeks for this report! What is the matter with you! @##."

Shame: "You are the only one on your team that has failed to produce results."

Boredom: "I'm not giving you any more assignments until you get this one finished. Don't even bother leaving your desk for any breaks until it's done."

Anxiety: "You're going to lose your job if your work doesn't improve."

Hopelessness: "I've given you everything you could possibly need to succeed in this job. You will never amount to anything. You're just a failure."

Emotions That Work

Hope: "I know we can accomplish this, you've been doing so well. You're almost there."

Pride: "You've done great work before. I know you can produce the high quality of work that we pride ourselves on here."

Excitement: "Completing this report will be a great achievement for all of us. It will take us to the next level."

How Can You Better Express Yourself?

The most important aspect in how you come across to others is authenticity. Unless you are an Academy Award winning actor, I don't recommend faking your emotional expressions. There's few things more disconcerting to your subordinates than being inconsistent in your communication with them. If you are delivering bad news, don't try and sugarcoat it. If you are celebrating success, be happy. Mixed messages only encourage confusion.

Your emotions, especially as a leader, are contagious. So if you want your workplace to be a happy, productive place, you as a leader will need to be happy or at least smile, as you make your way through the office, factory, or store. I once had a warehouse shipper tell me about his bosses as I toured a facility. He told me that the president and vice president both came through the warehouse at different times once a day. He explained that he really liked the vice president much better. When I asked why, it turned out that both the vice president and the president only had cursory conversations with him as they passed by, but the vice president was always smiling when he came through the warehouse. The small gesture of smiling did so much to spread a positive mood in employees.

Learning to smile is probably one of the least expensive and most time efficient interventions you can master. But you'll be surprised how noticeable it becomes once you start to use it. The first thing you'll notice is that others will start to smile back. Once they get used to you doing it more frequently, they'll be greeting you with a smile.

Asserting Yourself

Assertiveness is an important aspect of your self-expression. What we mean by assertiveness is the ability to express your thoughts, beliefs, and feelings in a constructive way. Think of two ends of a scale. On one side is passivity. That is, keeping things in or, close to the chest. Not really conveying where you stand on issues or what you feel about things. Leaders who are passive encourage their followers to guess what they might be thinking or feeling. Of course some people are prone to guess the worst scenario. So as a leader, silence isn't considered golden. It rather leads to conjecture, false hopes, negative attributions, and other misinterpretations.

On the other end of the scale is the aggressive leader—the bully. This is the bull in the china shop who causes damage throughout the workplace. This person overstates their thoughts and feelings often, to the point of micromanaging others. Being overly opinionated or giving unwanted advice, even though you are the leader, does not engender loyalty.

Daniel Ames and Francis Flynn at Columbia University carried out a study looking at how people viewed assertiveness in their leaders.[7] Interestingly, the relationship was not simple. In their study, they examined 213 people's ratings of their leaders, and it turned out that assertiveness was a double-edged sword.

The participants mentioned assertiveness (as good or bad) in describing their leader more frequently than intelligence, conscientiousness, or charisma. Managers who were described as too low, or too high, on assertiveness were seen as ineffective leaders. Moderate assertiveness was seen as a factor that facilitated success by opening the door to other positive behaviors. For example, moderately assertive leaders were seen as better at managing conflict, working with teams, motivating others, as well as overall leadership effectiveness and expected future success as a leader.

There was another important component to assertiveness. Leaders who were rated higher in assertiveness were described as better able to get things done. On the other hand, they were seen as lower in their social relationships at work. The leaders who were rated lower in assertiveness were reported as having better social relations but were less effective at getting things done.

One of the other important messages from the study was that assertiveness can be situational. That is, there may be times when it's important for you to be more assertive than other times. For example, when you need to get tasks done, you may be better increasing your assertiveness. This can be accomplished by giving more direction, explaining why you feel this task is important, and saying what your expectation is. Other times, however, team building may be more important, and you may have to step back and not say all of the things you would like to say. In these situations, it's possible that your words might cause conflict or reduce other people's motivation.

Assertiveness is a skill that helps us understand the difference between personality and emotional skills. People are often confused about the difference between personality and emotional intelligence. Research has found that personality characteristics, such as extroversion, neuroticism, and consciousness tend to be stable throughout one's lifetime. That is, if you were outgoing and extroverted as a child, you are likely to still have those traits today and likely will continue to be that way throughout your lifetime, perhaps with minor variation.

Emotional intelligence, however, consists of factors that change throughout your lifetime. In this case, assertiveness. While assertiveness tends to be positively correlated with extroversion, not all extroverts are assertive, and not all introverts lack assertiveness. Assertiveness, while more natural for some people than others, is a learned skill. It's also a critical managerial or leadership skill. This is one of the reasons why coaching, based on emotional intelligence assessment, can be so much more effective than personality testing.

How Assertiveness Impacts Leaders across Cultures

In our work with organizations worldwide, we have found cultural variations among many of the factors of emotional intelligence. One of the big questions in working with organizations across cultures has been how to adapt these factors, especially when we know they differ across cultures. There have been two points of views in working with leaders in different cultures. They are generally referred to as *divergence* and *convergence.*

People who believe in *divergence* feel that a country's national culture is the primary driving force in setting the values and beliefs within the organization. So, if you work in Mexico, or Malaysia, the most important thing is to understand their cultures before you can lead a workforce in those countries. This would hold true even though most multinational corporations have already transplanted people from various other countries into these companies.

There are actual studies that have looked at cultural variations in management styles and they report that between 14 and 35 percent of management style is due to cultural values.[8] The important question is that even though we know that these differences exist (which I'll soon demonstrate), how does that impact the nature of your leadership training for these locations?

The other point of view revolves around *convergence*. According to this point of view, globalization is impacting organizations everywhere. As a result, there are more similarities than differences in how organizations are run, wherever they are. In other words, the business culture overrides the local culture. Terms like "McDonaldization" or "Disneyfication" are used to describe this trend. So according to this view, the leadership skills taught in one country should be no different than the skills taught in any other country.

Before we get into some research that actually explores these two viewpoints in companies around the world, let's look at some of the cultural data on assertiveness. It's widely believed that assertiveness skills would be useful for leaders everywhere. In the MHS database we have taken a subsample of data on 52,974 individuals that have taken the EQ-i 2.0 Leadership Report. This report—specially designed for use with current leaders, people undergoing leadership training, and high potential leaders—evaluates their results against a sample, or benchmark, of a variety of organizational leaders. In this sample of data, we looked at assertiveness scores in countries where we have data on 200 or more leaders.

As seen in Figure 6.1, there is a rather large variation in assertiveness scores by country.

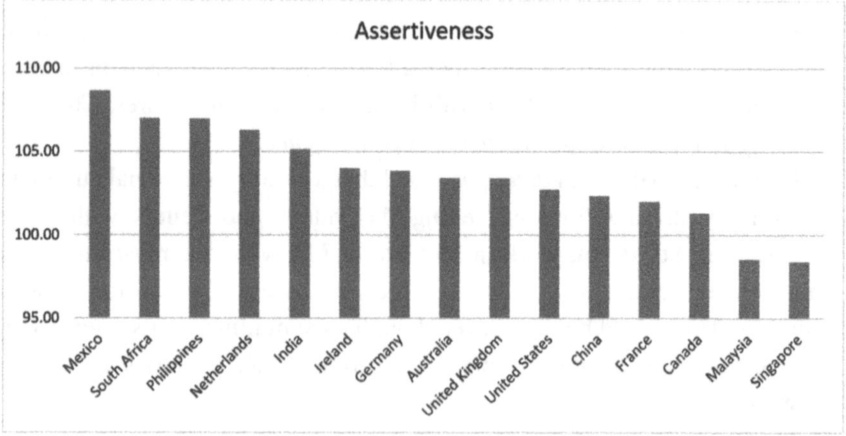

Figure 6.1 EQ-i 2.0 Assertiveness Scores of Leaders in 15 Countries

Source: Reprinted with permission of MHS, 2016.

These data are based on leader self-reports. The most assertive leaders are in Mexico, South Africa, and the Philippines, while the least assertive leaders are in Singapore, Malaysia, and Canada. The question remains, how does the leader's level of assertiveness affect their ability to manage?

William Gentry of the Center for Creative Leadership along with Alexander Patterson of the University of North Carolina and their colleagues carried out a study looking at three of the most important managerial skillsets across 30 countries.[9] On the basis of a detailed review of effective management, they identified three critical areas, which I'll call competencies, for effective management that were believed to be important for any company, regardless of location or culture:

1. Decisional: taking action, making decisions, and following through
2. Interpersonal: the ability of managers to build and maintain relationships
3. Personal Resources: possessing a determination or drive to excel and having the energy and ambition to find new approaches to resolve work-related issues

Interestingly, these competencies are all directly related to some of the factors, which I'll call basic skills, in our definition of emotional intelligence. Decisional is related to Assertiveness. Interpersonal is like our Interpersonal Relationship, and Personal Resources resembles our Self-Actualization factors. In terms, of culture, Gentry used the definition provided by GLOBE,[10] which is the "Global Leadership and Organizational Effectiveness" Forum developed by Robert House of the Wharton School of Business. They defined "culture" as "the collective programming of the mind that distinguishes the members of one category of people from another."[11]

Based on research of about 17,300 middle managers from 951 organizations in the food processing, financial services, and telecommunications services industries, this group looks at leadership from a cultural perspective. They developed nine cultural dimensions that make it possible to capture the similarities and/or differences in norms, values, beliefs, and practices among societies. One of those dimensions is assertiveness, which is defined slightly differently in their research from ours. Their definition ranged from non-assertive or passive at one end of the scale to aggressive at the other; whereas in the EQ-i 2.0 definition we range from nonassertive (passive or aggressive) at the low end to very assertive (direct, not passive or aggressive) at the high end.

Nevertheless, in their research as in ours, there is significant variation of assertiveness across cultures.

The interesting thing about Gentry's research was that he used the culturally variable dimension of assertiveness, something we know varies by country, and applied sophisticated statistical techniques to determine whether the three dimensions—decisional, interpersonal, and personal resources—also varied by country (or culture). They found, in fact, that these three organizational demands on leaders were universal. In other words, these values were shared by leaders in organizations everywhere.

What does that mean for leadership programs? Well, the good news is that the same three competencies can be taught to leaders of companies everywhere in the world. We don't need different curriculum that are focused on different competencies in each culture. However, since we know that specific skills, such as assertiveness vary by culture, you will need to take that into account in the implementation of those training programs. Assertiveness, for example, relates directly to the decisional component. Training leaders to be more directive in Mexico will be different from the same training in Singapore. Mexican leaders will need to be directive in less aggressive ways, whereas in Singapore leaders can be taught to assert themselves more, and not be as passive, when giving direction or expressing their thoughts and beliefs in order to maximize their leadership effectiveness.

Becoming More Independent

A big part of the decisional/action competency involves the emotional intelligence skill of Independence. Taking action, making things happen, and following up go beyond assertiveness (your verbal and nonverbal expression) and includes independent behaviors. Leaders need to be able to act independently. Smart leaders will seek out advice, do the necessary research, but then will act on their decisions.

Greg had been second in command of a division of a large manufacturing firm for five years. Alisa had led the division all of that time and had been a strong leader, successfully navigating the team through a number of challenges. She then got promoted to vice president of the company in another division. On her recommendation, Greg was made the new division leader.

There was no preparation or training offered to Greg for his new role, as he readily and excitedly took his place in charge of the division. As second in command, he felt that he knew exactly what his new job involved. Things started off well as he moved into his new office, got congratulatory e-mails from colleagues, and started settling into a routine. Then problems started to arise that were mostly unexpected.

He felt he could still call on Alisa for advice, but she was getting more difficult to reach, now caught up in her own avalanche of work. As he began to deal with various crises, small and large, he continued wondering how Alisa would deal with them. In the past, when she passed off work to him, it was just a matter of executing her instructions. Now he seemed stuck, not knowing how to tackle the entire problem. When unsure of how to deal with a situation he would write a note to himself and post it up on his board, hoping it might go away if he waited long enough.

Basically, Greg found himself in his new position facing an increasing number of new challenges, different obstacles, and unfamiliar situations. During this time, his dependency on others came into full force. He was unable to stand on his own two feet, as he worried about making errors, and was insecure about his own abilities. He became increasingly anxious and paralyzed. More and more tasks were piling up on Greg's desk and sticky note board. It's as though he was frozen and unable to act. People on his team were becoming more and more frustrated, not to mention his supervisors and customers.

Eventually Greg was let go. It actually came as a relief to him as the stress of not succeeding was too great. Unfortunately, getting promoted and not succeeding is usually a path of no return. This series of events may have been prevented in one of two ways. First, there could have been a focused interview with Greg prior to offering him the promotion where he would have been asked the right questions. Do you really want this job? What does it mean to you to be a manager? What skills do you have that will make you good at this? What have you done that indicates your capability of taking the lead? Are you prepared to step back from the work you've been doing up until now and manage other people's work?

You might want to see if the person has been a leader in activities outside of work—sports teams, volunteer positions, political campaigns, and so on. Of course you also need to know what others, who have worked with this person, think about their qualities for leadership.

Second, he could be offered training and coaching that includes specific skill development in managing other people. In this case, to be successful, personal coaching dealing with Greg's tendency to be dependent on others would need to be dealt with before introducing training in managerial competencies. Once ready to be independent, he'd be equipped for training in a combination of basic skills of emotional intelligence, as well as decision making, interpersonal, and personal resources, and leadership competencies.

What does it take to be an independent leader? The first thing you need is a high level of self-regard. It's important to be confident and take responsibility for the consequences of your actions. High independent leaders are not easily manipulated. Because they are not dependent on others, either for emotional or material support, they feel free to be their own person. They do not play to the crowd, just to get the applause. These are people who think for themselves and do not crave the validation of others. However, independence does not equate to isolation; independent leaders seek out advice, suggestions, and ideas from others. Not to do so would reflect arrogance or insecurity.

EQ Leader: Things to Think About

1. How expressive do you think you are?
2. Do you get the impression other people can read your emotions, and they know where you stand on issues by your expressions?
3. Do you prefer to be a poker player, one who doesn't like to reveal their emotional hand?
4. Do you consider yourself an assertive person?
5. Do you feel you stand up for what you believe in?
6. Would you confront someone who tells a sexist or racist joke at a dinner party? If so, how?
7. Do you express your opinions at work?
8. If you have subordinates, do you believe they can tell how you feel at work?

9. Are there people in your workplace who tend to be passive (don't really express themselves) or aggressive (perhaps too opinionated)?
10. How do you deal with aggressive people?
11. Do you take action when needed, or do you prefer to put things off?
12. Who do you confide in when making tough decisions?

PART III

Interpersonal Abilities and Leadership

Interpersonal Relationship
The ability to develop and maintain mutually satisfying relationships

Empathy
The ability to recognize, understand, and appreciate the feelings of others

Social Responsibility
The ability to contribute to society, to one's social group, and to the welfare of others

Chapter 7

Interpersonal

Creating the Bonds of Trust

Leadership is about empathy. It's about having the ability to relate to and connect with people for the purpose of inspiring and empowering their lives.

—OPRAH WINFREY

I was at a meeting with other CEOs of entrepreneurial companies where the topic of discussion centered on workplace challenges. One CEO, Ted, who owned a chain of restaurants, was concerned about the manager of one of his locations. As far as he was concerned, the manager was a good guy, had great business acumen, high standards, was honest, but Ted couldn't understand the high turnover rate of staff at that one location. It was more than triple the turnover rate at his other restaurants.

We suggested he go back and talk with the manager about the situation. Find out how the manager saw the state of affairs, whether he saw it as a problem, what it might be, and how he might deal with it. In addition, we suggested he meet privately with some of the staff and get a sense from them of how things were going.

It didn't take too long for Ted to get a clearer picture of what was happening. The manager thought things were just fine. He went on about the younger generation having no work ethic, not listening to him, and so on. The staff, on the other hand, detailed several examples where the manager was rude to them, didn't support them when customers were being unreasonable, gave mixed messages in his instructions to them, and generally was not pleasant to work with. What clearly came through was a problem in communication. The manager's lack of interpersonal, or relationship, skills caused a great deal of distress to the frontline staff.

Ted initially felt quite strongly that this manager had great leadership qualities. He had been a loyal part of the team for several years. He was strong, outgoing, opinionated, and had lots of ideas. In fact, to us, Ted was very protective of this manager. He wasn't seen as a problem until Ted looked at staffing patterns and happened to notice the turnover rate at the one location that was higher than all the others. Only then, with our prodding, was he inclined to look further and get to the root of the problem. The manager was subsequently let go, and the restaurant is now reaching or surpassing all the metrics with a new, more compatible manager.

To be a successful leader you need to be able to build relationships. Having good relationships, not exploiting or using people, and the ability to relate to different types of people, are key aspects of leading others. Not all the CEOs I know excel in interpersonal relationships. Some of them come from engineering, legal, or accounting backgrounds and are less comfortable with people. In some of those cases they have a 2IC (second in command) or general manager who is much more people-oriented.

The importance of interpersonal relationships in leadership is supported by the research as well. One study by Gary Yukl at the School of Business at the State University of New York in Albany and Leslie Kanuk looked at leadership and performance across a chain of 18 beauty salons.[1] What does it take to be successful in running a beauty salon? Success was determined by managerial effectiveness, which was defined by three criteria: (1) manager performance ratings (by two independent raters), (2) salon performance (profit margin), and (3) sales increase (over the year of the study). Managers were all rated by their subordinates on a number of leadership traits, including consideration, direction, planning, production emphasis, positive reinforcement, team building, work facilitation, and others.

The salons' profit margin was best predicted by production emphasis (manager's focus on improving productivity and efficiency) and direction (manager's focus on workers' duties, responsibilities, and goals). The sales increases were best predicted by positive reinforcement (manager's use of praise, recognition, and rewards).

However, the most important predictor of manager performance was team-building behavior. This requires a significant amount of interpersonal relationship skills as it includes encouraging subordinates to cooperate, being friendly with each other, sharing information, resolving conflicts, and encouraging others to constructively resolve conflicts. The managerial performance rating representing overall managerial effectiveness also has a major impact on the work climate, such that managers with higher ratings typically had healthier workplace climates.

Developing Your Interpersonal Skills

Like many of the emotional skills in our model there are different levels of development you can achieve. Initiating and maintaining relationships are very basic interpersonal skills that can be worked on and further developed. The next level of interpersonal skills for leaders involves networking ability. Networking is important for all leaders, and it tends to be more challenging for introverts; however, with the right attitude and interpersonal skill development it does get easier.

There are small steps that you can take right now to develop your interpersonal skills. For example, building contacts and expanding your base of potential customers, suppliers, and talent can have great advantages. Further, getting involved in industry associations and volunteering on nonprofit boards are two areas that I've found very rewarding in this regard.

If you are a leader or a CEO, there are many organizations you can join, such as the Young Presidents Organization (YPO), Tech, Vistage, Business Networking International (BNI), Innovators Alliance (IA), Young Entrepreneurs Council (YEC), Entrepreneur's Organization (EO), and others that provide opportunities to network and get peer support. Once again, there are many benefits you can get from involvement in these groups.

I find that some people seem to be a bit confused when it comes to networking. They think that it involves only connecting with people that can have an immediate benefit for them. This is not a good attitude to have when building up your contacts. You never know when someone you meet can be important for you. Your attitude going into any networking situation should be "this seems like an interesting person, I wonder what I can learn about them." You never know when a person you meet will give you an important tip or connection or may be in a position to advance your career.

For example, I've served on a number of nonprofit boards and have met many interesting people in that capacity. On one board I met someone who worked in public relations. It's an area I've had no previous interest in, but over time, and in numerous conversations with the person, I learned more about it. One day I talked to her about a new product launch we were planning and expressed some concern over the marketing costs and uncertainty of reaching our target market. She then gave me a brief course in public relations 101, and I was intrigued. We decided to include a public relations component in our launch, which was unheard of in our industry at the time, and it turned out to be a tremendous success. We reached a huge number of people that far exceeded anything that we achieved before, and it led to our best ever product launch and one of our most successful products.

The Importance of Influence

Leaders who excel in interpersonal relationships are able to inspire people, impact them, and be better negotiators. Today's workplace is characterized by unprecedented levels of change and complexity. Workplace realities, such as identifying shared goals, leading complex and often dispersed teams, working across occupational and international boundaries, coordinating matrixed projects, and integrating diverse people and interests, require the capacity to influence others in a way that has a positive and unifying impact. Whether you are leading, following, and/or collaborating you will need to influence others to be successful. The ability to influence effectively is emerging as a key leadership skill, especially for this new generation of leaders.

In fact, no leader can be successful without the ability to influence others. Whether it's closing an important deal, getting your subordinate to see things a bit differently, or getting your kids to go to bed at night, you need influencing skills. In many organizations, where teams prevail (and there may be no formal leader), you often have to influence others whom you have no authority over. Although there is little doubt about the importance of influence, the question remains: what does it take to be a better influencer?

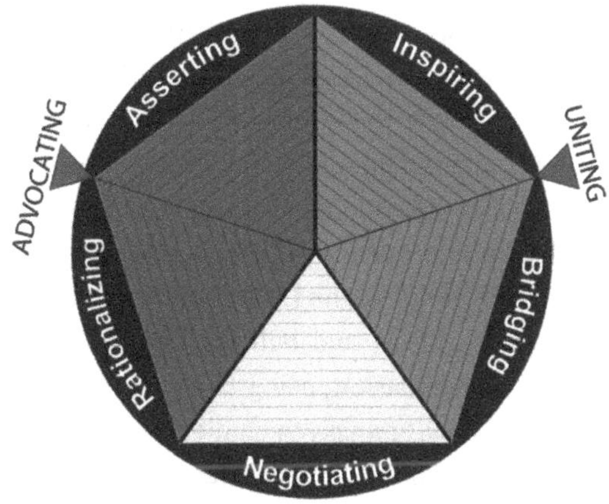

Figure 7.1 Influence Style Indicator Model

Source: Reprinted with permission of MHS, 2016.

Christopher Musselwhite and Tammie Plouffe have looked at all the current theories and practices on influencing others and have put together a model and assessment known as the Influence Style Indicator® that helps you understand your current methods of influencing others.[2] The model is shown in Figure 7.1.

Being a good influencer means you are effective at getting your opinions and ideas heard, recognized, and considered by others. It means that you are able to impact the ideas, opinions, and actions of others. There are several strategies you can use in influencing others that can include using your position and power, educating, encouraging, or collaborating. As Musselwhite points out, "When you influence effectively you increase trust, support, and ownership for your priorities. When you influence ineffectively you increase mistrust, intimidation, and resentment."

Effective leaders can influence people around them into accepting positive outcomes. From the perspective of the Influence Style Indicator model, influence is defined as the interpersonal skills that we use to have a positive impact on another person's choices.

We are all aware of some of the different influencing styles that people use. Some of these styles we instinctively understand and appreciate and others we may find confusing, unclear, and frustrating. Musselwhite and Plouffe's work has identified five styles of influence. Four of these styles fit into one of two orientations: Advocating and Uniting.

These five distinctive styles are Rationalizing, Asserting, Negotiating, Inspiring, and Bridging. Being aware of the characteristics of your influencing style, what situations your style works best in, when it may prove ineffective, and knowing how you can build your style flexibility to respond to a full range of situations, is essential to developing your leadership effectiveness.

The model starts with two overall influencing orientations.

The first is referred to as *Advocating*. This involves influencing others by pushing your perspectives, ideas, and beliefs. The techniques used include logical reasoning, rational persuasion, using facts and data, insisting that your ideas are considered, and a willingness to challenge the ideas and opinions of others. The two styles contained within the Advocating orientation are *Rationalizing* and *Asserting*.

The other orientation is *Uniting*. This orientation involves influencing by pulling people together and toward your point of view. You do this by rallying support, communicating possibilities, clarifying shared interests, building coalitions, and understanding the positions and interests of others. The two styles contained within the Uniting orientation are *Inspiring* and *Bridging*.

Let's look at each style in turn:

Rationalizing involves pushing your ideas, perspectives, and beliefs using logic and reasoning to convince others of your point of view. It includes using facts and figures, expert views, and historical data to support your arguments and persuade others. There are times when rational arguments are effective, such as when you are seen as having unique status or expertise. However, it may not work so well when people believe you are ignoring their emotions or feelings.

So, in trying to influence others to develop a strategic plan, a rationalizing individual may say something like, "based on the facts, your company's current performance, and where your organization is right now, you need to develop a strategic plan."

Using an Asserting style indicates that you are pushing your perspectives and beliefs by insisting that you are heard and indicating that you are willing to challenge the ideas of others. It means a willingness to promote ideas knowing that they may not be popular. It sets up the expectation of debate and respectful rebuttals. It indicates a willingness to use power, rewards, and consequences, as needed, to get a resolution. However, it can sometimes be seen as aggressive and challenging and may lead to deadlock.

So, one might say, "I'm 100 percent certain, based on my expertise with dozens of companies, that your organization needs to develop a strategic plan."

The Negotiating style indicates you are always willing to compromise and negotiate to reach an outcome. It includes bargaining and making compromises to get agreement. It's all about mutual agreement, trade-offs, and support. It's best used when there is equal power between the parties and both want an agreement. There are downsides to this approach as well. For example, one may lose sight of long-term goals for short-term compromise. You also may end up giving away critical interests. This style is not contained with the Uniting or Advocating dimensions.

Here you might say, "If you agree to create a strategic plan for your organization, I can offer you my services at half their usual cost."

The Inspiring preference tries to pull people together and toward your point of view. It involves advocating your position by encouraging others toward a shared vision and common purpose. It's about being enthusiastic and excited about the possibilities and helping others see the benefits of those exciting hopes and dreams. It often involves using stories and metaphors to communicate visions. This approach helps build shared interests between the parties; however, it doesn't work that well when there is a lack of trust between the parties and it may build suspicion. Also, if there is no common goal between parties the Inspiring style can be less effective.

Here you could say, "Just think of how your organization could grow and be even more successful if you developed a strategic plan."

Bridging involves pulling people together and toward your point of view. You do this by building coalitions and communities of interest based on common mutual interest. It involves listening to what others have to say and building a climate of trust. By acknowledging the needs and concerns of others you show appreciation for their issues and interests. This involves asking questions to ensure you are fully understanding the other's point of view. It draws out the intentions, goals, and positions of the other party, allowing both to move forward on shared interests. This may not work well when time is at a premium or when the other party views it as being manipulative or dishonest.

One could say, "It seems like we all agree on where we want this organization to go, so developing a strategic plan is the next step to getting us there."

Most of us tend to lean toward one or two different styles. The Influence Style Indicator helps you better understand where you fit on these dimensions. As you can see, no one style will be effective all the time. Knowing your preferences, your strengths and weaknesses, can help you be much better at influencing others. Regardless of your preferences, it is important to communicate influence with authenticity. One way to communicate authentically is to practice empathy, which I will examine in the next section.

What Leaders Need to Know about Empathy

I was getting a cup of coffee during the break of a presentation I was giving on emotional intelligence at a major law firm. There were more than 100 lawyers in the room, and they all seemed pretty engaged and tuned in to my message. Some of the younger lawyers provided great examples of the concepts presented. But just as I finished pouring my coffee, one of the senior partners pulled me aside.

"I seem to like a number of things that you were saying," he started.

"Thanks, that's great," I eagerly replied, waiting for the other shoe to drop.

"But there's some parts I find hard to accept," he said, as I felt myself tightening up, waiting for the bad news.

"Really, which parts?" I cautiously asked.

"Well, that empathy stuff. Do you really think we, as busy lawyers, have time for that? Law is about facts and arguments, I don't really see any value in getting emotional with my clients."

"I agree, it's not about *getting* emotional. It's really about understanding your clients and where they're coming from so you can serve them better."

There's a scene in the movie *Erin Brockovich* that I now show whenever I'm giving a presentation with lawyers in the room. It's the scene where Erin and the lawyer she works for, Ed Masry, are visiting the home of one of the residents of Hinkley affected by the chromium poison. Ed makes his case to represent the family as part of a potential settlement claim. But when the husband asks Ed about the cost, he replies:

"My fee is 40 percent of whatever you get awarded."

The silence is deadly as the husband quickly looks to his wife and then puts the paperwork back on the table, signaling the end of the discussion.

Suddenly, Erin pipes up, "Boy, do I know how you feel. The first time I heard that number I said, whew, you got to be kidding me, forty goddamn percent! I'm the one that's injured, and this joker sits at a desk all day and he gets to walk away with almost half my reward?"

At which point Ed, getting annoyed, tries to interrupt her.

But she continues, "But then I asked him what he makes if I don't get anything."

"Then I don't get anything either," he responded.

"Plus he's out all the costs, so I realized, he's taking a chance too."

Well, thanks to Erin, the husband reconsiders and decides to agree to be part of the group. In this case, she clearly saved the day. It's an example I often use with lawyers—to drive home the importance of empathy and how many lawyers, who stick with facts and arguments, seem to belittle its importance.

Empathy is one of the most misunderstood, yet most powerful, tools a leader can use. While there are several definitions of empathy out there, the most important thing you need to know is that empathy is not sympathy. Sympathy is mostly about *your* feelings about someone else's situation. For example, saying, "I'm really sorry about the loss of your relative," or "I feel so bad about your recent job loss," is demonstrative of sympathy, not empathy. While sympathy is a valuable emotion, and it has its place, it's not the same as empathy.

Empathy, on the other hand, focuses on the *other* person's feelings and thoughts. We often describe empathy as "your ability to walk in the other person's moccasins." It really means the ability to look at things from the other person's point of view. For example, saying, "you must be feeling really upset over what he just said to you," or "you seem pretty happy about her response to your e-mail," is demonstrative of empathy.

Empathy can be experienced toward groups as well. Some people, especially talented politicians (think Jack Kennedy, Bill Clinton), successful movie directors (think Steven Spielberg, Alfred Hitchcock), product developers (think Steve Jobs), have the ability to read groups of people—audiences, voters, consumers—and know their thoughts, needs, wants, and likely behaviors in certain situations. They can produce products, films, or campaign slogans that win the hearts and minds of people by understanding the emotions of people.

Empathy has been broken down into different components. The first is the ability to understand someone's feelings. People high in this form of empathy know what people are feeling when interacting with them. Regardless of what they may be saying to you, for example, "I'm fine, how are you?" they know they are not fine. They can read between the lines (tone of voice, facial expression, body posture) and know the person is really feeling upset about something. This is a very powerful aspect of empathy. Knowing how a person feels can signal the most effective way for you to respond to them at the time. If you get this right, you build trust and an ally, if you get it wrong or ignore it, you become just another person out there. Another number, or uncaring statistic.

The second aspect of empathy is cognitive. This refers to your ability to "read" the other person's thoughts. People who excel in this aspect of empathy are good at knowing where the other person is coming from. Think of situations where someone made a request of you. One of your first thoughts may have been along the lines of "why would she want that?" Perhaps, after a few seconds, it may have come to you, "of course, she thought it would rain and wants extra protection." Of course, the better we know someone the more likely we are to understand their thoughts and motives. But, once again, some people excel at reading and understanding others. As a leader, those who excel at reading other people instinctively know who will be motivated by a pay increase and who will be more enthused by a change in status or additional perks.

There is a third component that some people attach to empathy. This involves actively caring—wanting to help a person in need. So beyond understanding how a person feels and what they likely are thinking, there can be a drive to heal their wounds. I've seen this component of empathy in some CEOs I know. They have been quick to provide extra money to a loyal staff person who had a sudden, unexpected need. It's as though it was instinctual and happened without any thought of payback.

Empathy was strongly emphasized by the psychologist Carl Rogers when he developed his "client-centered therapy" approach that was popular in the 1960s. One of the benefits found with his approach was that clients experiencing it felt reassured, recognized, and accepted. It's important to understand that empathy is not just an intellectual exercise but involves personal involvement and imagination.

How Important Is Empathy in a Leader?

Empathy has been shown to be a key factor of leadership in corporations, public service, military, and sports. Take, for example, John Mackey, the founder of Whole Foods Market, one of the largest natural foods grocers in the world. He states that when selecting leaders, "I look for somebody who has classic virtues such as integrity, honesty, courage, love, and wisdom. . . . I also look for people who have a high degree of emotional intelligence—a high capacity for caring. . . . Good leaders need to be able to connect to all of those around them. This is especially true at Whole Foods, where we have a very team-oriented culture."[3]

Hiring for emotional intelligence may be one reason why Whole Foods Market is a 14-year veteran among *Fortune*'s Best Companies to Work For and was recently ranked number 24 on this list.

In the sports world, successful coaches have also used empathy to make their teams successful. Mike Krzyzewski, the coach with the best win record of all currently active American college basketball coaches, also known as Coach K, understands the important of empathy. His Blue Devils have won four NCAA national championships, and he led the U.S. men's national basketball team to a gold medal at both the 2008 Summer Olympics and the 2010 FIBA World Championship.

Coach K wrote a book called *Leading with the Heart*[4] where he powerfully illustrates the importance of empathy: "People talk to you in different ways—through facial expressions, moods, mannerisms, body language, the tone of their voice, the look in their eyes" and "as a leader, you must be able to read your players."

He also recognizes that to be an effective leader and coach, it is his duty to help his players regulate their emotions. "A good leader presents an image that gives confidence to his team. And I make it a point to transform that image to the players by encouraging them to walk right, to stand right, and to look good."

Empathy and Emerging Leaders

One of the topics that I get asked about a lot is how to spot emerging leaders. There have been many "high potential" programs set up in large organizations around the world and I have worked with some of them. I'll deal with this a bit more in the last chapter. But a question that arises is, how do we select and prepare these high-potential leaders to eventually take over?

There has been increased attention to the concept of emergent leadership. We've also seen this arise in the context of cross-functional teams. In many situations today, instead of appointing a team leader, it is expected that the leader of the group will "emerge" in some natural way. That implies that the cream will essentially rise to the top.

When we do select leaders, we tend to base our choice on certain preconceived criteria, for example, education level, experience, technical knowledge, IQ, personality, and so on. But there have been few systematic studies looking at who will make the best leader. We can measure leader effectiveness based on team member reports or performance indicators.

An interesting study looking at this idea of emergent leadership was carried out by Stéphane Côté and his colleagues at the Rotman School of Business, University of Toronto.[5] They were interested in how leaders emerge from self-directed groups or teams. For example, you form a team (often cross functional) and assign them a project to work on. How do things get done? What happens when no one is appointed the leader? Well, we know that inevitably someone does take charge. We've seen this over and over again. In fact, if the group remained leaderless the chances of it succeeding are slim.

So, the question becomes, who arises as leader? One might think it's likely to be the smartest one in the room. In leadership selection we tend to put a lot of emphasis on selecting for IQ. Or maybe it's personality that determines the leader? Perhaps the most extroverted one will take control. After all, they know how to talk and will keep things moving along. There may, of course, be a third alternative. Maybe emotional intelligence has something to do with it.

Well, Côté and his colleagues set out to explore this question. Teams of MBA students were randomly assigned to working groups. They then worked together on real world business problems for a period of 10 weeks. But before their assignment into groups, they were all administered a battery of tests by the researchers. These tests measured their IQ, personality, and emotional intelligence. At the end of the 10 weeks, each participant was asked to rate the leadership qualities of their group members. There was a clear consensus in each of the groups as to who the designated leader was.

The researchers then looked at the preliminary testing that was done to see if the tests were able to predict leadership in this context. In fact, the IQ and personality tests were not at all predictive of who emerged as a leader. It was the emotional intelligence test (in this case the MSCEIT), particularly the understanding emotions branch that predicted emerging leadership. That is, people who are good at reading other people's emotions and interpreting them, are the ones that rise to the top. After having seen how leaders are selected and trained in many organizations around the world, I haven't found any (before this study and other related research came out) that focused on empathy as a key leadership attribute. However, perhaps due to this research, there are now processes for using empathy to predict, select for, and develop leadership.

In fact, there is now growing evidence that people will respond to others as leaders if they show empathy and make them feel valued and understood as individuals. Outstanding leaders have been found to differ from less effective leaders in their ability to take into account the needs of their followers. Basically, by supporting people's feelings of self-worth, they begin to be seen more as effective leaders.

Empathy and Gender

In our international research on emotional intelligence, which I'll further discuss in Chapter 15, females universally score higher in empathy than males. How does that play out when looking at leadership?

In an interesting study Kristin Byron at Syracuse University[6] looked at the difference between managers who can accurately read nonverbal emotional cues and those who are more challenged in this area. She recruited 44 part-time MBA students who had supervisory roles in their regular jobs, along with 78 managers from different companies in the hospitality industry. From 112 of the managers, she obtained 284 performance ratings by their subordinates and 58 performance ratings from their supervisors. All of these managers were administered a standardized test that evaluated their ability to read emotional expressions in others.

She found that female managers who were better at reading emotional expressions had higher ratings of performance from their supervisors and higher satisfaction ratings from subordinates. Females who scored lower in reading emotions had worse ratings from supervisors and subordinates than the men with similar abilities to read emotions.

She also looked at how managers used emotional information at work. Basically, emotion was used to provide emotional support and also to be more persuasive. However, once again there were gender differences here. Women used emotions as a way of supporting others more than men did. Men, on the other hand, used emotions for persuasion much more than women. There was also a suggestion that for women, the ability to read emotions was closely related to their performance review by their supervisor. It's almost as though women managers are expected to be good at reading emotions and are rewarded for this ability in their overall performance; however, women who are less skilled in this area may be rated as less competent managers.

Empathy around the World

In a study carried out on leaders from around the world, the Center for Creative Leadership was able to identify empathy as an important factor in being a successful leader.[7] They looked at their data from 6,731 managers in 38 countries, as well as data from subordinates and the managers' supervisors.

As the significance of building and maintaining relationships in leadership has been recognized, the identification of empathy as one of the key skill requirements has been highlighted. Among their key findings is that empathy is directly related to a leader's job performance and that empathy is more important to job performance in some cultures than others.

Empathy, as rated by subordinates, was directly related to the manager's performance review rated by the manager's supervisor. However, they found that empathy was more important in what they referred to as high "power-distance" countries. In high power-distance countries, or cultures, people believe that power should be stratified and concentrated at the top. Typically these countries believe that power provides harmony, social order, and role stability. Examples of the countries include China, Egypt, Hong Kong, Malaysia, New Zealand, Poland, and Singapore. The leader-subordinate relationship in these countries is described as paternalistic. It's as though the leader is like a parent that needs to supply support and protection to the people under his or her care. The relationship between empathy and performance is the strongest in these countries.

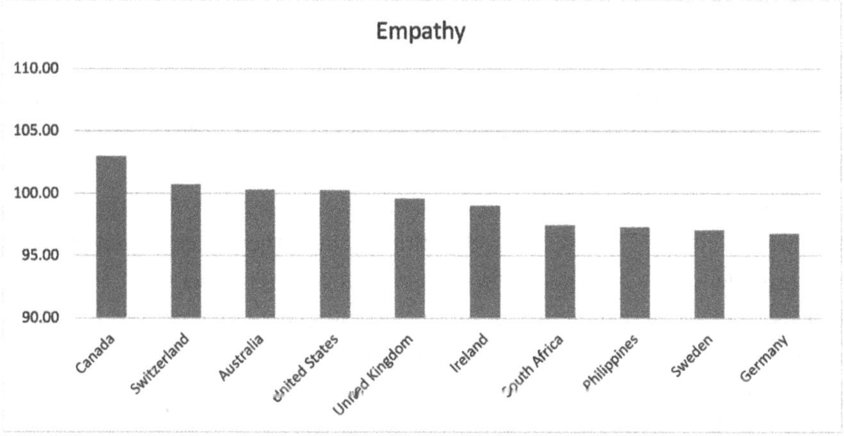

Figure 7.2 Leaders' Ratings of Empathy by Subordinates across 10 Countries

Source: Reprinted with permission of MHS, 2016.

Empathy ratings on leaders that we have collected at MHS in 10 countries are presented in Figure 7.2. This includes data on 41,555 raters rating 3,238 leaders. All 10 of these countries are regarded as medium power distance.[8] Leaders in Canada, Switzerland, and Australia are rated the most empathic while leaders in Germany, Sweden, and the Philippines are least empathic. Although there are variations in empathy scores across countries, all empathy scores are within a range of approximately 10 points.

Empathy: What Can We Do about It?

One of the questions that often arises when I talk about empathy is whether it's something you are just born with or without. Many people believe that it's instinctual, in other words, that people with empathy just meet someone and instantly understand what they're feeling and thinking. If you lack empathy, or you don't immediately "get" what's going on with someone, then it's something you don't have, and you might as well give up trying.

Well fortunately there's now research that has considered this question. In a study by Christine Ma-Kellams of the University of Laverne and Jennifer Lerner at Harvard University,[9] they explored this question in four related studies. In the first study, they looked at how ordinary people (not trained coaches), when put in a coaching situation, commonly approached the idea of increasing someone's empathy. Most people, as expected, believe that empathy is not only intuitive, but is hindered by our systematic, analytical thought process.

In their next study, they recruited working managers and supervisors enrolled in Harvard's executive education classes. They were placed in pairs and provided a few questions to be used with each other as part of an interview process. They then completed questionnaires rating both their own feelings and how they thought their partner felt during the interview. The researchers determined the participant's *empathic accuracy* by comparing each person's ratings of their partner with their partner's self-rating.

They had also been given a cognitive reflection test, which, although presented as a math test, measures whether you solve problems intuitively, or by systematic logic, using items that appear easy at first glance. For example, try answering the following question:

"A bat and a ball cost $1.10 in total. The bat costs $1.00 more than the ball. How much does the ball cost?"

Most people, who answer immediately and intuitively, say $0.10; the correct answer is actually $0.05. Choosing the immediate and reflexive, but incorrect, answer signals greater reliance on intuition and less reliance on systematic thinking.

After taking into account several variables, such as gender, their level of management, and social power, for example, they looked at which factors were related to empathic accuracy. They found that the only differentiating variable was the score on the cognitive test—in other words, whether they tend to use intuition or systematic analysis. Interestingly, the analytical subjects were more accurate at predicting emotions than the intuitive ones.

They then did another study with new group of Harvard executive students where they used the same cognitive test, but rather than a live interactive session, they had subjects rate photos of complex facial expressions. The photos they used had already been standardized and scored in many previous studies. Each person was scored based on their ability to correctly identify the complex emotion being expressed in the photos. This time subjects were also administered IQ tests. Interestingly, the cognitive test (intuitive versus systematic) was the best predictor of empathic accuracy, regardless of IQ, gender, age, or education level. The people who were systematically analytic were better at rating emotions in others than those who were intuitive.

The final study in this series looked at whether you could manipulate people's approach to empathy and affect the results. This time another 74 participants from the Harvard executive classes were recruited to participate. They were randomly assigned into one of two groups. One group was assigned the task of writing out the details of a situation where they used their intuition to solve a problem and where they had a good outcome. The other group was asked to write, in detail, about a situation in which they used careful reasoning and logic to work through a problem that led to a good outcome. They were all asked to use between eight and 10 sentences in their description.

They then went through the same process of the earlier study where they had to interview another participant using the three scripted questions. Following the interaction, they rated their own and their partner's emotions. Their empathic accuracy was then determined by the researchers. The groups that were asked to describe a previous situation where they used reasoning were significantly more accurate in rating emotions than those who were induced with an intuitive situation. Interestingly, unlike many other studies, this one used professionals and managers in three of the four studies. Using different methods these researchers were able to demonstrate that by using a reasoning approach, you could get better results in understanding someone else's emotions than by just using intuition. This supports the idea of being able to improve your ability in reading other people's feelings.

The good news is that empathy, like the other elements of emotional intelligence, can be developed and improved. Of course, motivation to change is always the first step. There have been many studies demonstrating that empathy can be learned and improved and for those of you interested in developing your empathy, there are suggestions at the end of the chapter that should set you on your way.

Some people find it more natural to be empathic. They genuinely care about other people and will often spend time with people learning more about them, remembering important details that have been shared, expressing concern when warranted, and feeling happy for them in times of celebration. Most leaders, however, are somewhat in the middle and are sometimes or somewhat empathic. The good news is that there are several approaches to increasing empathy. Leaders can increase this skill through coaching, training, or other developmental opportunities and initiatives. And, of course, there are those at the bottom, with little or no empathy. They tend to have the unhappiest, and perhaps most stressful workplaces. Even for leaders with little, or no, empathy these coaching interventions have been effective at increasing empathy.

To increase empathy, it's important that empathy be a shared value within an organization. For this to happen, leaders need to be committed to its importance. Empathy needs to be not only talked about and encouraged but also modeled. People throughout the organization should understand that empathy enhances performance and perceived effectiveness. If you need to benchmark empathy, the EQ-i 2.0 is a powerful tool for that.

The first part in teaching empathy is to focus on listening skills. Learn to pay attention to the nonverbal cues, and the meaning behind the words being spoken. By listening, and paying close attention, you learn how to better observe and interpret tone of voice, facial expressions, pace of speech, gestures, and body language.

You can become a better active listener. To be a better listener, you first must be willing to pay attention to the other person. You might have to bite your lip when they say something that makes you want to jump in and interrupt. That also means you should withhold judgment. Yes, he may be saying the stupidest thing you've ever heard, but let him finish. Then you can try to feed back or reflect what you think you just heard him say, "Do you mean that you get irritated when people ignore your ideas?" You must be willing to clarify if you don't quite get it, "Okay, tell me again exactly what gets you upset." Once again, you can summarize, just to make sure you got it right. Another technique is to share examples, "Yes, that sounds similar to how I felt when Beth ignored what I said and just carried on."

As a manager, it's important to try to consider the other person's personal experiences or perspective. The better you know where your employee is coming from, the better you'll be able to address their concerns. This can help you when solving problems, dealing with conflicts, or driving innovation.

You should also make efforts to demonstrate more compassion. When business decisions are made, think about how they may impact others. It doesn't mean you can't make difficult business decisions, but being aware of how it impacts others can help you better implement those decisions. Being empathic, even when you can't compromise on a tough decision, can be helpful.

Finally, support global managers. When working in new or different cultures, it's important to be empathic. You will be dealing with people who often have different perspectives and experiences and to lead them you will need to know where they're coming from. Empathy will show you have an interest in your subordinates as well as an appreciation of them. It makes for better working relationships. Increasing your awareness of others and their cultures will enable you to identify behaviors you can improve and be a better leader.

Social Responsibility and Work

There are some companies that have social responsibility as a core value of their organization. Probably the first company to have social responsibility as part of its business plan was The Body Shop. It published annual reports of its achievements in socially responsible activities. Its founder, Anita Roddick, led the company in championing many causes, such as self-esteem, environmental protection, animal rights, community trade, and human rights. The Body Shop has made significant contributions to many causes and, in many ways, has led the way for other organizations.

Advertising Age, a newspaper for professionals in marketing, has highlighted the top companies that excel in being socially responsible.[10] These include some that would be expected, such as Ben & Jerry's—who set up a foundation with 7.5 percent of their pretax profits going to charitable causes. Even after their purchase by Unilever, over $2 million is donated to charity. Other companies include Burt's Bees—supporting packaging sustainability; Method—safe, effective, environmentally friendly cleaning products; Ecomagination: GE—renewable energy and reduced carbon emissions; Starbucks Coffee—sustainable production of green coffee; Kenneth Cole—AIDS awareness and research, service volunteerism, and social change; Whole Foods—sustainable agriculture, reduction of waste, environmentally sound cleaning; and Toms Shoes—one pair of shoes donated to a child in need for every pair sold.

"But does it all really matter? Really?" That's what one CEO of a health tech company asked me after I mentioned the importance of a leader's social responsibility in a presentation. He was quite skeptical of corporate social responsibility and attributed it to one big marketing ploy, with questionable return on investment.

That sent me back to the research databases. I knew I had to justify corporate social responsibility even more now and make a stronger case. That's when I found an interesting study by Annebel De Hoogh and Deanne Den Hartog of the University of Amsterdam that shed some light on these types of leaders.[11] Their study included 73 CEOs of small and middle-sized organizations. The industries included service, manufacturing, construction, trade, transportation, information, and repair and maintenance. They interviewed the CEOs, had them complete questionnaires, and received more information from at least six subordinates in each of the organizations.

There was a strong relationship between a leader's commitment to social responsibility and the leader's observed ethical behavior. Socially responsible leaders were also rated as less despotic or authoritarian than their less socially responsible peers. Ethical leadership significantly related to the effectiveness of the top management team and subordinate's optimism about their future. Morality and fairness were key variables that characterized the high socially responsible leader-led organizations.

The authors had a very important practical suggestion for the selection of leaders. As we all know, we always want to select leaders who are ethical. And as we also know, integrity is extremely hard to assess in interviews and even in sophisticated tests. Most measures of ethical behavior and integrity are easy for people of average intelligence, and above, to fake. However, measuring leaders' social responsibility may be a much more benign way of getting at ethical behavior. There is less social desirability in responding to social responsibility items than to questions about ethical behavior.

The EQ-i 2.0 was the first measure used in the workplace that included social responsibility as a measureable factor. There was some skepticism about this in the early days, but now it's becoming more recognized as an important aspect of leadership. In fact, I have predicted for some time now that social responsibility will be an essential factor for the next cohort of corporate leaders.[12] I believe that this skill will become the signature strength of tomorrow's leaders. Just as steadfastness was important in the past, adaptability is today's key leadership strength, and tomorrow's best leaders will excel in social responsibility.

There are more studies showing the effects of socially responsible organizations on employee commitment. For example, Stephen Brammer, Andrew

Millington, and Bryce Rayton from the University of Bath in the United Kingdom surveyed 4,712 employees of a large financial services organization.[13]

They found that the more committed CEOs were to corporate social responsibility, the more that people in the organization were emotionally invested in, and committed to, the organization, in general. It reported that social responsibility was equivalent to job satisfaction as far as employee's motivation to work in the organization.

This desire for socially responsible workplaces is strongest among Millennials. In a survey composed of 7,500 working people that included older Baby Boomers, younger Baby Boomers, older Gen X, younger Gen X, and Millennials, respondents were asked about the importance of their employer contributing to social or ethical causes.[14] Nearly two-thirds of Millennials (63 percent) agreed that they'd like their employers to "contribute to social or ethical causes" that they think are important. Young Gen Xers agreed by the same amount (63 percent). Barely half of Baby Boomers (46 percent) and older Gen Xers (50 percent) felt the same way. Clearly, if you want to attract the younger workers into your organization, you will need to pay attention to social responsibility.

What about the Bottom Line?

Well, increasing employee commitment certainly can contribute to the bottom line. Measuring the effects of one intervention or another on an entire organization is difficult. However, a survey undertaken by *The Economist* attempted to answer that question. They surveyed 566 U.S.-based business-people and interviewed an additional 16 senior executives and experts in corporate citizenship.[15]

Among other things, they found that corporate citizenship can help improve the bottom line. The report noted, "Seventy-four percent of respondents to the survey say corporate citizenship can help increase profits at their company. Survey respondents who say effective corporate citizenship can help to improve the bottom line are also more likely to say their strategy is 'very important' to their business (33 percent) compared with other survey respondents (8 percent)."

We already know that several companies, as previously mentioned, primarily identified with social responsibility, are profitable. There are also many large companies that are perceived as socially responsible and recently ranked by *Forbes* magazine.[16] To find which companies have the very best reputations, with a focus on corporate social responsibility, *Forbes* worked with the Reputation Institute. 55,000 consumers across 15 markets were invited to participate in a study between January 2013 and February 2013 that ranked the world's 100 most reputable companies; all multinational businesses with a global presence. The leaders in their survey included, in descending order: Microsoft, The Walt Disney Company, Google, BMW, Daimler, Sony, Intel, Volkswagen, Apple, and Nestlé.

Social Responsibility Internationally

How do organizational leaders score in social responsibility on the EQ-i 2.0 around the world? In Figure 7.3, you can see the average national score of 15 countries based on the MHS data.

As can be seen, leaders in Mexico, India, and China see themselves as the most socially responsible, whereas leaders in the United Kingdom, Germany, and Singapore rate themselves as least socially responsible. It may be that in countries where there appear to be significant discrepancies between the

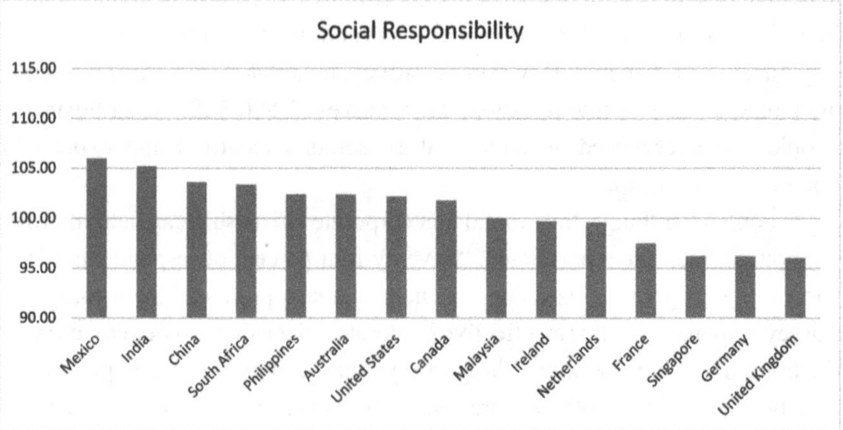

Figure 7.3 EQ-i 2.0 Leadership Social Responsibility Scores

Source: Reprinted with permission of MHS, 2016.

wealthy and the poorest, leaders are more likely to pay attention to social issues, and thus rate themselves higher. In countries with a larger middle class, social issues may be seen as less pressing and leaders may pay less attention to them.

Increasing Your Social Responsibility

Of all the areas that we measure of emotional intelligence, social responsibility is likely the easiest to change. Of course, I don't recommend that the solution to social responsibility is simply to write a check. You must be invested in the idea that being socially responsible has many benefits for you and your organization. There should be a commitment to participate beyond the donation of money.

There are a number of different ways to increase your social responsibility score. At MHS, for many years we operated like many traditional companies. We had an annual campaign for our local United Way and encouraged everyone to take part. There would be a set period of time each year where we would set up a number of different activities to involve our employees. There were corporate, as well as employee, donations. After a number of years, however, it felt that the energy and exuberance had been decreasing. It was almost turning into a chore to get involved.

We then hired a consultant and put together a small internal team that included managers and employees to look at how we could support meaningful charitable causes in ways that not only benefited the recipient charities but our staff as well. We wanted our people to be able to participate and be energized by the process. The criteria we looked for included finding a charitable cause that matched the mission and vision of MHS and would capture the hearts and minds of all the staff. It would also have to be a cause that works for our staff, not just at the head office, but also across Canada, the United States, and the United Kingdom.

The team came up with the Boys and Girls Club, which has branches in many locations. The club is based in inner cities and focuses on offering children and adolescents a safe, affordable, and enriching place to be, mostly between 3 PM and 7 PM, when they are at most risk for getting involved with unsafe activities and people. Our program, called Community 360, fits the MHS mission of helping professionals helping families. The Boys and Girls

Club provides more than 1,000 hours of healthy activities, individual fitness, team sports, and nutrition programming for at-risk city youth.

In addition to financial contributions, which are both staff and corporate initiated, we have many enriching opportunities. Staff raise funds through a series of company events that include table hockey competition, bake sales, potluck lunches, family feud competition, raffles (professional sports tickets from suppliers, gifts from credit cards from staff travel points), casual Thursdays, relaxation/massage chair sessions (available in office anytime), and many more creative activities.

But even more important, our staff volunteer with paid time off for a variety of activities with the kids and families served. We target 500 hours of staff time volunteering and often exceed this goal. In addition to ongoing activities at the club, staff can contribute their skills, which have included accounting, computers/programming, graphic design, ballet, improvisation, and more. In addition, we take two kids from the club to work as interns at MHS through the summer months. We have also sponsored a scholarship fund that has already enabled one youth to enroll in an out-of-town college to study his dream topic of geology, as well as take an internship in South Africa.

Social responsibility can provide benefits personally, for the organization, for the community, and to the world. As this message gets communicated to more organizations the effects can make a huge difference for people everywhere.

EQ Leader: Building Interpersonal Skills

1. What activities do you do to network? Where do you go?
2. Do you consider yourself as more introverted or extraverted when it comes to meeting new people?
3. What would make you want to meet a new person at a work/networking event?
4. What topics would you discuss with new acquaintances?
5. Do you really pay attention and focus on other people talking to you?
6. How do you show people you really listened to them?

7. Do people tend to confide in you, or are you usually the last person to find out about things?
8. Do you see yourself as socially responsible?
9. What do you do that makes you socially responsible?
10. What socially responsible activities are you involved in?
11. How can your organization become more socially responsible?

PART IV

Decision Making and Leadership

Decision Making and Leadership

Problem Solving

The ability to solve problems where emotions are involved using emotions

Reality Testing

The ability to remain objective by seeing things as they really are

Impulse Control

The ability to resist or delay an impulse, drive, or temptation to act

Chapter 8

Making Better Decisions: Emotionally

We simply attempt to be fearful when others are greedy and to be greedy only when others are fearful.

—WARREN BUFFETT

Trusting Your Instincts

It was December 13, 1961. Mike Smith and Dick Rowe were executives in charge of evaluating new talent for the London office of Decca Records. Mike Smith had traveled up to Liverpool to watch a local rock-and-roll band perform. After hearing them, he decided that the band had talent and invited them down to London to audition on New Year's Day, January 1, 1962.

The band made the trip down to London and spent two hours playing 15 different songs at the Decca studios. They then packed up, went home, and waited for an answer.

They waited for weeks.

And waited.

Not willing to wait any longer, the band's manager called Mike Smith and asked him what was happening.

"Not to mince words, Mr. Epstein, but we don't like your boys' sound. Groups are out; four-piece groups with guitars particularly are finished."

Decca's rejection of The Beatles made it to the top (or near top) spot on several lists of the worst business decisions of the twentieth century and the second worst business decision of all time by *Forbes* magazine.[1]

How could this have happened? I've been intrigued by this mishap for quite some time and through my work in the music industry, including volunteer training for early career musicians and musician managers through a nonprofit organization called Canada's Music Incubator (CMI), I've assessed the emotional intelligence, which includes a decision-making component, and entrepreneurship of many young musicians and musician managers, in their early career stages. In addition, I've asked several professionals involved with major record labels how this could have happened. The answer, it all boils down to, is a gut feeling. In Mike Smith's own words, "I went to the Cavern and I should have trusted my instincts as I thought they were wonderful on stage."[2]

Once an artist has a certain amount of talent and shows they can arouse emotion in an audience, it's then a matter of how much money and time the label is willing to invest to further develop the artist. Mike Smith and Dick Rowe somehow just missed that mark once The Beatles came to London. Something in their gut set them off in what turned out to be an unfortunate decision, although Dick Rowe did later sign the Rolling Stones.

Problem Solving

As a leader, making decisions is probably one of the most important things we have to do. When we think about making decisions our inclination is be rational and logical. Think of Spock from *Star Trek*. It's about getting together all the facts you can, putting them into categories, such as pro versus con, then adding up one side of the ledger followed by the other. Then we look at which side of the ledger is bigger, and go with it.

Somehow, we believe that the best decisions revolve around the arduous cycle of collecting facts, then more facts, and then again even more facts, until we know everything possible about the competing options that confront us. Fact checkers, in fact, should be the best decision makers we know. All of the information at their disposal should lead to flawless choices.

Every decision from choosing what car to buy, which sales manager to hire, when to get married, which new product to work on, which distributors to work with, which restaurant to go for dinner, and so on involve a series of decision-making processes. The method should be simple—identify alternatives, compare each against the others, and, on the basis of pure knowledge and rationality, make a selection.

Oh, if only life were that simple. Have you ever noticed that after pulling together all the facts about a choice you wanted to make, such as which car to by, you had to deal with your gut feeling? You knew that the red sports car convertible made no sense for you: it was bad on mileage, had less passenger room and storage space, a poor safety record, and cost more money; yet, you couldn't resist buying it.

How is it that our gut feeling—otherwise known as our emotions—so often overrules logical choices? Well, researchers have found a number of ways that our emotions affect the way we make decisions. By understanding the role of emotions in decision making, and being more proactive about *using* your emotions to make decisions, you can learn to make better, more *reasonable* decisions.

Let's start by exploring the relationship between emotion and decision making. First, there are two ways emotions affect your decisions. The first is referred to as *incidental*. This means you may be feeling a certain way—that is unrelated to the decision you are about to make. For example, you may be sad about a story you read, just before deciding on which of two sales reps to hire. Or, you may be the kind of person who is anxious much of the time. When things aren't going well around you, you worry that they will stay that way. And when things are going well, you're anxious that it won't last. So the emotion you happen to be feeling at the time can influence any kind of choice you are about to make, before even considering the rationality of the options.

The second way emotions affect your decision making is directly—in other words, the emotion you experience as a result of the choice itself, or from considering the options. Even if you choose to try to suppress your emotions (by being perfectly rational), research has shown that there will still be an emotional "tag," or imprint, on your decision making. For example, some aspect of the options you are considering will trigger an emotional memory. There is no Spock in the human condition (unless, of course, you have some sort of pathology, such as a disorder called *alexithymia*, where you don't experience emotions).

The Mood You're In

Let's begin by looking at the mood you're in. Whatever mood you happen to be in at a given point in time can impact your decision-making process. Researchers in the field call this "misattribution of incidental" feeling. In this case, you may be feeling a certain way because of one experience, but that feeling effects whatever decision you are about to make.

Psychologists Norbert Schwarz at the University of Heidelberg and Gerald Clore at the University of Illinois tested this out in an interesting experiment.[3] They wanted to see whether the way you felt about something incidental, such as the weather, would impact the way you felt about other, more significant things, such as yourself.

They randomly called 93 people during the months of April and May on only rainy days or sunny days. They told the person answering the phone that they were doing a research study. For some of the people they chatted about the weather right away—confirming that it was, in fact, raining, or sunny—before beginning the survey. All people called on the sunny days (whether or not they confirmed the weather) reported being happier than people called on the rainy days.

What was really interesting, though, was that people called on sunny days also reported themselves to be happy and satisfied with their lives in general. They reported having little desire to change anything in their lives at that time. People called on rainy days, however, said they were less happy than the other group, and reported being less satisfied with their lives. As well, these people said they wanted to make more changes in their lives.

Their study supports the idea that somebody who is happy and having a good day is more likely to have that happiness affect other aspects of their life at that time. Choices you make that day will be colored by your happy feelings. In the same way, making decisions while having a bad day will most certainly have an effect on the choices you make.

Another example of this can be found in a retrospective study carried out by Dr. Donald Redelmeier, a physician who spent 20 years as a researcher at Stanford University and University of Toronto medical schools.[4] After reviewing the results of success factors in 2,926 applicants admitted to medical school, he came across a startling result. Candidates who were interviewed on rainy days were significantly less successful in gaining admission than applicants interviewed on sunny days. Could it be that the gloomy weather affected the decisions of the judges? You might want to consider the weather before your next high impact interview.

When you encounter your next big, or even moderate, decision, take a moment to pay attention to your mood before you start in on your choices. Once you have a reading on your mood, then pause and contemplate how your mood might affect your dealing with the issue at hand. If your mood will have a neutral effect, that's good to know. If, however, your mood might adversely affect your ability to make a good decision (or your best decision), you might want to try changing your mood to something more neutral or positive. Alternatively, you might want to put off the decision until a later time.

The Mood You Create

Let's suppose you are quietly minding your own business, you're in your office either reading a report, writing something, or searching the Internet. You feel content and relaxed. Suddenly your phone rings. You answer it, and it's a salesperson trying to sell you ad space in their publication. Somehow, he got your direct number and wants you to advertise somewhere you've never even heard of before (something that happened to me, by the way, while writing the previous chapter).

The ringing phone took you out of your pleasantly relaxed state. You're not very pleased to be hearing from a salesperson, so your annoyance level starts to increase. After you tell him you're not interested, he starts telling you about this month's special rate that he has reserved just for you, upon which you become even more upset. Once he starts asking how many months you would like your ad to be placed, you lose your cool. In an angry tone, you tell him you don't want any ads and hang up the phone (not really how I handled it, but obviously thought about it).

In this case, your relaxed mood didn't spill over to the salesperson. However, the situation—phone ringing, unwanted caller, request for on-the-spot decision—all led to an unpleasant mood. This mood then affected the choice you made—basically to hang up on him. For example, you didn't consider whether the magazine might reach some of your target audience, or whether you should have just referred him to your marketing department; you decided to impulsively settle for the easiest (quickest) possible solution, regardless of whether it was the best choice. How often does this happen to you in other aspects of your life?

When you are confronted with your next decision, rather than ignoring your feelings, pay attention to your emotions as you approach the situation. Notice how you feel in your gut as you consider the various aspects of confronting your decision-making experience. Pausing and reflecting may help put you in a better frame of mind. If not, you might want to delay the decision making until a better time and a better mood is available.

How Those "Incidental" Emotions Can Affect You

As previously discussed, the way you feel, even before confronting a decision-making opportunity, can affect your decision-making ability. People who tend to ignore their feelings may be even more affected than others and this is largely because they try to ignore emotions. Emotions affect your ability to reason, and ignoring emotions leaves you not only affected by them but also completely unaware of their influence.

Most of your emotions, when the intensity increases, with the exception of sadness, cause your autonomic nervous system to be aroused. The autonomic nervous system controls your heart rate, breathing rate, digestion, perspiration, and a number of other bodily functions. Just think of how your body reacts when you get anxious, or when you're angry. Your heart starts to race, your breathing can speed up or get deeper, and you may start to sweat. These are functions that you don't usually control directly but come about because of your emotional state.

When your autonomic nervous system gets aroused (e.g., faster heart rate, sweating), research has shown that it has a negative impact on your memory. You become less able to remember information and it affects your ability to organize the information that you do recall. How might this affect your reasoning ability? Well there are a number of ways. For example, people who are anxious have more trouble remembering things than people who are calm. In order to reason you need to look at the various alternatives available and compare them. Anxiety also makes it difficult to organize the information that you do remember. What is remembered tends to be more confused, less connected, and not as useful in making decisions. Anxious people, when looking at alternative solutions to a problem, have also been found to be more careless when they scan the various options. Thus, just like in the telemarketing example before, they tend to make choices without considering the merits of other options.

It's also been found that when people are anxious they take longer to confirm the soundness of the inferences they make about a problem. So while in a calm state you may instantly know that a certain type of candidate for your sales position appeals to you; however, you may be less certain, or at least take longer to be sure of the same thing when you are anxious. So if you're making any kind of decision on the fly, or where speed is of the essence, being calm is to your advantage.

A very interesting study directly related to this was carried out at Cambridge University by John Coates, a former derivatives trader who now works as a neuroscientist, and his colleagues, and was reported in the *Washington Post*.[5] Their research looked at "interoception," meaning the ability to sense bodily signals, such as your current heart rate. Their study, published in *Scientific Reports*,[6] looked at how the ability to sense bodily signals affects the success of stock traders. They first looked at 18 male traders who bought and sold futures contracts throughout the day on the trading floor in the City of London and compared them to 48 nontrader males, who served as a control group. They had all subjects complete two standard heart detection tasks, which essentially looks at how well you can estimate, or count the number of heartbeats you experience over several brief intervals of time.

In the first series of studies, they found that the traders were significantly more accurate, on average, at counting their heartbeats than nontraders. But even more interesting, they also found that traders' precision on counting their own heartbeats predicted their profit and loss record, as well as the number of years they had survived in the market. In other words, traders who counted their heartbeats with greater accuracy tended to have greater profit and longer careers. The authors concluded, "Traders in the financial world often speak of the importance of gut feelings for choosing profitable trades. By this they mean that subtle physiological changes in their bodies provide cues helping them rapidly select from a range of possible trades the one that just 'feels right.' Our findings suggest that the gut feelings informing this decision are more than the mythical entities of financial lore–they are real physiological signals, valuable ones at that."

Something to think about when choosing your next money manager. As well, something to keep in mind when looking at prospective leaders, as leadership involves a great deal of decision making and, in some cases, high-risk decision making.

There's also research support for the finding that under certain emotional states, such as when people are aroused, they find it more difficult to process persuasive arguments. Trying to convince someone on the merits of your product, or why they should follow your ideas, will be much harder if that person is in a highly emotional state, such as anxious, angry, or sad. You are much more likely to influence someone if they are relaxed and focused.

In the same way, when we make decisions, we do a poor job of taking in the persuasive arguments being presented to us by advocates of the various options when our emotions get in the way. In other words, in order to make good decisions, we need to relax and focus on what the sales person for a product or idea is trying to sell us. That's when we're in the best position to separate the hype from the actual benefits of the product or service.

The Influence of Positive Emotions

A lot of what we know about problem solving in decision making is based on studies of negative emotions, such as anxiety and worry. We really don't know as much about the influence of more positive emotions. There is some evidence that intense emotions can have some benefit in completing tasks by narrowing down our focus. When we get emotional and there are a number of different cues that we need to pay attention to, we narrow down our focus to the most relevant or important cues. Someone in a burning building, for example, while stressed with how to react, may decide quickly to rescue the baby and leave everything else behind in order to survive.

There is also some support for the idea that being in a happy mood can help us make better decisions. It's not just the happy mood itself, but rather that the happy mood allows you to be more flexible. When you're more flexible you're willing to consider more options.

Think of the last time you planned a vacation. Generally, this is the type of activity we do when we're in a good mood. Just thinking about the vacation helps put us in a good mood. For many of us browsing through various vacation packages on the web, looking at the hotels, beaches, nightlife, shopping opportunities, and entertainment puts us in, or helps maintain a good mood. In fact, we tend to spend more time than expected browsing through packages, checking prices, and so on. We probably make good decisions in this area of our lives because of the time we spend making these comparisons.

Good moods have been found to have a number of other effects on our decision-making process. When we're in a good mood we tend to break our options into broad categories for comparison instead of focusing on each detail. So when comparing cars, instead of looking at 15 different features individually (e.g., safety, mileage, trunk space, seating capacity), we judge car A against car B on a few general categories, such as looks, price, and customer/expert ratings.

This was explored in a study by Joseph Mikels of DePaul University, Sam Maglio of New York University, and their colleagues who compared decision making using your gut versus deliberate decision strategies.[7] This has some similarities to the previous study described on empathy (see Chapter 7), although with different results. In this case subjects were asked to decide which one of four cars they would prefer after being shown a number of benefits and drawbacks of each one. This included things like, "gets good gas mileage," or "gets poor gas mileage."

They used several different manipulations with different groups of subjects. First, one group of subjects was instructed to make their decision by using their gut feelings while another group was told to focus on details. They were then presented with the positive and negative features for each car, one at a time. The dice were loaded, with one of the cars getting 75 percent positive features, two getting 50 percent positive features, and one getting only 25 percent positive features.

When there were a smaller number of features to choose from, there was no difference between gut and deliberate decision making in picking the best car. However, when the decision making became complex (12 attributes per car as opposed to just 4) people using their feelings did a better job of picking the best car. Not only that, but in replicating these results they also found that people using their feelings to make the decision were more satisfied and confident of their choice afterward than those who focused on details, and those that chose with their feelings had fewer second thoughts or regrets. Just thinking about the convertible I recently bought, I can wholeheartedly agree. I'm very happy with my choice.

When we're in a good mood, we're much better at generating lots of ideas. We become more creative in the ideas we come up with. We tend to do better in problem-solving tasks that require ingenuity or thinking out of the box. Being in a good mood can help us be better in reasoning, solving problems, making judgments, and in decision making.

But being in a good mood isn't always the way to go in problem-solving situations. It's also been reported that people in a good mood do worse than people in a neutral or sad mood when doing problems that involve reasoning. This includes the kinds of problems you encounter in many standardized tests, such as the LSAT, MCAT, GRE, GMAT, and so on. So, while being in a good mood may make you feel better while reasoning and solving problems, this good mood doesn't guarantee better results.

A good mood can also influence how we react to other people. For example, when we're in a good mood, we tend to overestimate the degree to which someone else's actions are due to personal factors as opposed to situational reasons. So if the car salesperson starts to tell us about his charitable activities, and we're feeling good, we may see him as a caring, socially responsible individual. This, in turn, may make it more likely that we'll buy a car from him. On the other hand, if we're in a bit of a sour, unpleasant mood, we are more likely to pass off his charity stories as a ploy he's using to try and close the sale on the car.

An experience I had while visiting San Francisco really drove home the power of this point. I was giving a presentation on emotional intelligence to a large group of professionals in the Bay area. As I sometimes do, I decided to come a bit early to spend some quiet time walking around and shopping in the city. With time to kill, I wandered into a few of the wonderful art stores near Union Square. Wearing my jeans and appearing somewhat relaxed and nonchalant, I was surprised at the interest one of the salesmen took in me. While there were other, better-dressed people in the gallery, he asked me questions about my preferences in the art I was viewing and gave me very detailed descriptions of the works.

I looked at art that was priced between a quarter million and five million dollars. I thought my expressions and actions were clear that these were out of my price range, plus I made it clear I was just looking around to pass the time. After some small talk about our families, he proceeded to tell me a story of one painting that had personal significance for him. It was a whimsical piece that had a burning house in the background and a rabbit with a match in its mouth in the foreground. He told me it was called *Bad Hare Day* and explained that his wife had gone through a bout of breast cancer, had chemotherapy, and had lost her hair a few years ago. It was a lithograph version of this painting that he used at home with his wife to keep her spirits up during this ordeal. Not quite the story you confide in to someone you've known for about 20 minutes.

Either this person thought we had bonded sufficiently in half an hour to get close and personal or he was taking a risk in revealing very personal information to a complete stranger in the hope of making a sale. At some level, I believe he intuitively used his emotional intelligence to tell himself that this was a safe thing to do at the time and would really give him an indication of how much I was really "with him" in the art adventure he took me through. Because I was in a good mood, I interpreted this story as a genuine attempt at connection and not a sales ploy.

Being in too good a mood can also impact our decision making when we're faced with situations that require complex decision-making processes. People in a good mood are more likely to superficially investigate the data when there's a lot of information to evaluate. Whereas, being in a foul mood makes you look at information more carefully and perhaps skeptically. Little wonder that so many business deals—from Hollywood films to New York acquisitions—are conducted over liquid lunches at exclusive restaurants. What better way to get someone to sign the dotted line than after a great meal, fine wine, and pleasant conversation.

People in a good mood tend to look at complex information superficially. They also look at things globally or in general terms. Rather than drill down to evaluate information and how it may apply to a specific situation, they will rely on stereotypes. When interviewing a potential investment adviser over drinks and a great meal, and listening to her accounts of great stock purchases and timely sales, you are more likely to see her as a savvy investor. This is especially true if she dresses the role and drives the Mercedes you've been dreaming about. Your good mood makes you reluctant to question the accuracy of her self-reported stories of success, get objective references, or double check her investment history.

In summary, being in a good mood while making decisions can be a mixed blessing. On one hand, you'll be more flexible and creative. On the other hand, you'll tend to base your decisions on more superficial, big picture, overall impressions and not dig down and be more specific or rely on data-driven evidence.

Interestingly, being in a negative mood also has its good and bad points. When you're in a sad mood you tend to be more careful when processing information. Also, you tend to rely less on generalities or stereotypes. We're much more logical and data driven when we're sad.

The Direct Effects of Emotion

What are the direct effects of emotion on decision making? That is, how do specific emotions affect you directly while you are making a decision? We know that if you make decisions while in an intense emotional state, such as in a high drive state (e.g., when you're hungry, thirsty, in pain, sleep deprived, sexually aroused), you are much more likely to make impulsive, not well-thought-out decisions. You're also more likely to bypass or overlook ethical boundaries. So, for example, when sexually aroused you may be more likely to cheat on your spouse or give in to temptation. You are also less likely to practice safe sex.

There are many examples of how these intense emotions can affect our behavior. Children are especially vulnerable to acting impulsively or at least with lower delays in gratification. Waiting until dessert for the pie and ice cream can be quite a challenge for the hungry tot who is less enthused about the vegetables that must come first. Or think about the dieters you've known who had to make it through the potato chips before controlled eating began in earnest (if at all). Relapse rates among smokers also show us how intense internal drives can control our behavior.

Other compulsions, such as compulsive shopping, also illustrate how intense drives seem to take over our common sense and control behaviors. Knowing that your credit card is significantly overdrawn, that you don't really need a 43rd pair of shoes, that you don't really have the time to shop—being aware of all this logic, can be overridden in a flash to meet those strong, internal "needs" to shop.

These same internal urges help explain decisions we make to the detriment of society or mankind—whether it's greed that directs us to hoard resources or material goods that could help others in need, or selfishness that prevents us from taking better care of our environment. Internal drives or emotions have a direct effect on how these socially responsible behaviors play out. For many people, it's more important to feel better in the short term than delay a gratification that may be in the interest of many others over the long term.

Your emotional state also affects your likelihood of taking risks. Certain emotions increase the chances that you'll take while gambling, making business deals, or having casual sex. For example, people who are angry, or fear being embarrassed are more likely to take long-shot, high-risk gambling moves over more secure "safe bet" gambles. Research has also found that people who are emotionally aroused will spend more money on lottery tickets. These same aroused people will choose to spend less on insurance to cover their losses. So if you're in the business of selling insurance to people, you're much better off dealing with people in a calm mood as opposed to an emotional state.

But not all negative emotional states have the same effects. When people are in a sad mood, they tend to choose options that are high risk with high-reward possibilities. On the other hand, when anxious, people tend to choose situations that are low risk and have low reward options. The thinking behind this is that when you are anxious, you are more likely to see yourself as having little control over situations and you see the outcome of any effort on your part as uncertain. So if you have so little influence over the outcome, why take a chance?

People who are sad, on the other hand, already see themselves in a loss situation. When you are sad it's generally because you've lost hope over something meaningful to you. In that case, you tend to go for broke. After all, what more do you have to lose? Alternatively, with anger, you tend to believe you have a high degree of control over the situation. In other words, you haven't given up yet. Angry people think they can still make a difference. They also take high risks. Interestingly studies have found that disgust tends to reduce the amount of risk you are willing to take.

What about the Object of the Decision?

Emotion plays a role in decision making based on your feelings toward the object or goal itself. If you have very good feelings about that car, the property you want to buy, a potential mate, or the lottery grand prize, that will affect your decision making. Likewise, when deciding on things that give you a bad feeling or vibe, such as whether to sit in a smoking section of a bar, eat food in a seemingly dirty restaurant, or go on a date with someone you've heard bad rumors about, your decision-making process becomes colored.

In some interesting research looking at this process, psychologists Richard Nisbett and Lee Ross in 1980 referred to a phenomenon coined the "vividness effect."[8] They wanted to understand how important the nature of the object being described would affect someone's choice to pursue it. They measured the consumption of beef in areas of France depending on how a recent crisis was described in the local newspapers. In regions where the papers talked about cows being stricken with a disease called Creutzfeldt-Jacob disease, beef consumption was significantly higher than where the papers reported on Mad Cow disease.

When risks are presented in an emotionally laden fashion, we are more likely to avoid or approach them for emotional reasons rather than using logical reasoning. Another interesting study looking at the effect of emotions on our decision-making process observed people's desire to dump their carefully chosen investment broker following a bad investment result. Rebecca Ratner of the Kenan-Flagler Business School, University of North Carolina in Chapel Hill, and Kenneth Herbst of the Erivan K. Haub School of Business at St. Joseph's University, in a 2005 study looked at people who invested with a broker who had a reputation for having a very strong track record.[9] When they experienced a disappointing outcome they tended to "overreact" and focus on their emotional response to the loss. As a result, they were most likely to switch to another broker with a poorer track record. A single-occurrence loss would override a long-term track record and result in a decision that would have poorer long-term consequences. Is it because losing money is an emotionally laden event that led people to dump a broker with a good long-term record?

When we have strong emotional feelings about the perceived outcome of a decision, we tend to be overemotional in our decision-making process. This becomes more of a problem when we overreact to an object or outcome based on an initial gut feeling or impression. What happens next is that we try and support or justify our emotional reaction with reasons. So instead of using our logic to make the best decisions, we use our logic to justify or build up a bad case that supports our decision, which was based on an emotional feeling.

This may help us begin to understand what goes on with some of our politicians or athletes who have been caught in extramarital sexual exploits. The object of their attraction is so beautiful, and makes them feel so good, that they start to justify the attraction. "After all, it's just a fling, who will ever find out? I can keep it under control. Other people I know have done worse." The arguments on the other side, "This might be unethical. What if my wife found out? How would this play out in the newspapers? Might this cost me my marriage? Would there be financial costs? What about my reputation?" Somehow, very smart people we've all read about and trusted as politicians or athletes have been able to make the first set of arguments, yet somehow overlook the second.

Another interesting effect of the emotion of the object guiding our behavior can be seen in a study published by Eric Johnson, John Hershey, Jacqueline Meszaros, and Howard Kunreuther of the Wharton School of Business at the University of Pennsylvania in 1993.[10] They looked at people purchasing life insurance with two different descriptions of what the insurance covered. In one policy, the insurance covered "death due to any reason." Another policy was written so that it specified "death due to any act of terrorism." People were willing to pay more money for the insurance that mentioned the emotionally laden concrete threat of terrorism than the other policy (with the same coverage) but only spoke of a higher probability but less concrete threat.

Immediate Gratification: What about the Brain?

Another important aspect of our decision-making process has to do with our ability to delay pleasure and the effect of emotion on our brain. Brain imaging studies have shown us that when certain parts of our brain, specifically the limbic system, are activated, we are prone to immediate gratification. It's as though the emotional excitement feeds our brain, which then signals us to hurry up and make our choice. Our emotions may then push us to conclude our decision before we've even considered all the options.

This is one of the reasons we're exposed to a lot of sensory information in those Las Vegas casinos. The bleeping machines, flashing lights, clanging slot machines, and screams from the crowd help stimulate our brain, specifically activating the limbic system. As a result, we tend to make quicker (although not as well informed) decisions than usual.

Making Decisions: Feelings versus Calculations

How many times have you been asked to donate to a charity to save impoverished children, endangered species, and victims of floods or earthquakes? How do you base your decision when confronted with multiple charities? Are you more convinced by the flood that killed 1,300 people or the earthquake that left 5,000 people homeless? What are the salient features that convince us where to allocate our limited resources? Is it the tragedy itself, or does the way in which the tragedy is portrayed make the difference?

A creative series of studies looking at people's patterns of donating to save the endangered panda was carried out by psychologists Christopher Hsee and Yuval Rottenstreich at the University of Chicago in 2004.[11] Subjects were asked how much they would donate to save either one or four panda bears. When asked simply by the numbers, people tended to donate more to save four pandas. However, when vivid and emotional descriptions were added to each of the requests, there was no difference in the amount people were willing to donate. In other words, it may not be the number of people we are potentially helping that influences our decision to donate; rather, it is the quality of the emotional description attached to the cause.

In a variation of this study, they asked students how much they would pay for five and then ten used Madonna CDs. The students had been selected to be in one of two groups. One group, the calculation group, had been primed earlier in a seemingly unrelated task in which they were asked a series of math-oriented questions. They had to deal with questions such as, "if an object travels at five feet per second, then by your calculation how far will it travel in 360 seconds?"

The other group was primed to consider their feelings. For example, they were asked, "How do you feel when you hear the name George W. Bush?" Then, half of the students in each group were given a chance to buy five used CDs and the other half were given a chance to buy 10 used CDs. The calculating group was willing to pay $28.81 for 10 CDs and $15.10 for five CDs, on average. This makes logical sense as you might expect to pay close to double for twice as many CDs. The feelings group, however, was willing to pay $19.77 for 10 CDs and $22.64 for five CDs, on average. Not very logical, when you think about it. In other words, by being more emotional at the time of purchase, people in this group were willing to pay a higher price for five

Madonna CDs then they would pay for 10 CDs. This was when emotions were primed at only a moderate intensity.

The authors suggest that, if the subjects were more highly emotionally charged, the price paid may have been even more skewed. Think about a CEO looking at a merger or acquisition. If it's for a company that has a high emotional appeal (for the leader), as opposed to strategic value, the price paid is likely to be much higher than the actual value.

Will gut feelings override logic when it comes to probabilities? Suppose you have a chance to make some money by picking jelly beans out of a bowl. You can select from one of two bowls and you'll get $1 every time you pick a red jelly bean (as opposed to a white one). One bowl has 100 jelly beans and another has only 10 jelly beans. The smaller bowl has a 10 percent chance of picking a red jelly bean, while the larger bowl has a 5 to 9 percent chance of picking a red one. Which bowl would you pick from?

Well, according to a study by Veronika Denes-Raj and Seymour Epstein at the University of Massachusetts, most people, when confronted with the two bowls, go with the larger one.[12] Even though they *knew* the probabilities were lower, people *felt* they had a better chance with the larger bowl. If you've spent any time at summer fairs or carnivals in the games section, you've seen how carnival operators have taken advantage of this aspect of human nature for years. Much money has been made by getting people to bet on their "gut" rather than looking at the probabilities.

One more way that you've seen people "bet with their gut" is through the millions of lottery tickets that get purchased. People will often pay a lot of money to go from a zero probability of winning (no lotto ticket) to a minute possibility of winning the big prize (buying one or many tickets). The emotional excitement of winning far overrides the actual probability that your ticket will be picked. However, this rarely stops someone from continuing to buy these tickets of chance.

How Subjective Are Our Feelings?

As you look at the effect of feelings on decision making you may be wondering—but aren't feelings just subjective states of mind? If I feel a certain way in a situation, would that feeling be the same for someone else in that situation? Don't we all interpret feelings differently? Well, yes and no.

There are some variations in how we feel that are due to our attitudes, beliefs, and the things we tell ourselves about the situation at hand.

On the other hand, there is some consistency in our feelings. You may have been taught that "beauty is in the eye of the beholder." But research has shown that there is a great deal of consensus on what is beautiful and what isn't. People consistently see the same people, and even physical features, as examples of beauty. This has been the case for generations as we still admire pieces of art created hundreds of years ago. It's also been found that beauty is consistent across cultures.

There also seems to be a high level of agreement over emotions experienced with respect to music. Regardless of musical taste, most people will agree that a specific excerpt of music made them feel sad (such as the theme from *Schindler's List*), charged (think of the theme from *Rocky*), or anxious (think of the music from the movie *Jaws*).

People, for the most part, also share feelings about various wrongdoings done by others. In a study by Daniel Kahneman of Princeton, David Schkade of the University of Texas, and Cass Sunstein of the University of Chicago, they looked at how people judge damages when presented with information about a personal injury case.[13] They found that for the most part people would independently agree on the outrageousness of the defendant's action, as well as the appropriate severity of punishment that should occur. At some level, it seems, people universally agree on their perceptions of beauty, emotions evoked by music, and perceptions of justice.

Deciding with Feelings or Logic

Another big question is around which decisions are most likely to stick. Will you be happier choosing a piece of art that appeals to you emotionally, or would you be happier after carefully analyzing its potential investment value, history of the artist, and various other "logical" factors about the painting?

An interesting study by Timothy Wilson and his colleagues at the University of Virginia looked at this issue.[14] Forty-three women were asked to choose which one of five art posters they would receive. Two were reproductions of Impressionist art and three were humorous posters. They were divided into two groups. One group was asked to consider the reasons for their choice—the attributes of the art. The other group chose the piece that appealed to them emotionally.

When all the women were contacted three weeks later and questioned about their satisfaction with the poster, the ones who chose based on various reasons or attributes were less satisfied with their choice than those who used emotion to choose. They were also less likely to have the art hanging on a wall in their home than those who used emotion to choose.

This doesn't only happen with art. Some interesting research shows it's true with other purchase decisions, such as electronic equipment—think smartphones, digital cameras, large screen TVs, camcorders, and computers. People who are really excited about a high-tech gadget are more satisfied for a longer period of time than people who carefully compare and weigh the benefits of one type of gadget (such as a camcorder) over another.

Going with our feelings when it comes to choosing certain material goods gives us longer-term satisfaction. We're happier with our choice both in the short term as well as over time. We're also more willing to overlook any imperfections that arise over time if our decision to buy was an emotional one.

Emotional Decision Making and the Brain

How many times have you heard someone at work asking people to leave their emotions at home? Perhaps on the way to some important strategic planning session? Those pesky emotions could sure get in the way, couldn't they?

Well we now know a lot more about how emotions, the brain, and our ability to make decisions interact. In fact, we now know that emotions are critical to our ability to make decisions. The work of world-renowned neuroscientist Antonio Damasio has helped us get a better understanding of this process.[15] He demonstrated, for example, how emotions are critical to our ability to make decisions. Going after hunches is an important part of decision making. In fact, emotion is just as important as reason when it comes to decision making. Domasio examined how people with damage to their prefrontal cortex, specifically the orbitofrontal cortex, a small region just behind the eyes that's linked to emotions and our understanding of reward and punishment, are affected in their ability to make decisions.

Domasio found that people with damaged orbitofrontal cortexes struggled significantly when making the simplest decisions. That's because they were unable to use their gut feeling for guidance.

That emotional pull, or gut feeling, that helps us make so many decisions in our lives is what Damasio calls a "somatic marker." Decisions can be made more efficiently using somatic markers rather than having to take the time to reason out every choice we make. In other words, hunches are a shortcut to good decision making according to Damasio.

On the other hand, impulsive thinking, or acting on emotions, can also be dangerous because it's the default mode we often go to when making choices. According to Daniel Kahneman, who won the Nobel Prize for his work on the psychology of judgment and decision making, the brain operates under two systems: System 1 and System 2, also known as fast and slow thinking.[16]

Fast thinking, or what Kahneman calls System 1, happens almost automatically with little effort or voluntary control. System 2, on the other hand, involves reasoning and careful consideration. "One of the tasks of System 2 is to overcome the impulses of System 1." He describes this as System 2 overseeing self-control. But more about impulse control later.

Making Strategic Business Decisions

More research on the importance of emotions in making "rational" decisions can be found in some pioneering brain research reported in the *Harvard Business Review* by Roderick Gilkey, Ricardo Caceda, and Clinton Kilts.[17] In their report, they write about how many companies treat strategy and execution as separate worlds. However, separating these two functions, according to their research, does more harm than good. People typically think of strategic reasoning as a high level executive function of the brain whereas tactical thought is believed to be a lower-level brain activity.

However, Gilkey and his colleagues showed that the two types of thinking are linked in a very important way. They both require social-emotional reasoning. They reported that strategic thought requires as much emotional intelligence as it requires IQ.

Together with Diana Robertson and Andrew Bate of the Wharton School of Business, they asked a number of managers to react to fictional strategic and tactical management dilemmas. As they worked on these problems, their brain activity was measured through functional magnetic resonance imaging (fMRI). In doing so, they went beyond studies that just looked at which parts of the brain "light up" and looked at how regions of the brain interacted.

The prefrontal cortex—top front of the brain—is the area that has been associated with strategic thought, a part of executive functioning. Executive function refers to our ability to plan or anticipate things, recognize patterns, evaluate probabilities, estimate risks, and think abstractly. These are skills that leaders typically use to solve problems.

These researchers discovered that when executives engaged in these kinds of executive tasks, there was actually less activity in the prefrontal cortex than there was in the areas that are associated with "gut" responses, empathy, and emotional intelligence. These emotional areas of the brain are referred to as the insula, the anterior cingulate cortex, and the superior temporal sulcus. What this means is that the conscious executive functioning was actually downplayed. The real calculating that went on had more to do with subtly processing emotions.

The results went even further. They found that the strongest performers' tactical reasoning was also affected by the insula, used in emotional processing, and the anterior cingulate cortex, used in making new choices based on assessing past outcomes. However, in addition, it used the part of the brain reserved for understanding sensory information and anticipating other people's thoughts and emotions—the superior temporal sulcus. This part of the brain helps an executive understand how the action plans would be perceived by the people in the organization who are responsible for carrying them out.

So it would seem that we still need our IQ or cognitive intelligence to carry out strategic and tactical tasks, but our emotional skills play a much more important role than we ever believed. Our emotions influence how decisions are made while the prefrontal cortex makes plans so that our decisions can be executed. So now you can rephrase that old saying to "make sure you bring your emotions to work."

Decision Making and Reality Testing: Which Emotions When?

Decision making involves your ability to notice and process cues from the environment around you, your own emotions, and your perception of the feelings of others. Your mood, together with your ability to attend to cues, can have a profound impact on the outcome of your decisions. An emotionally intelligent person recognizes the need to engage specific emotions in order to process relevant sources of information. In other words, your ability to manage change and solve problems depends on your ability to match your emotions with the demands of the specific situation. Your ability to realistically evaluate people and situations comes into play.

Our emotions dictate the intensity of our mood, which in turn directly influences our thoughts and behaviors. As previously outlined, emotions have differing effects on our decision-making process. Both our positive and negative emotions—whether we're happy or sad—directly influence both our thinking and physical resources allocated to the decision-making process needed to finish tasks.

So when we experience positive emotions, such as happiness, elation, and exuberance, we tend to overestimate the likelihood that we'll have a positive outcome and underestimate the chances that we'll have a negative outcome. The opposite of this is also true. When we're in a grounded state of mind we'll most likely be at our best in solving interpersonal and personal problems and managing change.

Being emotionally intelligent means you'll have the ability to successfully distinguish the emotions best suited to a particular situation from those associated with other parts of daily life and use those emotions to navigate the decision-making process. For example, a task, personal encounter, or problem that evokes emotions with a negative tone signals that there is a problem going on or coming up. The subdued mood that you get with these emotions is best suited to manage this situation. This mood sets you up for using a more detail-oriented approach to solving the problem.

On the other hand, experiencing positive emotions can be linked to the acceptance of a safe, nonthreatening environment. As a result, your positive feelings make you more creative and quicker at making decisions—often using past experience as a guide.

Subdued emotions are better for detailed information processing, while positive emotions increase your creativity, rapid thinking, and decisions based on past experience. Here are some reasons why better emotional intelligence will make you more skilled at decision making:

1. You'll be able to successfully recognize when you need to activate the right emotion for the right task. So, when you need to make decisions that

involve a lot of detailed attention to your surroundings you'll know you should be in a more subdued emotional state.
2. You'll be able to manage change and solve problems of a personal and interpersonal nature based on your emotional state. For example, when in a good mood, you'll be better able to make decisions that rely on past information and knowledge that you've stored in memory. This is when your "gut reaction" best applies.
3. You'll be better aware of the "problem" and the appropriate emotional response. Emotions affect your decision making in many different ways. One good example is when you are buying something new that you're excited about. The positive emotions from all that excitement can overshadow the detailed evaluation of a savvy purchaser sometimes leading to buyer's remorse. However, when you're better able to manage your emotions you are more likely to ask more informed and useful questions to guide your purchase decision.

Impulse Control and Decision Making

David was a leader who liked to take control. While he encouraged his senior team members to come up with solutions to problems, he always managed to engineer the outcomes his way. He was also known for making quick decisions, some of which had to be eventually reversed for the good of the company. Like many entrepreneurs, he verged close to being ADHD (attention deficit/hyperactivity disordered). While he was never professionally diagnosed, he seemed to display many of the signs and symptoms.

So it was no surprise when the team was confronted with a decision involving the hiring of a new sales manager, that David would present some resistance. Everyone had been presented detailed profile reports from the search firm that was used, and all the senior staff, except for David, had interviewed the final three candidates. There was agreement among the senior team that Virginia was the best candidate based on almost all the selection criteria, including best fit within the company. Each of the candidate's results was to be presented, one by one, by Elinor, the HR director, along with the final recommendation.

After listening impatiently through the first few minutes of the presentation, David blurted out, "Yes, but didn't Leo work for our biggest competitor?"

"He did," Elinor explained, "but let me first review each of the candidates, so we can make the most informed decision. Besides, that alone doesn't mean he was the best qualified for the job."

"That may be, but we can get customer lists, inside information on their operations. Why wouldn't you just hire him?" David continued.

Rudy answered, "Look David, we looked at each choice carefully, just let us review the findings and . . .

"And what?" Dave interrupted, "I don't see why you wouldn't just grab him."

"As I was saying, we looked at each choice carefully. That included the pluses and minuses, and we all agreed, after looking at everything, that he wasn't our best choice for this job. In fact, if you let Elinor finish, you'll see why Virginia is the best overall choice for the company," Rudy replied.

Not only does David's impulsiveness disrupt the flow of information, it also sends a message that he doesn't trust those around him who were given responsibility for these kinds of decisions. It doesn't mean that David can't ask questions about the choice or the process leading up to it, but rather that he should respectfully hear them out first. Once the case has been presented, he can more tactfully respond with his questions, such as:

> "Did you consider Leo's previous employment?"
> "What does Virginia bring to the table that Leo doesn't?"
> "What were the factors that weighed most in your decision making?"
> "In what ways do you see Virginia as a better company fit?"

By learning to control his impulsiveness, David could be a much better contributor to the success of the organization and much less of an obstacle. I have often seen managers or senior leaders who can't help but interject into a well-functioning process. Whether it's because of the ADHD, impulsiveness, or simply the ego-based fear of not being in control, a lack of impulse control and poor interpersonal skills are one of the biggest derailers, or causes of failure for leaders.

The EQ Leader: Things to Think About

Coaching these leaders has often involved giving them tasks—mental or physical—to perform while letting others take the floor. Some techniques that you can use with leaders, or if you are a leader with this issue include:

1. Using a pen and paper and simply taking point form notes of what other people are saying. The leader cannot respond verbally until a predetermined time after the discussion has run its course.
2. Having the leader focus on key words while other people are talking. The focus is on words that strike you in a positive or negative way.
3. Some leaders need to keep themselves physically occupied to not interfere. That's when either pad and pen, or other objects, such as a small toy, can be useful. However, smartphone or tablet should not be used as it is more likely it will draw attention away from the task at hand.

Things to keep mind when making decisions:

1. Pay attention to your emotions, and practice determining whether they are positive or negative.
2. Once you know whether you are getting positive or negative vibes in a situation, focus on those feelings. Let your mind follow the emotion and see what thoughts are triggered. Try not to fight the emotion, do your best to try and understand it.
3. Once you have a sense of the thinking "attached" to the emotion, come back to the decision at hand. Then ask yourself questions about your thoughts.
   a. Was my emotional response reasonable based on my thoughts?
   b. How important are those thoughts in this decision?
   c. Am I overblowing the importance of some fears from some past, perhaps similar situation(s)?
   d. Are there more pieces of information I need to consider for this decision?
   e. Basically, overall, am I getting a good or bad feel about the decision I'm about to make?

PART V

Stress Management and Leadership

Stress Management and Leadership

Flexibility

The ability to adjust their feelings, thoughts, and actions to changing, challenging, or unfamiliar conditions

Stress Tolerance

The ability to remain calm and focused and to constructively withstand adverse events and conflicting emotions without caving in

Optimism

The ability to maintain a realistically positive attitude, particularly in the face of adversity

Chapter 9

Stress Management and Leadership

Only three things happen naturally in organizations: friction, confusion, and underperformance. Everything else requires leadership.

—PETER DRUCKER

More companies die because of the rigidity of their leaders than any other single cause, according to an article in *Forbes* by Dina Gerdeman.[1] She points out that less than 0.1 percent of firms in the United States make it to the age of 40 years. Amazingly, only 10 percent of firms founded in 1976 were still operating in 1986.

In addition, we are all well aware of those large, longstanding, seemingly infallible companies that collapsed: Polaroid (started in 1937), RCA (which was twice the size of IBM in 1955), Blockbuster, RadioShack, Borders, and many others. The lack of agility of the leaders in these organizations, perhaps combined with poor planning and execution of strategies for changing markets, led to their downfall. Gerdeman cites the work of Harvard Business professor Michael Tushman and Stanford Business professor Charles O'Reilly III who concluded, "The leaders of these companies were rigid in one way or another—unable or unwilling to sense new opportunities and to reconfigure the firm's assets in ways that permitted the company to continue to survive and prosper."[2]

Of course, they also present examples of companies whose leaders were successfully able to make these transitions. For example, IBM started out in 1913 as a mechanical tabulating machine manufacturer and is now a $100 billion company that gets 85 percent of its revenue from software and services that didn't even exist 50 years ago. Amazon, which began as an online bookseller, is now the largest web retailer and a major player in cloud-based utility computing. In order to succeed, these authors talk about leaders needing the ability to *run today's business* while simultaneously *working toward the future*. You need different skills and an adaptable mind-set to accomplish both tasks. Also, you must define your organization in a way that allows for both *exploiting* existing products or services and *exploring* new products and services. IBM has been able to define itself in a way that transitions itself over time:

IBM's own website states, "IBM's character has been formed over nearly 100 years of doing business in the field of information-handling. Nearly all of the company's products were designed and developed to record, process, communicate, store, and retrieve information—from its first scales, tabulators and clocks to today's powerful computers and vast global networks."[3]

This constant state of innovation is described by IBM CEO, Ginni Rometty as, "Digital is the wires, but digital intelligence, or artificial intelligence as some people call it, is about much more than that. This next decade is about how you combine those and become a cognitive business. It's the dawn of a new era."[4]

In other words, she's prepared IBM for the next decade and its continued exploration. By narrowly focusing on your current activities you run the risk of future disruption. Often it's the anxiety about change that keeps us locked in our present day mentality.

I started MHS as a narrowly focused test publishing company. We began by computerizing traditional paper-and-pencil psychological tests into the newly released (at the time) Apple (II and 2e) microcomputers. We soon discovered that psychologists were not on the leading edge but rather the trailing edge of technology. If they were to adopt computers at all it was most likely for office management purposes, not for putting their patients in front of. We then created a mental health office management system (called SHRINK) that was fairly successful. However, during that process we also ended up creating a paper version of our most popular computerized psychological rating scale at the time, the Conners' Rating Scales®, the first assessment used for ADHD.

Subsequently, as technology (and the times) changed we had to move (meaning rewrite the code for) our computerized assessments from Apple DOS on to MS DOS, MS DOS Networks, Windows (and each subsequent upgrade), SDK's (software development kits, for large institutional and state-wide orders), online (web-based), APIs (Application Program Interfaces), and cloud-based operating systems and platforms.

As well, we had to redefine ourselves as an organization. Over time, we no longer thought of ourselves as simply a test publishing company, but rather as an organization that helps professionals transform people's lives. In our clinical and educational division, for example, we help psychologists, psychiatrists, and other mental health professionals more accurately assess and diagnose ADHD, autism, depression, anxiety, and other disorders in children and adults so that patients get the right treatment that helps them cope better in life.

In our public safety division, where we measure risk assessment, we help probation and correctional officers keep our streets safe and ensure that offenders get the right amount of supervision. In other words, our assessments are used to ensure that we don't fill our jails with people who don't need to be there, and that we keep the dangerous people under lock and key.

In our talent division, we help human resource professionals and organizational psychologists identify the right people for the right job and develop leadership skills in high potential employees and new leaders. Our assessments offer actionable strategies to clients, thereby enabling people to reach their potential and giving organizations the means to function better.

Not only does redefining your mission help you find more purpose in your work, it broadens your vision, and leads to greater people engagement. By redefining what you do as something purposeful and meaningful to employees, customers, partners, and the community at large, you gain many advantages. Not the least of which it helps you stay relevant, as the world around you changes. It also makes disruption of your industry more difficult. To effectively lead organizations through change requires flexible leadership.

In terms of the vision of the organization, just as Ginni Rometty sees IBM as becoming a "cognitive business," I see MHS as being in the business of scientifically predicting human behavior. By having a broad vision we don't stay focused on narrow tasks.

If MHS, for example, stayed narrowly focused on publishing psychological tests for psychologists on the computer system of the day, we likely would have disappeared as a company long ago. In fact, back in the early 1980s, when we started MHS, there were a number of such companies in my industry—Psychometrics, Psychologistics, PsychSystems, PsychoMeter, Software Office Solutions, and many others whose names I now forget. The point, however, is that they have all disappeared. Fortunately, we were flexible enough to enable the company to expand into new areas, with just the right amount of risk taking.

Leading an organization when times are good and things are going well is not when one thinks of flexibility. However, when times get tough, or we encounter challenges, that's when the need to be flexible as a leader arises. Even when those challenges seem far off in the distance, the importance of flexibility comes into play because flexible leaders are typically skilled at sensing potential sources of disruption.

The ability to remain flexible in times of stress or crisis is a skill that leaders can develop. There has been a fair bit of research on flexibility during difficult times, much of which is summarized by Gary Yukl of the University of Albany and Rubina Mahsud of Seattle University.[5]

They identified the following steps flexible leaders take in anticipation and management of stressful events:

1. Become aware of early warning signs of crises that can affect your organization. Do not become complacent and ignore or minimize these warning signs.
2. Quickly analyze and better understand any immediate problems or crises.
3. Be receptive and open to new information or anything you may have overlooked as you confidently direct the response of your team.
4. Respond in a way that is consistent with the core values of your organization and high standards of corporate social responsibility.

5. Plan on how to avoid serious problems and make contingency plans for those problems you can't avoid.
6. Keep everyone informed about the problem and how it is being resolved.
7. After the crisis ends carry out a review session to determine what was done well, what mistakes were made, and what lessons were learned.

Stress Tolerance and Leadership

Craig was having a hard day. He is the CEO of a medium-sized technology company and he had been experiencing a high turnover rate among his software developers. He has several projects underway, but the deadlines keep slipping away due to the staff disruptions. In one case, because of the high customer demand, they prematurely released one of their cloud-based business management products. It had been rushed through their quality assurance process without proper vetting.

Between the high number of customer complaints over errors in the financial management program and staff resignations, Craig was stressed out. He felt uneasy in his stomach each morning as he entered his office building. Just flipping through the high number of service tickets registered by his tech support department made his head spin. Craig's stress level was getting to the point that it affected his basic functioning. His decision making was becoming questionable.

Sometimes the stress of running an organization can be overwhelming. This is especially true when the organization faces problems. If a leader struggles with the problems at work when they're relatively small and manageable, it can only get worse when the difficulties start to escalate. There's likely more than one issue at play in Craig's case. The first is whether he has the ability and right competencies as a leader to work through the problems his company is facing. He may need a skilled manager that can take charge of his product development and customer support issues. He also needs an experienced human resource person to manage his personnel issues. Next, he needs to be able to manage the stress he is experiencing. It is highly unlikely that he can properly focus and come up with solutions to his problems when distracted by the effects of stress.

Craig reached a point where he had to deal with his stress. It was consuming all his time and taking over his life. He realized, with some help from a CEO peer group he belonged to, that he needed to redirect his energy. The group encouraged him to engage a senior, experienced executive coach. It was important for Craig to gain some self-awareness of his current emotional strengths and challenges. The coach administered a Leadership EQ-i 2.0 to Craig and debriefed him on his results. His low scores on Stress Tolerance, Problem Solving, and Impulse Control provided the coach with direction in how to frame the intervention.

As part of the coaching initiative Craig learned more about his strengths and weaknesses, both emotionally and management-related. He learned to be more in control of his emotions and was more comfortable handing over control of a number of business functions to senior staff. By learning how to better manage others, and giving up his command and control style, things started to improve. He brought in and empowered an HR director and project manager to take over some tasks that he wasn't managing well. These tasks were a source of pain for him.

Over the course of a year there were significant improvements in Craig's company. Turnover was down, and projects weren't being released until there was a proper quality assurance process in place. Customer satisfaction went up dramatically, and revenue and profitability improved.

Managing stress is an important part of leadership success. Being a leader of an organization used to mean putting in long hours of continuous work, taking little time to enjoy life, family, or anything else. Most successful leaders I know today have learned how to balance their lifestyle. If they are putting in too many hours at work it usually means they don't have a strong team working with him or her.

I find it's important to schedule recreational and family times in my calendar just as I schedule product development and marketing meetings. Whether it's my band practice, time to work out, an evening at the theater, or an event with my grandson, I like to see it on my calendar.

When it comes to managing stress, there are many options to choose from. However, not everyone is comfortable using every technique available and no one method works for everybody. I recommend mindfulness and meditation to a lot of people, and I find it works for many of them. But, in all honesty, it doesn't work well for me. I find that I can feel much more relaxed after an hour's practice on one of my saxophones because playing and listening to music is a great relaxer for me. Some people do well going out for a half-hour walk or working out in the gym. I worked with one executive who enjoyed putting on boxing gloves and sparring with a punching bag. There is no one size fits all. You really need to find out what works best for you. If you are unfamiliar with mindfulness, meditation, or yoga, you might want to sign up for a trial class to experience it and see if it works for you.

How Can You Better Manage Your Time?

For many leaders, I see the attempt at even trying to manage their time as stressful. Using checklists and schedules may be helpful, but to really get control over your time I find that being values based helps a lot. So rather than starting with activities—time-limited occurrences at specific points in time—I like to start with values. I have leaders rank order the most important things in their life, such as:

1. Family
2. Work
3. Fitness
4. Health
5. Social activities
6. Friends
7. Vacation
8. Tennis
9. Dance
10. Travel
11. Live theater
12. Movies
13. And so on

Once you've established the values and activities that are most important to you, you can then set goals within each one. You can also specify a frequency and amount of time you want to spend in each area:

Working out—3 times/week for 1 hour each time

Senior Team meetings—1 time/week for 1 hour (Mondays)

Check on product development—1 time every 2 weeks

As you go through the exercise your priorities will become much clearer. You can move from there to scheduling the ideal dates and times for you to execute each of your activities. Of course, you must build in some flexibility, but try and stick with your plan. For example, I have band practices booked weekly into my schedule and my assistant knows not to book any meetings for that time. However, things happen: I travel, we get an out-of-town author or business associate visiting us, and so on. So be prepared to adjust (flexibility) and reallocate your time.

The Half-Full Glass

Imagine Bryan, the company CEO, coming out to address 50 of his staff at a town hall meeting after having the worst financial quarter of the company's ten-year history:

> Unfortunately, I'm here to deliver some bad news. As you all know it's been a tough few months. We lost out on some major bids and we lost a couple of our long-term customers to our competition. We also lost a couple of our sales reps. It's been a bad quarter. In fact, this has been the worst quarter in our entire history. I don't really know what we can do to get out of this. I was hoping to deliver better news. But I can't. We're just going to have to tighten things up. We'll have to cut back on expenses. We'll do less travel. Our sales are really down. We have to get them up somehow. I just don't know how yet. I think we all should just work harder. I don't know if we can get out of this downward spiral. I guess we'll have to try and see what happens. The future doesn't look good.
>
> Okay, let's go out there and win!

Now if you read that again, but slower, how does it make you feel? Does it inspire you? Are you ready to go all out and win for the company? I know of one case where a similar speech led to people dusting off their resumes and starting their job search.

On the other hand, what if Bryan had delivered the following speech?

> Hi everyone. I know it's been a difficult few months. We've had a tough quarter. Things didn't go quite as we expected. But you have all worked hard, and as managers, we really appreciate your efforts. We had a few rough breaks, but I'm confident that we, together, can overcome that. We've seen some tough times before. I've been meeting with the senior team, looking at ways to turn this around. Together with the senior team we've already

> thought of a few things that can make a difference for us. As well, we'll be putting together a cross-company team with someone representing each department, to get together and brainstorm some new ideas that we can go forward with. With everyone's help and all of us pulling together I am confident we will break out of this. We have the talent and will to have a great year. Together we're going to make it happen. Let's all work together to get there. I'm proud of you all and I know we can do great things.
>
> So, let's go out there and win!

How do you feel after that speech? As a leader, I know that speech is more likely to get the results you need. As with most leaders, I've been in that place, where sales were down and things were tough. I've had to give a speech like that one. And, in fact, we did pull together and get out of the hole we were in and were able to rise to a much better place.

Optimism is much more than saying the glass is half full. Optimism, as we see it and measure it in emotional intelligence terms, is more about resilience. It's not just seeing the world through rose colored glasses. It's acknowledging the reality of where we are, and having a vision of where we need to get to. It's the confidence of maintaining that vision even though the going gets tough sometimes. If you lead an organization, as I have, then you know how scary it can be having responsibility for the financial welfare of other people and their families. The risks that you take can affect not just your own wellbeing, but that of dozens, or hundreds, of people and their families who are depending on the success of your organization. On the other hand, I feel great pride when I see people in our organization buying a new car, getting a new house, growing their family. One of the real joys of leading a successful company is knowing that something you created has given so much, both emotionally and materially, to the people who have contributed to it. It gives me a great sense of gratitude.

There are several studies demonstrating the importance of optimism in leadership, but one that still stands out for me, over the years is the study carried out by Dr. Marian Ruderman of the Center for Creative Leadership (CCL) in Greensboro, North Carolina.[6] Founded in 1970, the CCL is a world-famous, nonprofit, top-rated global provider of leadership development. It's ranked by the *Financial Times* as one of the top five worldwide executive education programs.

Several years back, when the concept of emotional intelligence was still relatively new, I received a call from Marian telling me about their programs and about how leaders from all over the world came to their center. She pointed out that while they had many top-level, excellent leaders coming to enhance their skills, they also had some struggling leaders who, in fact, were one step away from being dismissed from their positions if they didn't shape up. This, she explained, was a great opportunity to see if emotional intelligence was important in leadership. Their group had reviewed the various measures of emotional intelligence available and had decided that the EQ-i was the best validated tool to use for this. As well, the EQ-i model of emotional intelligence would be a good fit for organizational leaders.

Of course, I jumped at the opportunity. In those days, I hadn't really thought very much about the potential impact of emotional intelligence and leadership. Here was a world-class organization willing to do an independent study on our tool, which was selected as the best among the various emotional intelligence tools starting to crop up. In the CCL study, 302 leaders and senior managers, ranging from very successful to barely struggling along, were tested for emotional intelligence with the EQ-i. They were also assessed for their on-the-job performance with Benchmarks®, a tool designed to get a clear picture of leadership performance from superiors, peers, and subordinates.

One of Dr. Ruderman's findings was that emotional intelligence, as measured by the EQ-i, accounted for roughly 28 percent of leadership performance. This finding is consistent with other studies that have used the EQ-i 2.0. The findings, comparing high-performing, average, and low-performing leaders can be seen in Figure 9.1.

Three of the areas that significantly differentiated the high performing leaders from the unsuccessful leaders were Interpersonal Relationships, Stress Tolerance, and Optimism. While poor interpersonal relationships were found to be the best predictor of leader derailment, optimism is a good predictor of leadership success. Good interpersonal relationship skills enable leaders to manage all of the people aspects of the business. The ability to manage stress enables a leader to remain grounded and confident, even when dealing with crises. A confident leader, even in difficult times, is reassuring to others on the team, and allows them to deal with what they need to do more effectively.

There have been many similar studies carried out, some published and some kept within the confines of the organization carrying out the research. They

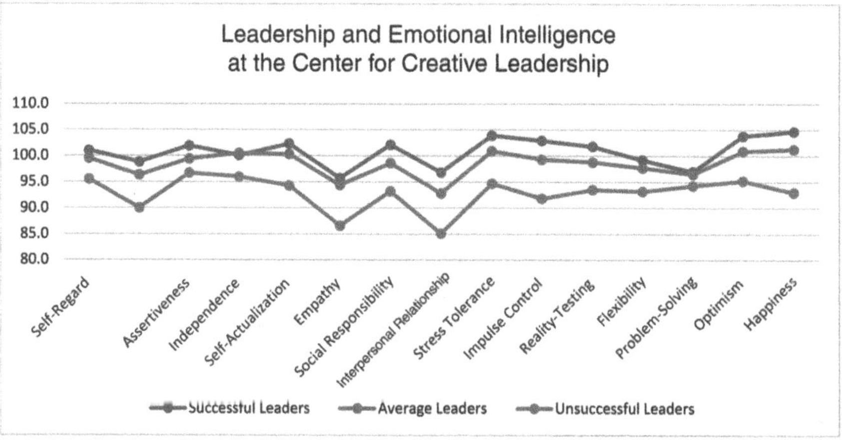

Figure 9.1 EQ-i Scores of Leaders Participating in Leadership Training at the Center for Creative Leadership

have spanned across different types of organizations, industries, and geographic locations. Consistently, the EQ-i (and EQ-i 2.0) has helped differentiate the more effective leaders from the less successful ones.

Cheryl Meredith at Capella University carried out a study of executive leaders across several nonprofit, faith-based organizations based in Colorado.[7] The leaders of these organizations were assessed for their transformational leadership style, as well as their emotional intelligence with the EQ-i. Transformational leadership styles were, once again, highly correlated with emotional intelligence. Further analysis revealed that five components of emotional intelligence accounted for over half of the variation in transformational leadership behavior. The five were (1) optimism, (2) self-actualization, (3) empathy, (4) problem solving, and (5) assertiveness. The leaders scored higher than the general population on all of these scales except for empathy. The study concludes by highlighting the importance of training leaders in emotional intelligence to maximize their effectiveness.

In summary, we all have preferred ways of managing our own stress. Our ability to be flexible, tolerate stress, and be optimistic all contribute to how well we can lead others through stressful situations and have the potential to influence the long-term health of our organizations. Developing these skills, which can be effectively accomplished through a professional coach, is an important part of leadership development.

The EQ Leader: Some Things to Think About

1. Do you consider yourself flexible?
2. Think of some of the major changes and adaptations you have made career wise. How easy or difficult did you find these changes?
3. How have some of the leaders you've worked with managed change?
4. When changes happen at your workplace do you tend to be an early adopter or do you have more of a "wait and see how this turns out" approach?
5. How do you normally deal with stress?
6. What is your most effective way of "de-stressing" yourself?
7. When there's stress at work, are you seen more as a calming influence or do you tend to get caught up in the mayhem?
8. Do you tend to think that things will always work out or do you focus more on how bad a problem is?
9. An exercise we have trained people in at MHS is to come to their manager with solutions, never with a problem. So, whenever something has gone "wrong," you should have two or three possible solutions, with one recommendation on how to go forward.
10. How can you train yourself to be more (realistically) optimistic?

PART VI

The Four Pillars of Successful Leadership

Development of the Model

Authenticity

Lead authentically to inspire and motivate others:

Commands esteem and confidence, inspires fair and moral behavior, and acts as a role model

Coaching

Support employee's needs and nurture development:

Operates as a mentor, responds to concerns and queries, and supports employee needs

Insight

Communicate with purpose, meaning, and vision:

Communicates a purpose, meaning, and vision, hopeful view of the future, compels employees to reach and exceed goals

Innovation

Foster ingenuity, imagination, and autonomous thinking:

Understands the importance of taking risks, spurring ingenuity, imagination, autonomous thinking, values knowledge, and challenges seen as learning opportunities

Chapter 10

The Four Pillars of Successful Leadership

Developing the Model

By being authentic, supporting employees' needs, communicating with purpose, and fostering ingenuity, you can become a successful leader for the future.

—STEVEN J. STEIN

What is it that makes a successful leader today, and how can you get there and stay there? While research and real-life experience continues to teach us what makes leaders great, as well as why leaders fail to succeed, this chapter combines what we've learned from the literature with our own original work in this area. The talented staff at MHS has contributed a great deal in the compilation and execution of this work. In this chapter, I will present you with how we arrived at our Four-Pillar Model of leadership. In the next four chapters, I'll provide you with steps you can take to increase your own leadership style along the lines of this model. As well, the model is intended to be used by professionals who work with leaders in their development.

Most of the previous chapters have dealt with the basic (emotional intelligence) skills we believe are important for leaders. These skills are important parts of our model. Developing these skills is an ongoing, perhaps even lifelong process.

In this chapter, I intend to deal with the competencies of leadership. Being successful at mastering the competencies implies that you have some basic abilities at the skill level. Each competency is composed of a cluster of basic emotional intelligence skills. So, assuming you have mastered each of the basic skills to a level comparable to other leaders (which can be measured in the EQ-i 2.0 Leadership Report), you are ready to develop the competencies of high EQ leaders.

Developing the Four-Pillar Model: Theories of Leadership

We began with an exhaustive review of the literature surrounding emotional intelligence and leadership to determine which leadership dimensions were most applicable and practical for leadership experts—trainers, facilitators, coaches, organizational psychologists, as well as aspiring and experienced leaders themselves. The philosophy behind our leadership research was to arrive at a succinct set of leadership dimensions that underpinned most any leadership model and provided a framework for organizing the EQ-i 2.0 subscales in a way that effectively highlighted leadership development areas for aspiring and current leaders.

We found that there are a variety of different leadership models and tools in use today, but many had common themes, particularly in leadership theories that have emotional intelligence behaviors at their core. In addition, we surveyed the many thousands of consultants and learning and development professionals that we work with, who are actively involved with organizations (both internal and external). Many of them have their own customized leadership competency frameworks and models for what successful leadership looks like within their organizations. Therefore, it was important that our model's language and leadership dimensions support these frameworks as well.

The review of the literature, and our survey work, led to the arrival of four common leadership dimensions (or pillars) that were inherent to most definitions and models of leadership: Authenticity, Coaching, Insight, and Innovation. To validate that these four areas of leadership were related to our model of emotional intelligence (EQ-i 2.0), data collection efforts were undertaken that were validated with measures of effectiveness in these four leadership areas.

Much of the leadership and emotional intelligence research centers around the model of transformational leadership.[1] As its name implies, transformational leadership looks at the process of changing and transforming individuals. James Burns, a leadership theorist,[2] described transformational leadership as a process in which leaders and subordinates raise one another to higher levels of morality and motivation. Transformational leaders motivate individuals to perform beyond baseline expectations, arouse dormant needs in their subordinates, and can regulate their own emotions.

Transformational leaders often seek to empower subordinates, which increases subordinate commitment. An effective transformational leader knows how emotions affect others' interactions, whom others will follow, and how to make decisions. Transformational leaders are also able to understand and manage their own emotions, making it possible for them to be flexible and creative in their decision making, consider alternative approaches, and have the self-confidence needed to act.[3]

Emotional intelligence plays a particularly important role in transforming others. There are a number of research studies (some cited in previous chapters) that associate emotional intelligence and transformational leadership, and show positive relationships between the two constructs.[4]

There are several other leadership theories we examined, as well, including:

Authentic Leadership: an approach to leadership that emphasizes building the leader's legitimacy through honest relationships with followers that value their input and are built on an ethical foundation. Generally, authentic leaders are positive people with truthful self-concepts who promote openness.

Charismatic Leadership: the process of encouraging certain behaviors in others via force of personality, persuasion, and eloquent communication. Charismatic leaders inspire their followers to do things, or to do things better; this is done by conjuring up enthusiasm in others for a stated vision or goal.

Twenty-First-Century Leadership: a perspective of leadership intended to respond to the unique challenges and opportunities of today's world. It is a multidimensional and integrative view of leadership that is based in relationships. It is oriented toward being inclusive, collaborative, and of service, to individuals, the social good, and ecological sustainability.

Developing the Four-Pillar Model: Collecting and Analyzing the Data

We started data collection with 221 leaders derived from a variety of organizations throughout North America who completed the EQ-i 2.0 and the Multifactor Leadership Questionnaire (MLQ).[5] The MLQ assesses different leadership types, such as passive or avoidant leadership (i.e., laissez-faire leadership), leaders who focus on an exchange relationship and use rewards/punishments to get the job done (i.e., transactional leadership), and the gold standard of leadership (i.e., transformational leadership; engaged leaders who are adept at harnessing employee potential), which includes behaviors akin to the four leadership dimensions presented earlier.

Correlational analyses were used to determine which EQ-i 2.0 subscales were related with the most widely used transformational leadership measure (MLQ). This was done to determine which EQ-i 2.0 subscales help fuel success in each leadership dimension. Subsequent analyses also correlated the EQ-i 2.0 with laissez-faire leadership to see which subscales contributed to leadership derailment. These results were used to support the theoretical underpinnings for the current Four Pillars leadership model.

The participants, who reflect current leadership census in organizations, were mostly male (64.7 percent), white (79.2 percent), with at least a bachelor's degree (85.5 percent). The average age was 46.8 years. The most highly represented position, as seen in Figure 10.1, was CEO (29.0 percent), followed by Director (19.9 percent), and Manager (19.9 percent). Most leaders (44.8 percent), as seen in Figures 10.2 and 10.3, worked in large organizations (i.e., more than 400 employees), with an annual revenue exceeding $10 million (57.5 percent).

While this represents our current, overall reference sample, we are also examining the different profiles represented by successful female, African American, Hispanic, Asian American, and other leaders of special interest. In addition, we are collecting data worldwide looking at the cultural variations of leaders (some of which is reported in a later chapter). We are also looking at differences in leadership styles across different industry sectors (e.g., manufacturing, retail sales, financial services, pharmaceutical, airlines, government, nonprofits, military, police forces, high tech, mining, oil and gas, consulting companies, accounting services, legal, distribution, and others).

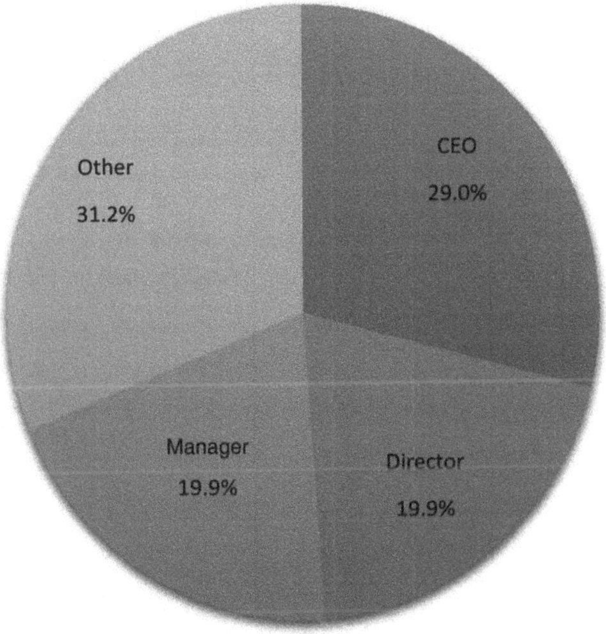

Figure 10.1 Role in Organization

Source: Reprinted with permission of MHS, 2016.

Our starting premise was that if leaders score higher in emotional intelligence than the general population, it would support the idea that high emotional intelligence is a key characteristic of leaders. Scores in our leadership sample were compared to scores from the EQ-i 2.0 general population normative sample. As expected, the leaders' scores were significantly higher than the North American norm group (general population). The leadership sample's scores were also higher than the normative group on all subscales (see Figure 10.4). All the details of the analyses, for those readers who are into the minutiae of data analysis, are available from MHS.[6]

From our results, we then separated the leaders into two groups: (1) those who were classified as high in transformational leadership and (2) those who were classified as taking a more transactional (or less transformational) approach.

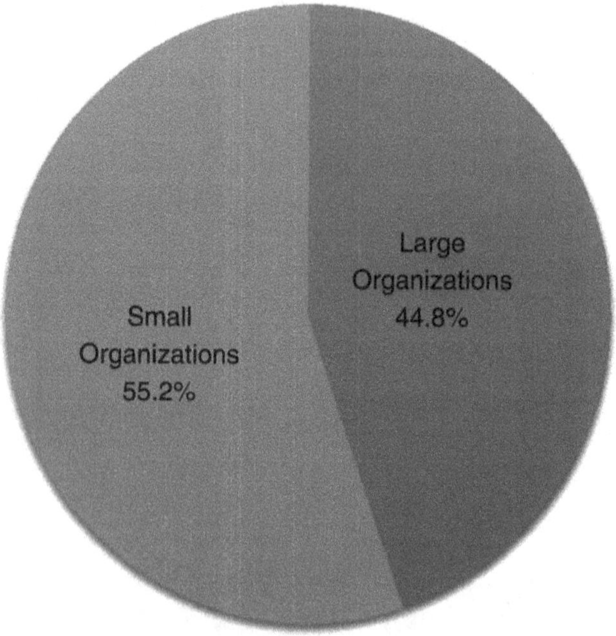

Figure 10.2 Size of Organization

Source: Reprinted with permission of MHS, 2016.

The results indicated that those with predominantly transformational leadership styles scored significantly higher in emotional intelligence than those with predominantly transactional leadership styles. Transformational leaders also had substantially higher scores on virtually all the subscales (with the exceptions being Assertiveness, Independence, and Problem Solving). The meaningfully higher scores found in transformational relative to transactional leaders provides preliminary validation for the idea that leaders whose approach values transforming and growing their teams have higher levels of emotional intelligence than those who are more transactional in nature.

A strong positive relationship was found between EQ-i 2.0 subscales and aspects of transformational leadership. Except for Impulse Control, all EQ-i 2.0 scores correlated strongly with all transformational leadership characteristics.

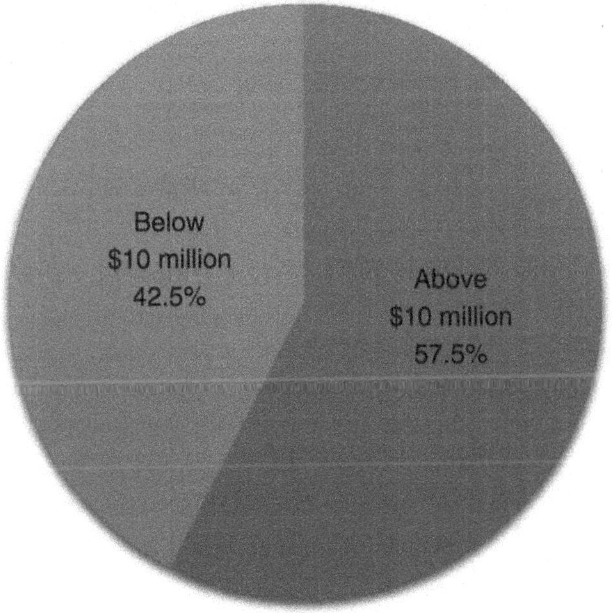

Figure 10.3 Size of Organization Based on Earnings

Source: Reprinted with permission of MHS, 2016.

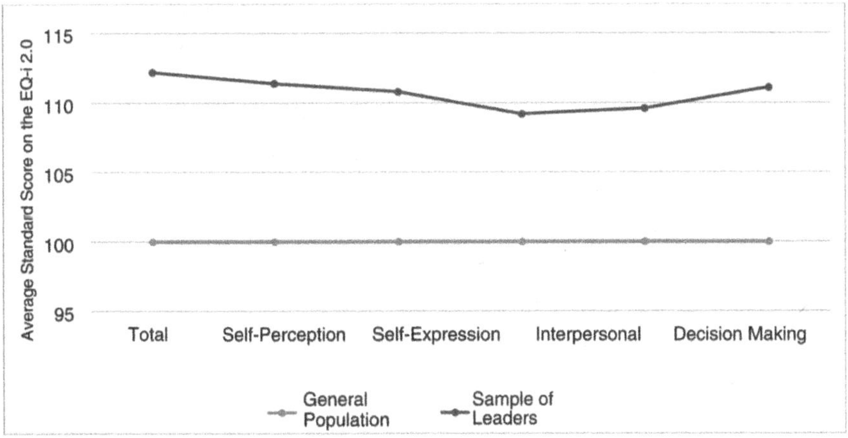

Figure 10.4 Differences in EQ-i 2.0 Scores between Our Leader Sample and the General Population

Source: Reprinted with permission of MHS, 2016.

Authenticity	Coaching	Insight	Innovation
• Self-Actualization • Reality Testing • Self-Regard • Emotional Self-Awareness • Social Responsibility • Independence	• Self-Actualization • Empathy • Reality Testing • Interpersonal Relationships • Assertiveness • Emotional Self-Awareness	• Self-Actualization • Optimism • Self-Regard • Social Responsibility • Interpersonal Relationships • Emotional Expression	• Self-Actualization • Independence • Problem Solving • Assertiveness • Flexibility • Optimism

Figure 10.5 EQ-i 2.0 Loadings on the Four Pillars of Leadership

Source: Reprinted with permission of MHS, 2016.

The correlations, along with theoretical considerations, were used to inform decisions about which subscales to assign to the four leadership dimensions. These groupings are shown in Figure 10.5.

The Four Pillars

Authenticity

The first competency, or pillar, we identified has to do with being authentic or real. Today's best leaders must be viewed as credible, fair, and "real." For these leaders, humility is a strength. Bombast, "putting on airs," and dominating people are out. Acting arrogantly or not showing integrity can be the kiss of death in today's world. The new Internet-saturated business environment of transparency and accountability means it is becoming harder to disguise self-serving behavior. Morally dubious individuals can still reach high positions, but it has become harder to do and—it's getting much tougher to hide transgressions when you're at the top.

Above all, those who do not project the traits of authenticity and humility will be at an increasing disadvantage. People will respect you more and go the extra mile for you, if they think you are real.

If they don't see these traits, they won't follow you. They'll punch the clock, but they won't go to the wall for you.

Authentic leaders:

1. Act as role models.
2. Inspire fair and moral behavior.
3. Command esteem and confidence.

Coaching

The second pillar we identified is coaching. For generations, the role of leaders has been to "check up on people." Today's more equitable workplaces run on collaboration and mentoring, not policing. Coaching means going out of your way to make sure people realize their full potential. Generation X workers especially, will leave a job unless they feel they are getting something out of it.

The best leaders coach their teams through tactics as simple as town hall meetings, "management by walking around," department lunch dates, and one-on-one meetings where they listen to employees' concerns, offer feedback and guidance and take responsibility for removing any roadblocks that prevent employees from achieving success.

Coaching leaders:

1. Operate as mentors.
2. Respond to concerns and queries.
3. Support employee needs.

Insight

The third pillar, which we call insight, combines two essential leadership skills:

1. Truly understanding the organization—its vision, mission, goals, and values.
2. Communicating those messages in a form that will inspire employees, customers, and suppliers.

At great organizations, everyone knows the purpose of the organization and what it stands for. More and more companies are realizing they are not in business just to make money or produce a certain product. Developing a sense of higher purpose (for example, Google says its mission is "to organize the world's information and make it universally accessible and useful") heightens engagement and motivation for employees and other stakeholders, which helps attract and retain the right people.

Companies such as Apple, Google, Tim Hortons, apparel makers Roots Canada Ltd., Timberland, and Canada Goose are companies whose brands resonate with mission. That's what makes a company exciting. You can be good operationally, you can get by and do well, but if you want people lining up to work for you, you have to have a meaningful purpose.

Insightful leaders:

1. Communicate a purpose, meaning and vision.
2. Express a hopeful view of the future.
3. Compel employees to reach and exceed goals.

Innovation

The fourth pillar is innovation. Leaders today need to be innovative. More and more success will accrue to organizations that encourage all their employees to think creatively and champion new procedures, products, and services. That doesn't mean everyone gets their own research and development (R&D) budget, but it does require that leaders give their people more autonomy and license to explore changing customer needs and that they provide a fair, safe, and encouraging hearing when employees propose new ideas. They also need to be understanding when new, but risky ideas, don't succeed.

Many organizations used to create a climate of "Don't make mistakes. Just get your quota, and don't take chances." In today's faster-moving markets, companies need all their creative resources moving forward together.

Innovative leaders:

1. Realize the importance of taking risks.
2. Spur ingenuity, imagination, and autonomous thinking.
3. Value knowledge.
4. See challenges as learning opportunities.

Here are the definitions we use for each of these competencies:

Authenticity: An authentic leader serves as a role model for moral and fair behavior. A transparent approach commands esteem and confidence from employees.

Coaching: A leader who coaches effectively is seen as a mentor who supports employee growth. Employees are nurtured toward achieving their highest levels of performance.

Insight: A leader provides insight by sharing a purpose and hopeful vision for colleagues to follow. Employees are compelled and inspired to exceed goals.

Innovation: An innovative leader focuses on taking risks, spurring colleagues' ingenuity and autonomous thought. Knowledge is valued, and challenges are viewed as learning opportunities.

Regardless of leadership role, or leadership theory, one could argue that without the ability to coach, to innovate, to communicate a compelling vision, and to serve as an ethical role model, leading an effective team would seem nearly impossible. Using these four leadership dimensions as a lens can help you hone in on the EQ-i 2.0 subscales that may require development and the leadership areas that may be the most affected.

The Four-Pillar Model also shows you the impact certain EQ-i 2.0 subscales have on your overall leadership performance. For instance, Self-Actualization is a key facet of all four leadership dimensions, while other EQ-i 2.0 subscales may only directly affect one or two dimensions.

Emotional Intelligence and Derailers

We also examined possible "Leadership Derailers." That is, the factors that have been shown in the research literature to be the most important in the failure of leaders. If emotional intelligence is positively related to transformational leadership, are there any subscales that, if lacking, relate to leadership derailment? To answer this question, EQ-i 2.0 subscale scores were correlated with the Laissez-Faire score. Laissez-Faire leaders demonstrate avoidance of responsibility and action; they are essentially leaders by the nature of their position in the organization, and not by their presence, ability to motivate, or positive impact that they have on others. Research has shown that this type of nonleadership is, at a minimum, not related to positive outcomes[7] and, at most, destructive—contributing to distress, role ambiguity, and conflict.[8] As predicted, the EQ-i 2.0 showed strong negative correlations with Laissez-Faire leadership. A negative correlation here suggests that as emotional intelligence increases, the risk of avoiding leadership responsibilities decreases.

Lower scores in any EQ-i 2.0 subscale may make it more difficult for a leader to be inspirational, visionary, innovative, and able to motivate their team to outperform expectations. Lower scores across the profile may suggest that you avoid leadership responsibilities altogether, or that you have a good chance of derailing from influential positions of leadership.

Although all subscales are important to prevent leadership derailment, to provide development focus, four subscales are emphasized in our reports due to their stronger connection to leadership derailment (Laissez-Faire leadership). These four subscales were chosen based on both practical significance and statistical importance:

- Impulse Control
- Stress Tolerance
- Problem Solving
- Independence

From this data, we designed a Leadership Report that allows you (through your coach) to compare your results to those of the top leaders in our leadership sample. Only the top leaders, those scoring in the top 50 percent of our sample on the EQ-i 2.0, were included in this comparison group. This means you can be compared to those exceptional leaders who demonstrate high emotional intelligence.

High Emotional Intelligence and Leader Success

Leadership research, much of which has been discussed throughout this book, suggests that high levels of emotional intelligence in some areas can help predict leadership success, while low levels of emotional intelligence in other areas can help predict leadership derailment (i.e., unsuccessful, if not catastrophic, leadership). We've identified and included these factors in the EQ-i 2.0 Leadership Report—an assessment of the factors of emotional intelligence that are empirically linked to specific behaviors of successful leaders. As such, it is a useful tool for all those who assess leadership effectiveness and/or aptitude within organizations, including human resources personnel who are responsible for the selection, development, and promotion of adept leaders.

There is ample support for the theory that leaders score higher on emotional intelligence skills than the general population. Some of these data have already been presented in this chapter. In another study (discussed in more detail in Chapter 16) my colleagues at MHS and I published earlier,[9] top executives of entrepreneurial companies (e.g., members of Young Presidents Organization, Innovators Alliance) significantly differed from the general population on the EQ-i in 8 of 15 EQ-i subscales, scoring higher than the general population. Moreover, leaders who demonstrated higher levels of empathy, self-regard, reality testing, and problem solving were more likely to generate high profits for their companies.

Because of often changing market forces, a volatile environment, and pressures to accomplish more with fewer resources, leaders require more than technical knowledge to succeed in their role.[10] Researchers have noted that emotional skills are important for successful performance at the executive level,[11] and become more critical (as compared to IQ or technical savvy) as employees progress through the organizational hierarchy.[12]

David McClelland, the late Harvard psychologist, demonstrated that division presidents with higher levels of emotional intelligence factors outperformed performance targets by 15 to 20 percent and had a 94 percent retention rate.[13] On the other hand, division presidents who rated lower on emotional intelligence competencies underperformed by 20 percent and had a 50 percent retention rate.

Further support for the role of emotional intelligence in leadership can be substantiated by two independent meta-analyses. A meta-analysis is a "study of studies" that helps to remove the subjective interpretation around inconsistent research findings. In the first two meta-analyses, a strong positive relationship was found linking emotional intelligence to leadership.[14] In the third meta-analysis conducted by Peter Harms and Marcus Credé of the University of Nebraska, Lincoln, and SUNY-Albany,[15] the link between emotional intelligence and leadership was also found when both constructs were independently rated.

One of the reasons I decided to write this book now is that the support for emotionally intelligent leadership, the EQ Leader, is now substantial. Since the early 1990s it has been an almost uphill struggle to establish this concept. There is now enough momentum, published research studies, practical examples, and corporate acceptance that there really can be emotional intelligence in the workplace and in leadership. While there are still pockets of resistance among some academics and other curmudgeons, the horses have long ago left the barn.

The real questions will be around which coaching and training methods will be the most effective in preparing our future leaders in these skills. This is an area we are currently researching at MHS. We have developed half-day, full-day, and two-day leadership programs in emotional intelligence with an ongoing coaching component for leaders and high potentials that are being evaluated in several Fortune 100 companies. Stay tuned.

EQ Leader: Something to Think About

1. What does it mean to you to be authentic as a leader?
2. Have you ever had to work under someone who wasn't very authentic?
3. What behaviors of this person stood out?
4. Think of what things you can do to be more authentic.
5. Have you ever worked for a leader that coached you at work?
6. What do you see as the qualities of a good coach?
7. Is there anyone at work that you currently coach?
8. Do you feel that your work has purpose?
9. What can leaders at your organization do to instill more purpose in the work of employees?
10. Can you state your organization's vision? Or its mission?
11. Do you feel you work in an innovative environment?
12. Think of some innovations that have occurred at your workplace.
13. How could you make your workplace more innovative?

Chapter 11

Pillar I: Developing Authenticity

The supreme quality of leadership is unquestionably integrity.

—DWIGHT D. EISENHOWER

Authenticity

Authenticity Definition

Lead authentically to inspire and motivate others:

Commands esteem and confidence, inspires fair and moral behavior, and acts as a role model.

Now that we've identified four competencies—(1) authenticity, (2) coaching, (3) insight, and (4) innovation—that are believed to be important for successful leadership, where do we go from here? In this chapter, I hope to guide you along a pathway to continue improving your capabilities as a leader. The focus of this and the next three chapters will be on the four pillars identified in the previous chapter.

Simply reading leadership books like this one can only go so far in developing you as a leader. They can help shed light on areas you may not have considered before, reinforce ideas that you may have had, and provide you with a road map for change. However, it is crucial to remember that there is no "one size fits all" approach to developing leadership. People become great leaders through a variety of means. Some people take to it more naturally—the right skills come to them more easily through the rough and tumble of everyday life. It can be a trial-and-error experience.

Others have had a mentor, a wise leader in their life that skillfully guided them along. Some leaders, more and more these days, use a personal coach. This is someone who can walk them through the trials and tribulations of their day-to-day challenges. A good coach starts off with an assessment (like the EQ-i 2.0 or EQ 360) to quickly get a picture of the individual's strengths and weaknesses. As well, this provides the leader with some additional self-awareness, which is a significant first step toward change. Then, over time, the coach and leader together develop strategies that set the leader on course for improvement.

Leadership development courses are another route to change, and we have developed some that are being used by organizations for both high-potential, emerging, or future leaders, as well as current, or newly minted, leaders. These courses are often individualized to the organization's needs, but use the basic tenets of emotional intelligence as described in this book. Some of these courses use hands-on experiential exercises or simulations to emulate real-life leadership challenges that have been faced by organizations.

Becoming a More Authentic Leader

In the previous chapter, I presented our definition of authentic leadership:

> An authentic leader serves as a role model for moral and fair behavior. A transparent approach commands esteem and confidence from employees.

The emotional skills that load on this competency are:

Self-Actualization
Emotional Self-Awareness
Reality Testing
Social Responsibility
Independence
Self-Regard

Authentic leaders have been described by different leadership experts in a variety of ways. While the original concept dates back to ancient Greek times and the philosophy of "know thyself," the more modern perspective is attributed to Bill George, the former CEO of Medtronic, and his book *Authentic Leadership*.[1]

Summarizing the many characteristics of authentic leaders that have been proposed by a variety of leadership theorists, Kevin Kruse, in *Forbes* magazine, broke it down into four attributes[2]:

1. Authentic leaders are self-aware and genuine.
    - They are described as self-actualized individuals with an awareness of their strengths, their limitations, and their emotions.
    - They show their real selves to their followers.
    - They act the same in private and in public.
    - They don't hide their mistakes or weaknesses out of fear of looking weak.
    - They know that being self-actualized is an endless journey, which is never complete.
2. Authentic leaders are mission driven and focused on results.
    - They can put the mission and the goals of the organization ahead of their own self-interest.
    - They do their job in pursuit of results, not for their own power, money, or ego.
3. Authentic leaders lead with their heart, not just their minds.
    - They have no fear of showing their emotions, or their vulnerability.
    - They connect with their employees.
    - Showing emotions does not make them "soft."
    - Communicating in a direct manner is important for successful outcomes.
    - They use empathy with others.
4. Authentic leaders focus on the long term.
    - Bill George, for example, focused on long-term shareholder value, not on just beating quarterly estimates.

- Leaders realize that to nurture individuals and to nurture a company requires hard work and patience, but the approach pays large dividends over time.

In addition, authentic leaders: (1) act as role models, (2) inspire fair and moral behavior, and (3) command esteem and confidence.

One of the best comments about authentic leaders is from Mark Bonchek in the *Harvard Business Review* where he writes, "being authentic is a bit like being cool—sometimes the harder you try, the less you are."[3]

Becoming More Authentic

How does one become more authentic as a leader? Let's look at some of the key emotional intelligence factors and how you can further develop them to improve your ability to demonstrate authenticity.

Self-Actualization

Self-actualization is a significant factor that loads on all four of our pillars of successful leadership. Self-actualization is strongly related to overall work success and performance. It can be summed up in three words: pursuit of meaning. While this may sound philosophical, as a leader it means finding purpose and enjoyment in your role and performing to your fullest potential. When you have a higher sense of accomplishment and resolve, then you are motivated, both as an individual and as an influencer, for your team or organization to strive for greatness.

Leadership Implications A self-actualized leader is perceived as a role model and as someone who is striving to learn, develop new skills, and willing to grow to fully optimize their talents. Strong self-actualized leaders permeate the entire organization as employees may emulate their approach. This drive for self-fulfillment stimulates higher productivity and greater employee satisfaction.

One Step at a Time To develop your self-actualizing skills, you should have an action plan. You should have specific goals that are personal, professional, leadership oriented, and organizational. Transcribing your objectives is a great strategy to solidify your action plan as you work toward greater self-actualization. By writing your action plan on paper or sharing it with a colleague, you solidify your goals. Choose one small strategy for making your life more enriching and share this with a colleague or place it in your calendar. Alternatively, consider whether there is there a way you can get your whole team involved in adding more meaning to the workday. Research clearly demonstrates that the likelihood of successful goal attainment increases by the mere fact of simply writing down your goals.

Capitalize on Strengths

You are already aware of your passions, though at times you may not realize it. List tasks in which you excel (e.g., chairing meetings, producing comprehensive financial reports, sales, presentations), and try to incorporate these activities throughout the workday. If you feel unsure of your areas of strength, pinpoint pursuits in which you receive many compliments, or ask your colleagues for feedback. These activities will reinvigorate your zeal for work and improve your productivity.

Authentic people are seen as competent and demonstrate expertise in their chosen field. So, it's important to keep up your expertise and stay current in your chosen field. If you are a professional, it doesn't mean you have to be as hands on as someone practicing in your profession (lawyer, engineer, scientist, etc.). But it's helpful to scan and keep up to date with the latest developments in the field. You will likely rely on experts in these areas, but it's good to know what questions you should be asking them.

Be Real/Transparent

As a leader, you are under constant scrutiny. People all around—employees, customers, shareholders, partners, frenemies, competitors, even your own family members—are watching you. Not that you should be paranoid, but that's the reality. Some people look up to you; they're on your side. Others watch you, looking for slip-ups or failures, especially in this digital age when slip-ups are more visible than ever before. Whether it's Twitter, YouTube, or Instagram, there are endless channels on social media with the potential to expose you to millions of people (if you do something really egregious). These are mostly people you never had any desire to know or for them to know you. Reputations that have taken decades to build, today, can be destroyed in nanoseconds.

Transparency, for a leader, has always been important. But in today's world the rules have changed dramatically. What was passable language, or behavior, in the days of the TV series *Mad Men* no longer flies today. What's acceptable, or "politically correct" in today's world fits within a new, narrower band of rules. You can cross these rules if you choose, but beware—there can be consequences.

For example, University of Toronto professor Jordan Peterson decided he would choose the pronouns he wanted to use when addressing transgendered students in his class, rather than have them be dictated to him.[4] While framing the conflict as a freedom of speech issue, Peterson made a number of salient and rational points. However, his YouTube video on the subject, with more than 165,000 views to date, has become quite controversial. The topic, not central to his previous areas of research, has now consumed much of his life. In fact, for tens of thousands of people he has now been defined by this conflict. This example should illustrate the point that standards for behavior are consistently changing and leaders should be aware that, in presenting your views on social media, you can quickly lose control over the dialogue. This, in turn, may turn your original argument into something that is more harmful to you and others than you ever intended.

While there are few saints among us walking around today, as a leader, if you want to be successful, you will need to carefully choose your public battles, if at all. While we all want the world to be a better place, you will need to decide whether there is a cause for which you are willing to put aside much of what you have already built as a leader. It is rare that you will support a cause that is universally accepted and, although your support may benefit your organization and you as a leader, you must be willing to defend your actions. Especially if your stance is political, getting involved in causes can have unpredictable consequences.

The more you can be yourself, that is, live in your own skin, 24/7, the less you need to worry about transparency. Not that you behave the same when you are directing your employees at work as when you are with your family at home, but you should be your natural self in both cases. We don't put on a Superman or Superwoman suit before we head off to work and leave Clark Kent or Kristen Wells behind. Also, putting on an act for long periods of time does not work well. People see through it, and if they feel you are fake with them, well, they tend to be fake with you. As a leader, you need to be honest and transparent in your behavior with others.

Emotional Self-Awareness

If you have a solid understanding of what brings about your emotions, it is much easier for you to regulate your behavior and control the impact your emotions have on employees in your organization. Authentic leaders are more conscious of their emotions and the impact they have on performance than most people. Emotional self-awareness will enable you to lead with composure and a full understanding of your impact on others. As well, it will be more likely that you will choose a course of action based on your gut feeling in time-constrained situations.

You will more easily generate respect, admiration, and honesty from employees when you are viewed as highly self-aware. One step in getting there is to take time to contemplate your behaviors instead of acting rashly, thereby considering your own emotional response as well as those of others.

Leadership Implications As a leader, you need to develop a thorough grasp of your emotional triggers and reactions. This in-depth understanding will help you develop a more streamlined decision-making process as you incorporate your emotions into your role as a leader. Knowing your emotional triggers and reactions will enable you to use this emotional knowledge to effectively navigate through challenging or difficult situations.

Organizational Implications Your capacity to grasp subtle emotional nuances will help you take calculated risks that support the organization in meeting its strategic goals. Once you are comfortable with, and know your emotional triggers and reactions, you will be better able to lead with authenticity, and with an open approach, helping you gain credibility and buy-in from employees. You will be able to manage tense and perhaps overwhelming situations with ease, and you will be able to use and recognize your full spectrum of emotions.

Be a Role Model

Once you are better able to manage your emotions, you can be innovative, successfully take risks, and gain the trust of your employees. The most prominent leaders have an aptitude for remaining composed in competitive situations and under mounting pressure and duress. Your ability to be aware of your emotions will serve as a model of composure and ensure that employees feel secure and content to overcome any potential challenge.

As you become better at emotional self-management, talk about it with employees. Welcome presentations or seminars at your workplace on the topic. You can hire an expert to teach employees about understanding emotions and the impact of their emotions on others.

Weigh the Evidence

As you become more skilled at understanding your emotions, you may tend to be overly reliant on your emotional barometer to make decisions. Be mindful to incorporate objective evidence.

Intuition can only carry you so far. While a deal may feel right, data may not support the intended strategy. Be sure to seek counsel from colleagues, involve members of your team, and emphasize facts to support your proposed course of action.

Reality Testing

Your ability to be realistic can impact your perception of being authentic. Reality testing is a key contributor to how you make decisions as a leader, and whether your approach is seen as grounded, objective, and in touch with the work environment, or disconnected and biased.

It's important to be tuned in to your team and the organizational landscape. You may habitually deal with everyone in the same way, not always adjusting your approach to individual needs. You may set goals for yourself and others that are unrealistic. You can benefit from creating goals based on data and reasonable expectations.

Leadership Implications As an authentic leader, it's important to convey an appropriate level of objectivity for your direct reports to see you as a fair, accurate, and in-touch leader. Your leadership style can be even-keeled, particularly if you have good impulse control. However, you should be aware that there may be times, particularly when under stress, when your emotions and personal biases can cloud your objectivity.

Organizational Implications You may have great and inspiring aspirations for the organization, but matching possibilities with capabilities will create the buy-in you need. You need to set realistic goals and ensure that others, particularly those in other teams, can trust that your decisions are rooted in evidence. Leaders who can accurately size up external events and solve problems based on this assessment tend to be capable of greater achievements.

Fearing the Worst, or Sugarcoating Reality?

Under times of stress, some leaders rely less on reality testing skills and fall victim to fearing the worst-case scenario or sugarcoating reality. Which of these two extremes best describes you when you are not seeing things realistically?

If you worry about catastrophes, remember that sometimes the best actions involve risks. Don't be stymied by worst-case scenarios that may never occur. Is there evidence that there is real danger? Try running your catastrophe hypothesis by a third party to see whether it has any truth. If you tend to sugarcoat reality, try playing the role of devil's advocate, and find data to more accurately describe the current situation. Also, watch other's reactions to your positivity; if there is hesitation in their voice or body language, they likely see your positive outlook as unrealistic.

Opening the Books

Keeping up-to-date data at your fingertips will ensure you have objective information ready to fuel strong decisions and goal-setting processes. Provide yourself and your team with critical business unit or departmental data (e.g., profit and loss, sales, product development costs) to make intelligent decisions with your team. Information is a form of power and can combat the tendency to color reality with our own personal biases. Instill this power in your team. Validate theories and assumptions and avoid targets that have no basis in hard data.

Encourage your team to take the pulse of the organization by constantly listening and responding to what they hear so they can serve the needs of their people.

Be Socially Responsible

Socially responsible leaders are authentic leaders. Social responsibility calls for leaders to act in a moral and responsible manner, promote the greater good, and be a strong voice in their teams, organizations, and communities. A socially responsible leader takes most, if not all, opportunities to help the team and the organization. Their concern for others, whether at work or in the community, is demonstrated through the selfless contributions they make. They are receptive and engage in nonjudgmental listening. These leaders also keep their word and deliver what they promise.

To be a socially responsible leader you should consistently demonstrate your social conscience and coach those you lead. You can be a Good Samaritan who helps others without expecting anything in return. This type of leader gains fulfillment from a variety of sources, including activities outside of work.

Leadership Implications Socially responsible leaders believe in coaching and serve as champions for their team and community. You will need to uphold the moral and ethical compass in your leadership approach and often place your team's goals ahead of your own agenda. You may also want to consider contributing to a charity, or involving your team in fundraising. Be mindful that being helpful to the point where you do all the work is not truly helping or coaching; allow your direct reports to spread their wings and grow on their own.

Organizational Implications Get involved in a variety of social and leadership pursuits both inside and outside of the workplace (e.g., charity involvement, fundraising). You need to consistently promote employee engagement, morale, mentoring, and other development practices that help build talent in your team and others in the organization. One note of caution is to be wary that such involvement may involve taking on too many responsibilities, which may adversely impact the quality of your work or personal well-being.

Reflect and Focus

Being a successful leader is not a solo activity. Real success comes from helping your team members reach professional goals and individual improvement. Always supporting others, however, can take away the time you need to spend on yourself as a leader. Try to ensure that you are not avoiding your current emotional state, goals, and functioning by focusing too heavily on others. This can be made easier by active reflection.

For example, reflect on how you spent your time last week. What activities and tasks did you spend your time on?

Which of those tasks were for the betterment of yourself, your family, your work, those you lead, and others? If you are over involved in any area, adjust your schedule for the next month and refocus your efforts.

Inspiring Initiative

Inspiring others to be socially responsible can create an overall feeling of meaning while contributing toward the greater good. Leverage your passion for causes you care about by reaching out to your team and organization (e.g., setting up a community support group within the organization). Brainstorm several activities that you, your team, or the organization as a whole can engage in. Ensure these activities are in line with your organization's vision and are of benefit to the employees.

As a first step, identify a plan of action to build social responsibility within your organization; identify specific roles and a time frame in which to complete the plan of action.

Independence

Being independent means you are capable of feeling, thinking, and working on your own, a critical skill that all great leaders have in common. When this skill is well developed, you are willing and capable of holding your own ideas and making necessary decisions required for your team on your own. You are unlikely to be swayed by popular opinion, which can help you maintain an established direction for your team.

You should be comfortable providing direction and working on your own. You should be able to work without emotional dependency on others, and not require their reassurance. You should be accepting of responsibility for your decisions, knowing that at times people will disagree with you.

Leadership Implications An independent leader does not depend on others to make important decisions. Being self-directed, you can analyze a situation, formulate a response, and move into implementation mode without second-guessing your decisions. This skill is crucial for a leader, especially when difficult decisions need to be made and direction is limited. At the same time, be careful not to neglect the emotions and opinions of your team, which could possibly leave them feeling alienated, and eventually disengaged.

Organizational Implications You should be able to voice your thoughts and opinions, adding your own perspective to the discussion table and influencing the direction of your organization. Be an active participant in generating ideas rather than a passive receiver. Keep a close eye on how often you go off in your own direction rather than building coalitions. Teams that strive for the same values and goals build strong organizations.

Stay Connected

While being emotionally independent is important for leading a team, being completely autonomous can hurt the amount of buy-in you receive from them. Keep the lines of communication open with team members.

There is always a risk of being *too* independent. If you find that you are displaying any of these four qualities, then it may be time to scale back your independence:

Ignorance: Are people feeling like I am ignoring facts in an effort to pursue my own agenda?

Know it all: Do I think I know everything, and thus my team's advice is not needed?

Detached: Am I hurting collaborative relationships and engagement by not including others?

Closed door: While I have an open-door policy, is my behavior distancing myself from my team?

Listening to Feedback

To ensure that you do not hurt any key relationships throughout the organization, balance self-directed thought with the ability to seek advice and feedback. You do not have to be a fan of an idea to entertain the thought process of others and explore different perspectives. Doing so can help gain the support of others and perhaps even generate new possibilities.

Examine a few of your past decisions. What did your decision-making process look like? Who did you connect with to seek advice or a differing point of view? How well did you follow along the input that was given to you?

Next time when you are seeking advice from your team, note the different perspectives before presenting a counterthought. Then reflect on those notes and think through the feedback and the possible impact on your decision.

Summary

Authentic leaders know themselves. They are self-aware. They really know their strengths and limitations by being honest with themselves. They don't have to worry about how they will come across to others. Their persona is the same, whether in private or public. They don't have to worry about how they've presented themselves in one place or at one time, and whether they will come across congruently with the same people in a different time or place.

Authentic leaders are not ego driven, nor are they driven by power or money. They are more interested in learning, self-improvement, and helping others. Authentic leaders focus on results—setting both short-term and longer-term goals. They are not afraid of looking vulnerable and can own up to mistakes. These leaders can be comfortable showing emotions, when and where appropriate. They find it easy to connect with employees and are trusted by them.

Being present is an important part of being a leader. While there is no shortage of activities that can keep leaders busy today, it's as important as ever to get away from your computer screen and smartphone and interact with the people in your organization. Getting to know people, having casual conversations adds to your being seen as a regular person, someone employees can relate to. Communicate directly with everyone in your organization and behave genuinely regardless of formal job titles. As a role model who pursues excellence and continues to grow, it is important for you, as leader, to offer employees ample opportunities for training and development.

As an authentic leader, you will want to develop these distinct qualities:

- Self-Awareness: Continuing to self-reflect and better understand your strengths, challenges, and values
- Relational Transparency: Open sharing of your thoughts and emotions, balanced by an appropriate emotional expression
- Balanced Processing: Welcoming opposing points of view and being fair-minded about them

- Internalized Moral Perspective: Having a strong positive ethical foundation demonstrated in relationships and decisions that are resistant to outside pressures

Example of Authentic Leadership

Who Is Authentic?

One leader that has been described as authentic in his leadership style is Howard Schultz, the former CEO of Starbucks. Schultz was born to a family with a truck driver father and grew up in a blue-collar household. He escaped his surroundings through involvement in sports and the Boys & Girls Clubs of America.

In a number of media interviews, Schultz stresses what has been his "passion." His passion, however, has not been coffee but, rather, about "building a company that treats people with dignity and respect." He said coffee is what Starbucks makes as a product, "but that's not the business we're in."[5]

Schultz, in an interview with Oprah, talked about his father who struggled with a series of blue-collar jobs, never able to find meaning or fulfillment in his work. He reported a breaking point when his father was injured on the job, with no health insurance or workers' compensation. Schultz recalled that the experience left a lifelong impression on him.

"It was not the calling of coffee, but the calling to try to build a company that my father never got a chance to work for," said Schultz. "When we began Starbucks what I wanted to try to do was to create a set of values, guiding principles, and culture." According to Schultz, Starbucks was the first company in America to offer comprehensive health insurance and ownership in the form of stock options to all of its employees, including part-time workers. Schultz demonstrates authenticity by not masking what his passion is, by demonstrating care for all employees, and by committing his business to the development of a better world through meaningful employment.

Among the awards Schultz has received are the FIRST Responsible Capitalism Award and the Rev. Theodore M. Hesburgh, C.S.C., Award for Ethics in Business at the Mendoza College of Business at the University of Notre Dame.

Being Real and the Culture of Reality TV

One of the more dramatic influences on our perception of being authentic or "real" today has been the influence of reality TV. While the readers of this book are not likely to be the main audience for this form of entertainment, many of the people you work with are. If you don't believe me, just check out the statistics.

The ratings among viewers 18 to 49 during a specific period in the summer of 2016, that looked at both broadcast and cable TV, showed that:[6]

- Nine of the top 10, and 16 of the top 25, broadcast shows were reality TV.
- Three of the top five shows were *Big Brother* episodes.
- ABC had seven unscripted shows in the top 25, Fox had three, NBC had two (not counting Olympics), and CBS had one (though *Big Brother* shows up three times).
- Sixteen of the top 25 shows on cable—not including wrestling—were unscripted.
- Nine of those 16 cable shows were documentary *Shark Week* specials on Discovery.
- The top three cable series were reality TV: *Love & Hip Hop Atlanta*, *Keeping Up with the Kardashians*, and *Black Ink Crew*.

A Canadian TV ratings poll for 2016 reported that the top three of the four most-watched TV shows in Canada were reality shows:[7]

1. *The Amazing Race Canada*
2. *MasterChef Canada*
3. *Murdoch Mysteries*
4. *Big Brother Canada*

Wearing another of my hats, I'm the psychology consultant, and help screen candidates for many reality TV shows. In addition to the three above (*The Amazing Race Canada*, *MasterChef Canada*, and *Big Brother Canada*), I also have worked on *Real Housewives of Toronto*, *Game of Homes*, *Scare Tactics*, *The Bachelor Canada*, *Intervention Canada*, *Panic Button*, and many others. I've screened and worked with many hundreds of people who want to be on reality TV shows.

Probably the most asked question I get about reality TV is, "isn't it fake, don't they script it?" Actually, no. While I'm not at liberty to give examples from shows I work on, I can shed light on this issue by commenting on Andy Cohen's, creator of the *Real Housewives* franchise, interview in the *New York Times*.[8] In the interview, he talked about the "reality" of reality TV. One of the most-watched episodes of *Real Housewives of New York* was when one of the housewives, Aviva Drescher, got angry at Le Cirque and threw her prosthetic leg, in what was described as a last-ditch effort to make her onscreen presence more interesting. Well, that was the last we saw of Aviva, she was eliminated from the show.

In explaining the experience of reality TV, and that particular outcome, Cohen stated, "It is very real to them, and by the way, when it's not, they're off the show." In reality TV, the best scenes are real experiences of emotion—anger, fear, excitement, panic, revenge, passion. While situations are often created, with all the cameras around, you just can't fake the emotion; trying to fake it is like trying to be cool—it just doesn't work.

Why Is This Relevant to Leadership?

One of the lessons that can be learned from reality TV has to do with being real, in other words, being your authentic self. Although the situations in reality TV may seem less than realistic, viewers remain engrossed with the actions of characters that are viewed as the most authentic. Whether they are "good" or "bad" characters is often secondary.

As an interesting aside, these shows can give us a bit of insight into some of our cultural differences. For example, the show *Big Brother* is produced in about 40 countries. In the U.S. version, some of the most popular and winning characters include Dan Gheesling (known for backstabbing, lying, and dominating the house), Dr. Will Kirby (Evil Dr. Will, built people up, then tore them down), "Evel Dick" Donato (used loudmouth tactics to get what he wanted), and Rachel Reilly (an emotional train wreck). You may start to see a pattern here.

In the Canadian version, some of the most popular and winning characters are Emmett Blois (outgoing, friendly, social, an adventure seeker), Jon Pardy (friendly, social, big drinker, goofy Newfie), Sarah Hanlon (great social player, several friendmances, gets along with everyone), and Gary "Glitter" Levy (social player, funky, outgoing, fabulous).

These choices may be a reflection on our societies and may help us better understand our choices in leaders. For example, Canadian Prime Minister Justin Trudeau is known for being friendly and outgoing.

Our fascination with authenticity goes far beyond reality TV: consider this—while at least half of Americans found many of Donald Trump's behaviors distasteful, he still managed to captivate his audience, and many people argued that this was due to his authenticity. Once again, if you find that hard to believe, look at the data. Here were the TV ratings of the 10 most watched TV shows in the United States in 2016 per Nielsen.[9]

No.	Show	Viewership (in millions)	Date	Network
1	Super Bowl 50	111.9	Feb. 7, 2016	CBS
2	First presidential debate	84.0	Sept. 26, 2016	CPD
3	Third presidential debate	71.6	Oct. 19, 2016	CPD
4	Super Bowl 50 post-game show	70.0	Feb. 7, 2016	CBS
5	Second presidential debate	60.3	Oct. 9, 2016	VOA
6	World Series Game 7: Cubs vs. Indians	40.5	Nov. 2, 2016	FOX
7	Vice presidential debate	37.0	Oct. 4, 2016	CPD
8	Redskins vs. Cowboys	35.1	Nov. 24, 2016	FOX
9	Donald Trump RNC acceptance speech	34.9	July 21, 2016	VOA
10	88th Academy Awards	34.4	Feb. 28, 2016	ABC

Compiled by Wikipedia.

Notice that four of the top 10 most-watched shows featured Donald Trump, and one his running mate. While Hillary Clinton was also featured in three of these, her media coverage was nowhere close to Trump's. And even though many of Trump's behaviors were distasteful to some, voters continually praised his authenticity (perhaps using terms like "politically incorrect"), which was a quality that many people found lacking in Hillary Clinton.

Although Trump's perceived authenticity may have been a critical factor for voters, it remains to be seen how his authenticity will translate in the longer term as president regarding the actual results achieved. While this chapter encourages authenticity in leaders, it also notes that leaders who don't fulfill promises will eventually see their credibility damaged. Going forward, I encourage leaders to practice authenticity. In most cases, followers will be vigilant and take to task leaders who promise more than they can deliver or fail to make good on promises.

EQ Leader: Things to Consider

1. How important is authenticity in a leader for you?
2. Have you experienced leaders that you just couldn't trust?
3. How do you determine if someone is trustworthy?
4. How have you responded to leaders you didn't trust?
5. As a leader, do your subordinates find you trustworthy?
6. What can you do to be more authentic?
7. Can being too authentic ever work against you?
8. Do you feel you are the same person at work and at home?

Chapter 12

Pillar II: Developing Leader Coaches

You get the best effort from others not by lighting a fire beneath them, but by building a fire within.

—BOB NELSON

Coaching

Coaching Definition:

Support employee's needs and nurture development:

Operates as a mentor, responds to concerns and queries, and supports employee needs.

One of the big changes in leadership over the years has been the expanding role of coaching. Leadership, in the past, was mainly about telling people what to do, then monitoring whether or not they have done it. However, as times have changed, and organizations have become less hierarchical and more collaborative, our ways of getting things done has changed.

Relationships have become much more significant at work since so much of what a leader does is through other people, not just direct reports. The ability to get along, for example, is now required for teams to run smoothly. As well, when it comes to getting things done correctly, with the increased emphasis on quality control, coaching becomes even more important. Coaching has become much better defined over the years with specific skills being identified that can enhance your success in this area.

Just how prevalent is coaching in today's organizations? The use of coaching for employees, throughout the corporate chain, has grown dramatically over the past decade. The Human Capital Institute (HCI) together with the International Coach Federation (ICF) surveyed over 300 organizations about their coaching practices.[1] The companies they surveyed were worldwide, and ranged in size from less than 100 employees to more than 50,000, and covered over a dozen different industries.

They found that 65 percent of organizations use external coaches, 57 percent use internal coaches, and 84 percent use their own manager/leaders for coaching. They also reported that organizations with a strong coaching culture have higher employee engagement (60 percent of employees rated as highly engaged compared to 48 percent of all other organizations). As well, organizations with a strong coaching culture report higher revenue growth (63 percent report being above their industry peer group in 2014 revenue compared to 45 percent of all other organizations).

In another report, produced by the same group,[2] they found that 81 percent of the organizations surveyed planned to expand their scope of managers/leaders by investing in efforts to develop their coaching skills. By way of comparison, they planned a 72 percent increase in the use of internal coaches and a 35 percent increase in the use of external coaches.

How important do managers and employees view coaching? In a study MHS did together with HCI,[3] we surveyed 784 individuals from 500 organizations as part of looking at how emotional intelligence initiatives were implemented. We asked about the importance of various training initiatives, including coaching. As you can see in Figure 12.1, there were large differences in how managers and employees viewed coaching.

While 49 percent of employees felt coaching was an important skill for leaders, only 27 percent of leaders believed it was important. We found this to be the biggest leadership-employee gap among the areas surveyed. This is an area where employees are grasping its importance, but most of their managers haven't caught on to it yet. Interestingly, 50 percent of leaders felt that training in interpersonal skills was important. Of course, interpersonal skills are an integral part of coaching.

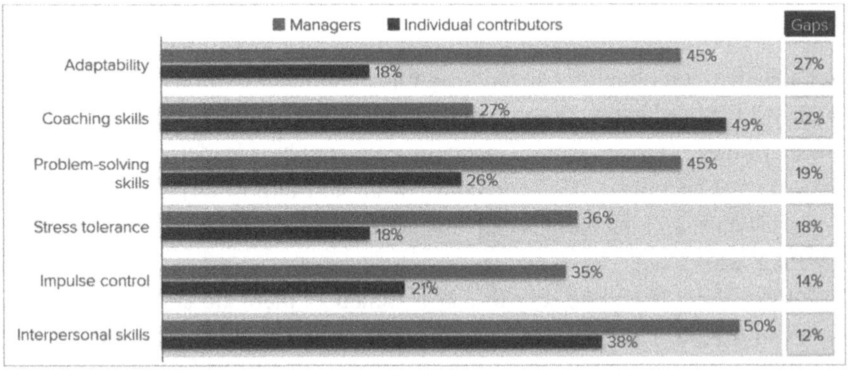

Figure 12.1 Critical Skills: Two Perspectives

Source: Adapted with permission of HCI, 2016.

Also, in the same study, we found a great deal of dissatisfaction with current leadership development programs. Many respondents told us that their leadership development efforts need immediate improvement. More than half of survey respondents think the current leadership development efforts at their organizations are less than effective. Good coaching is clearly a form of development that employees are looking for.

What Is a Coaching Leader?

So, what does it mean to be a leader who coaches employees? Our definition of a coaching leader is:

> A leader who coaches effectively and is seen as a mentor who supports employee growth. Employees are nurtured toward achieving their highest levels of performance.

The emotional skills that contribute most to coaching leadership include:

Self-Actualization
Empathy
Reality Testing
Interpersonal Relationship
Assertiveness
Emotional Self-Awareness

Better Conversations

As a leader, you hopefully spend a significant amount of time communicating with your subordinates. When coaching, it's important that you become more aware of these conversations. Coaching, delivered by a leader, doesn't have to be a formal encounter. You can coach your staff almost anywhere. That can include while walking along a hallway, getting a cup of coffee, or even popping by their workspace.

While there is no one way to coach someone, there are certain guidelines you can follow. There are also specific (emotional) skill sets, as noted above, that help make you a better coach. Furthermore, coaching does not need to be a daunting task; some of the rules you follow when having a good conversation can apply in a coaching situation.

Writing in *Forbes* magazine William Arruda offers several guidelines for leaders to follow when coaching subordinates.[4] He interviews several highly experienced coaches who advise on how better conversations lead to better relationships. Better relationships, in turn, lead to better outputs. They recommend that you, as a leader, see yourself as a thought partner. In your conversations with employees, you should listen for potential of both people and ideas. You do this by asking questions. Keep your questions open-ended and pay attention to the answers. For example, "if there were no limits, how would you solve this problem?" This way you remove the people (or blaming) out of the equation and keep the solution problem-focused (as opposed to people-focused).

Promote self-discovery by encouraging your subordinates to find their own answers to their own challenges. Recommending that people come to you with solutions, not problems, is one way to do this. Pay attention to the person in front of you, not just the issue. You may be tempted to respond negatively to a suggestion or an idea, but that could discourage further dialogue. So be patient, and accepting. That doesn't mean you must accept every idea presented.

Expect that the person can find the best approach. Be positive. Have faith that they can succeed. You can empower the other person to succeed by removing obstacles and providing resources. Finally, maintain accountability, celebrate effort and results. You want to reinforce the conversation so that it continues. Acknowledging success also helps that happen.

In a feature article in *Forbes* magazine, pulled together from the Forbes Coaches Council, an invitation-only group of professional coaches, several coaching skills are presented specifically for leaders.[5] Their first recommendation is for leaders to show empathy. As one of the emotional skills I've already identified, this will be elaborated on later in this chapter. In line with the previous recommendation to ask questions, they suggest that leaders remain curious. By being curious, you're likely to discover things that you didn't know before.

Develop Strengths

It's important for you, as a leader, to recognize strengths. Traditional forms of leading—such as, find and fix what's wrong—have changed. While issues that may derail leaders and potential leaders must be addressed (more on that later), your initial focus with others should be on finding and reinforcing strengths. It's about giving someone his or her best chance of succeeding. If, of course, there's persistent lack of performance, a different conversation should be on the table.

A great leader can be compared to a great sports coach. It's about being out in front, pulling for your team member's success. It's not so much about directing people, but rather partnering for success. You need to create an environment where "team members are heard, their experience is valued and validated, and difficult decisions are embraced by the team." As leader, you want to be seen as a partner who wants the team to win.

A leader can both give and receive feedback. When giving constructive feedback to others, or receiving it yourself, it can be an emotional experience. Stay calm. Some people are overly sensitive to anything perceived as criticism. It's important not to get drawn into an overly emotional state in these situations. Be fully engaged, and remain objective and nonjudgmental when receiving feedback. If needed, take the information received with you and calmly and honestly consider it later.

As a leader you have the opportunity to create transformational opportunities and guide people to them. A true sign of a leader is the ability to create transformation and set visions for others to reach for and achieve. In this way, you can inspire others to do their best work. Remember, as a leader you have an opportunity to smooth the way through change by removing barriers for your team.

Aligned with our view on self-actualization, the *Forbes* article goes on to state, "the ability to coach means the ability to know, apply and teach effectively. It also means taking ownership of the results for yourself and others. In other words, if your client does well—celebrate. If your client doesn't do well, other than say they simply aren't doing the work, examine what you can do better, more effectively or differently. That way, you are always improving and growing."[6]

And along the same lines as our work on empathy, the coaches advise on the importance of listening, while pointing out that it's only half of the communication equation. Along with how you listen, you need to pay attention to what you say, how you say it, and when you say it. All of these steps affect whether your message hits its target and whether you get the results you are looking for. Leaders who carefully listen to both the words and the meaning behind the words, and who respond with "inclusive language, pace, and tone (i.e., this report seems to be more difficult than we thought, I see why you're frustrated)" can both improve performance and increase enjoyment at work.

Emotional Skills

Self-Actualization

Self-actualization, more fully described in the previous chapter, is also a key component for effective coaching. Self-actualized leaders are perceived as role models and as someone who is striving to learn, develop new skills, and willing to grow to fully optimize their talents. Strong self-actualized leaders permeate the entire organization, as employees may emulate their approach. This drive for self-fulfillment stimulates higher productivity and greater employee satisfaction. It also makes for a more effective leader-coach.

Empathy

As a leader, the ability to manage relationships is your medium for transforming your team and taking the organization to new heights. Empathy, the ability to recognize, understand, and appreciate the way others feel, is a crucial component in building these strong interpersonal relationships. Good leader-coaches lead with empathy, grasping what another individual is feeling, even if it is much different from what you as a leader feel. Having an empathic nature makes you an approachable leader and allows your team to feel safe while sharing thoughts and ideas.

Furthermore, good leader-coaches are "tuned in" to how others are feeling. They care about the thoughts and feelings of their team. Under times of stress or moments of defensiveness, you may be tempted to adopt a less empathic approach, possibly making decisions without considering the needs of your team. Nevertheless, try to be aware of how your actions may impact others.

Leadership Implications For the leader-coach, empathy is a daily active process when resolving conflict, managing change, or making tough decisions. Your ability to show empathy usually allows you to come across as an authentic leader who can gain the trust and respect of your team. In order to be even more effective in inspiring and coaching your team, be aware of instances where your empathic demeanor may crack (e.g., when you are feeling stress, or anger) and cause an emotional disconnect between you and your employees.

Organizational Implications Whatever your current level of empathy, working to increase it will benefit both you and your organization. The need to feel heard and understood is in the core nature of all human beings. Further increasing your level of empathy to provide this validation will help dampen defenses in conflict management and gain the commitment you need to achieve common goals.

Kick It up a Notch

Successful leaders have the ability to adopt others' perspectives and can understand how different people experience emotions. Take the time to understand each member of your team. Prior to your next meeting, you might want to prepare by:

- Listing all attendees and what needs and expectations each bring to the meeting.
- Predicting how they will act during the meeting. What issues do you need to be sensitive toward?
- Generating a number of questions that you can use during the meeting to further understand your team members' needs.

- Keeping a journal that records your correct predictions (hits) and incorrect predictions (misses) of the issues and actions that would be brought forth. You can reduce the number of misses by understanding individual team members on a deeper level.

Watching a Pro

Find someone you know who is an empathic, and yet efficient communicator. Observe their communication style in practice, taking note of how they balance their ability to remain empathic and respectful with meeting organizational demands. Think about how you can leverage your interpersonal skills to develop empathy.

Interpersonal Relationships

Leadership cannot exist without strong relationships. While you may have solid technical skills, your ability to form strong relationships in your team is also important, especially to help weather difficult times. Place an emphasis on building strong relationships and, even more than most people, model what it means to be a team player. Your leadership style will need to use people and relationships to get the job done, by gaining buy-in and commitment, building integrity, and attaining the resources your team needs to succeed. Try to understand your team's hidden, and visible, strengths and weaknesses. Strive to understand each team member individually. Consistently reach out beyond your team to a build a network of support that can buffer you from the negative effects of stress.

Leadership Implications As a leader, you should value maintaining confidences, team harmony, and open communication in your relationships. These features of authentic relationships help you engage the hearts and minds of your team. You need to build loyal relationships where you know people at a very personal level. By maintaining a strong rapport, you can motivate and inspire others toward innovative and challenging goals.

Organizational Implications You should be committed to forming healthy interpersonal networks throughout the organization and be able to share the benefits of these connections with those you lead. The consistent and natural effort that you invest in relationship maintenance provides you the opportunity to influence the organizational stage by leveraging the people you know to get the job done.

Balance Recognition with Constructive Feedback

Remember to express recognition on a regular basis and to coach your team by delivering constructive feedback. As a leader, you are in an ideal position to inspire, coach, and motivate your team to reach their individual and group potential. Do you know what kind of recognition your team prefers? Not everyone likes a reward given in front of their peers or "Happy Birthday" sung at their desk.

Leverage your empathy skills to understand the types of recognition that motivate and inspire each of your team members. Find opportunities where you can help your team members unlock their individual potential; the most successful leaders develop their employees.

Take the Extra Step

Building resilient and trusting relationships with all types of people, regardless of your personal feelings toward them, is crucial to navigating the political landscape of your workplace.

You can:

- Identify an individual outside your team whose relationship with you is superficial, at best.
- What can you do to earn their trust and their willingness to help you?
- List what you think this person needs from you.
- Meet with this person to confirm your perspective.
- Emphasize the importance of understanding mutual needs and arrive at an action plan to support one another on common goals.

Assertiveness

Another key emotional skill you should develop as a leader-coach is assertiveness. Picture a line between the words passive and aggressive. At the middle point of this line lies assertiveness, a place where you work with your team by finding the right language at the right time to express your feelings and thoughts. It is helpful to articulate your thoughts in a clear and confident way. You should be firm and direct when making decisions. You can guide your team toward your goals by articulating your needs and protecting their resources. As well, you should view your rights, and those of your team's as sacred.

Leadership Implications At times, such as when meeting resistance from others, you may need to pull on strong emotions and convictions to state your position. This is a crucial skill to have when leading a team as it helps in gaining your team's buy-in and inspiring them toward innovative solutions. Further, a high level of assertiveness helps to gain the resources your team needs and can proactively clear obstacles in the path of your team's success. While such situations require you to be an assertive leader, others may require you to be more flexible in your thinking. Becoming too rigid in defending your position may result in unproductive, stubborn, or aggressive behavior (refer back to Chapter 9 for consequences of inflexible leadership).

Organizational Implications Leader-coaches are skilled at getting their point across in a clear and confident manner. This skill helps them resolve conflict, leverage organizational resources, openly voice their opinion, and contribute to the success of the organization. Leadership competencies are especially visible when you are assertive because you create a strong platform from which to showcase your talents, and those of your team. Watch that when you defend your position, you do not miss important information or feedback that may alter your perspective.

Knowing Where You Stand

In order to move toward a decision, and ensure your team works collaboratively, highly assertive leaders need to have a clear understanding of where they stand and the points on which they are willing to concede.

For your next meeting with an individual or team:

- Note down the ideal outcomes you would like to achieve.
- Review the outcomes you identified and separate the core outcomes that are essential to progress.
- Then, identify the information you need to hear from others to concede on these points.

Knowing the core outcomes that are essential, and the idealistic outcomes on which you are willing to be flexible, will help you stay focused on the goal, and not become paralyzed in rigid debate.

Crossing the Aggression Line

Leaders with a high level of assertiveness make decisions more easily. This likely provides direction for your team to work toward project goals. It is important to be mindful of your behavior crossing the line into aggression. Ensure you spend the time truly listening to the input of others when making decisions. Maintaining a culture of open and respectful communication in this way can help immensely in inspiring others to reach new heights. This is invaluable for the leader-coach.

Emotional Self-Awareness

In the last chapter we dealt with the importance of emotional self-awareness in being an authentic leader. Well, it's also important in becoming a good coaching leader. Having a solid understanding of what brings about your emotions, makes it much easier for you to regulate your behavior and control the impact your emotions have on employees in your organization. Coaching leaders are conscious of their emotions and the impact they have on the performance of others as well as themselves. Being emotionally self-aware enables you to lead with composure and to develop a better understanding of your impact on others. As well, it will be more likely that you will choose a course of action based on your gut feeling when needed.

You will more easily generate respect, admiration, and honesty from employees when you are viewed as highly self-aware. One step in getting there is to take time to contemplate your behaviors instead of acting rashly, which requires considering your own emotional response as well as those of others.

Example of Coaching Leadership

One leader who is currently seen as committed to coaching and seeing improvements in others' performance is Sheryl Sandberg. Sandberg is the COO of Facebook, previously served as vice president of Global Online Sales and Operations at Google and before that was chief of staff for the U.S.

Secretary of Treasury. She is the author of the best-selling book *Lean In*. She was ranked number 16 on *Fortune*'s 50 Most Powerful Women in Business list, and she was named one of the 25 Most Influential People on the web by *BusinessWeek*.

A quote she identifies with is "Leadership is about making others better as a result of your presence and making sure that impact lasts in your absence" (Harvard Business School definition of leadership).[7] After *Lean In* was published, she spent considerable time on what has become a movement encouraging women to discuss their work-life situations and how to succeed. Sandberg values ambition and personal fulfillment so highly that she hopes to use the *Lean In* movement to help others overcome their fears and succeed.

Being able to influence change in others involves taking time to understand one's personal values, which Sandberg has spent considerable amounts of time doing. She has been reported as someone who processes feelings effectively, efficiently works in teams, communicates openly, and is persistent in seeking growth.[8]

The greatest leaders know that the only way that they can achieve their vision is to involve others. Sandberg knows that if she wants to realize her dream of placing more women in more senior positions, she has to involve others, and she has done that by encouraging women to be more proactive in their career by stepping up, leaning in, and owning their own success.[9]

She has gone so far in helping others that she has created Lean In Circles, which are online communities offering community for female professionals.[10] The movement also helps women form groups of 8 to 10 people that then become support groups.

Sheryl Sandberg's view of coaching, or mentoring is somewhat less conventional. She advocates asking people, both senior and junior, to help you for *specific* advice to solve a problem. In her view, this encourages much more productive relationships than a simplistic, general plea for mentoring.

In today's world, with the fast pace of work and travel, it is much more challenging to maintain an effective mentor/mentee relationship. Also, traditional mentor relationships may suffer from a lack of clear need and purpose. A more purposeful approach to asking for help, as Sandberg advocates, makes a lot of sense. Along with that is the idea of creating your own "advisory board" and being able to seek and provide value and advice to others based on your needs, unique strengths, and experience.[11]

Another concern Sandberg has with traditional mentoring is that it has the potential to create dependency on others. She compares the search for a mentor as being the "professional equivalent of waiting for Prince Charming." Again, she supports the view that one can have more than one mentor (mentor = trusted advisor) by developing relationships with several trusted advisors at any one time. Additionally, why go looking for "a mentor"' when a number of "trusted advisors" will naturally appear throughout one's career. It is this contrived seeking out Sandberg objects to, rather than having a mentor per se.[12]

In any event, while some of Sandberg's proposals have been met with controversy, she remains a strong advocate for the importance of coaching in leadership. For those of you looking to develop your own leadership, this chapter provides many actionable steps that you can take to develop your own coaching behaviors. If you need further guidance, consider the questions in the following section.

EQ Leader: Things to Think About

1. Have you ever experienced having a good coach?
2. What about them made the experience good?
3. Have you had someone you would consider a mentor?
4. How would you differentiate a coach from a mentor?
5. What skills do you have that would make you a good coach?
6. Do you see coaching as part of your job?
7. How much time do you devote to coaching others?
8. What skills could you coach someone in?

Chapter 13

Pillar III: Developing Insight

Being the richest man in the cemetery doesn't matter to me. Going to bed at night saying we've done something wonderful, that's what matters to me.

—STEVE JOBS

Insight

Insight Definition:

Communicate with purpose, meaning, and vision:

Communicates a purpose, meaning and vision, hopeful view of the future, compels employees to reach and exceed goals.

What does it mean to have a purpose-driven leadership? The origins of leading with purpose can be traced back to the psychiatrist and Holocaust survivor Viktor Frankl. Following his release from the concentration camp, Frankl set about writing his masterwork, *Man's Search for Meaning*.[1] Camp survivors, Frankl had observed, were those who believed their lives had meaning and purpose amid the starvation and degradation. The nihilists and cynics perished.

Being a purpose-driven organization has huge advantages today. There's a major push on among companies around the world to become more purpose driven. In a recent *Harvard Business Review* article, it was written, "academics argue persuasively that an executive's most important role is to be a steward of the organization's purpose. Business experts make the case that purpose is a key to exceptional performance, while psychologists describe it as the pathway to greater well-being."[2]

Mark Bonchek, also writing in the *Harvard Business Review*, describes three kinds of purpose.[3] First, purpose can be about values—who you are and what you stand for. Second, it can be about value—what you do and how it benefits others. Ultimately, you want your values and value aligned. What you do should reflect who you are. What you stand for should guide what you offer or produce.

Third, purpose is about your shared values with others. And your value to the community should enhance your value to customers and shareholders. This is an important aspect of corporate social responsibility.

The idea is to conduct your business operations in a way that makes your customers part of your purpose. They should want to *share* your purpose. It should also be their purpose. They want to be there *with* you, and not just *for* you.

Purpose is not the same as a mission statement, although a good mission statement implies purpose. By way of example, Bonchek compares the Adidas mission statement to Nike's.

> Adidas: The Adidas Group strives to be the global leader in the sporting goods industry with brands built on a passion for sports and a sporting lifestyle.
>
> Nike: To bring inspiration and innovation to every athlete* in the world.
>
> *"If you have a body, you are an athlete."

While Adidas emphasizes value and values, the Nike statement goes further. It addresses not just your interests but who you are. While Adidas is *for* you, Nike is *with* you.

Craig and Snook surveyed their students and executives at Harvard Business School and found that less than 20 percent of leaders have a strong sense of their own individual purpose.[4] These authors describe leadership purpose as knowing who you are and what makes you distinctive. They see purpose basically as your brand, what you're driven to achieve. It's not so much about what you do but, rather, why you do it.

Discovering Your Purpose

While there is an organizational purpose, there is also a personal purpose. Identifying both of these can make you a better leader. How do you identify your purpose? Think of your purpose as your lifelong core, strengths, values, and passions. What are the passions that energize you and bring you joy?

There are specific questions that can help you find your purpose. Start by thinking of things you loved doing as a child. You may remember certain activities you had to stop doing, and how you felt as a result of that. Challenging life experiences that you have had may also lead you to a life purpose. Finally, think of those things that you've always enjoyed doing, and that keep you passionate. You may want to get the opinions of others who are close to you on how they see you in these areas.

Once you have gone through this exercise, try completing the following statement for yourself: "My leadership purpose is ________________."

Understanding your purpose, or what motivates you, enables you to redefine your role. By better understanding your personal goal, you are better able to establish the purpose of the organization. Craig and Snook outline a five-point plan to getting there. *Your first step is to create a purpose statement.* If your passion has been music, for example, it could be to create tunes that energize and excite people.

Then you explain your purpose. You always loved music. You learned to perform on an instrument when you were young and played in a band. You created tunes that sounded great and people loved your music. By working together with your bandmates, and paying attention to your audience, you experienced the success of exciting an audience. You learned how to manage your bandmates and keep them focused on getting the job done, whether it's writing a song, creating the arrangement, or performing on a live gig. At the same time, you were fully aware of what your audience would want to hear.

Third, you set three to five-year goals. Create the best and most innovative products or services that your customers not only are really looking for, but that moves them emotionally. Define how you do it; the steps you take. Get your internal team focused on the goal. Pay attention to the trends in your customers' world. Try out your innovation with a small, trusted audience. Then practice and do your best when you release your work to the biggest and best audience you can find.

Fourth, you can set two-year goals. You start by stating the goal: Have your product, for example, attain best-selling status. Then you can lay out the steps for how you can get there. *Fifth, and finally, you can set your one-year goals along with the steps for getting there.* You can then set six-month goals as well as 30-day goals.

Communicating the Purpose

Once you've established a purpose for your organization, it's important for you, as a leader, to communicate that purpose to the people within and outside the company. Working for an organization with purpose is especially important for Millennials, and they need to hear your message. Specific steps on communicating purpose were presented in an article by Jeff Boss (Boss, 2016).[5] It's important to realize that expressing purpose is not simply giving a motivational speech or using some inspirational words now and then.

Your company purpose should be exciting and challenging. It needs to be realistic and believable in order to be effective. If it's too audacious it may become overwhelming. You need a stretch goal that people can really believe in.

Your purpose should be clear but not too prescriptive. There needs to be enough freedom for people to choose how to reach the goal set. Being the "best in the world" or adding "value" to your existing product or service does not qualify as a good statement of purpose. These types of statements are too vague as well as uninteresting. Jeff Boss gives the example of Southwest Airlines, whose purpose is, "To connect people to what's important in their lives through friendly, reliable, and low-cost air travel." This type of statement helps employees decide how to handle certain challenges when they arise because saving the customer costs is a priority in decision making.

Realizing your organization's purpose should fill a need for employees. Now, more than ever, people seek meaning from their work. People need to feel a sense of pride in their work. Working for a purpose that matches personal values is tremendously energizing for people. Purpose not only gives direction to the organization, but it gives direction to the people working there as well.

What Is an Insightful Leader?

There are a number of basic emotional intelligence skills that contribute to leadership insight. Some of these have already been discussed in relation to the previous pillars of leadership. They will be briefly touched upon in this chapter for their relationship with insight.

Our definition of an insightful leader is:

> A leader provides insight by sharing a purpose and hopeful vision for colleagues to follow. Employees are compelled and inspired to exceed goals.

The emotional intelligence basic skills associated with this leadership style are:

Self-Actualization
Optimism
Self-Regard
Social Responsibility
Interpersonal Relationships
Emotional Expression

Self-Actualization

Self-actualization is a significant factor on all four of our pillars of successful leadership. Further, self-actualization is strongly related to overall work success and performance. It can be summed up in three words: pursuit of meaning—directly related to this third pillar, insight. While this sounds quite philosophical, as a leader it means finding purpose and enjoyment in your role and performing to your fullest potential. When you have a higher sense of accomplishment and resolve, then you are motivated, both as an individual and as an influencer, for your team or organization to strive for greatness.

Self-actualized leaders are perceived as role models and as someone who is striving to learn, develop new skills, and willing to grow to fully optimize their talents. Strong self-actualized leaders permeate the entire organization, as employees may emulate their approach. This drive for self-fulfillment stimulates higher productivity and greater employee satisfaction.

Optimism

Optimism, the ability to remain positive despite setbacks, is a crucial differentiator between successful leaders and unsuccessful leaders in the workplace. Optimism permeates almost every application of emotional intelligence, from helping you persevere, to motivating and inspiring colleagues. As a leader, you need to view your work and life in a positive light.

Some characteristics of optimistic leaders are:

- They approach leadership with enthusiasm and gusto.
- They motivate colleagues to achieve success, help them set stretch goals and reach for greater heights.
- They believe that setbacks are temporary and that they can overcome them.

Leadership Implications An optimistic leadership style helps you view most situations as malleable and controllable. By further developing a sense of optimism, when you encounter adversity, you will be able to overcome the challenge, learn from the situation, and inspire others to do the same. You will be able to set an inspiring mission and vision for the organization that produces results and productivity.

Organizational Implications By having an optimistic outlook, your colleagues can emulate your disposition and use you as a role model when encountering tough situations. For the most part, the organization prospers under uncertainty, and these situations are viewed as transient and easily overcome.

Modify Your Language

If you are looking to develop optimism, you can monitor your speech, as the words you use can either create a positive or negative ambiance. For example:

- In a meeting, take note if you play the role of devil's advocate. Do you often criticize others' ideas or solutions without weighing the evidence?

- The next time a colleague proposes an initiative, take the time to consider their perspective and their contribution.
- Temper your initial reaction with positive statements (e.g., "that sounds promising," and "did you consider the alternative?") to help boost your positive mind-set.

Self-Regard

Leaders with high self-regard respect themselves and accept both their personal strengths and limitations while remaining satisfied and self-secure. A self-confident leader also understands both their personal strengths and weaknesses. Self-regard can include having a strong character that does not compromise values. It is important to ground your self-assuredness by using your reality testing skills and by continually seeking feedback.

You may:

- Exercise your considerable influence on key, strategic decisions.
- Demonstrate courage to stick by your convictions even in the face of dissenting viewpoints.
- Use a leadership approach that leverages your strengths and delegates tasks in your weaker areas.

Leadership Implications High self-regard leaders are driven to surpass organizational targets, create an atmosphere of excellence, and demonstrate a strong sense of confidence in their leadership capabilities. The challenge is that they can lose touch with a realistic appraisal of their capabilities. It is important to draw on reality testing behaviors and feedback from their team to maintain a healthy self perception.

Organizational Implications The ability to understand and accept one's strengths and weaknesses is perceived as a genuine approach to leadership. Higher confidence leaders can help others in a variety of capacities. They serve as a role model, and their higher expectations of themselves and their employees lead to better-quality decisions and greater productivity. High self-regard leaders are advised to use external validation to avoid any attempts at self-aggrandizement and to maintain a realistic appraisal of their talents.

Be Mindful of Your Weaknesses

Awareness of shortcomings helps circumvent an inflated self-concept and tempers an exaggerated self-image. Nobody's perfect; our flaws make us human. The key is to be cognizant of your limitations and ensure that they do not impinge on organizational performance. Develop strategies to improve your limitations. For example, if you are impatient and anxious when deadlines are not met in a timely fashion, you may want to refocus and practice relaxation techniques (e.g., deep breathing). You are only limited by the power of your imagination. Awareness leads to action and meaningful change. Be mindful that change does not occur overnight, but with persistence, transformation is possible.

Focus on Your Strengths

Capitalize on your talents to introduce positive emotions in your way of thinking.

Every leader is endowed with strengths and weaknesses. The key is to focus on your strengths. For instance, if you are adept at public speaking, volunteer to deliver presentations at the next meeting.

When appropriate, delegate tasks in which you do not excel to your colleagues who may be more specialized in a certain area of expertise. By focusing on your strengths, you are better able to leverage your skills to their full extent, which will aid in fostering a positive outlook.

Modesty Is the Best Policy

While it is important to feel good about your strengths, do not overinflate them. Watch that you don't fall prey to arrogance; demonstrate humility and be humble in your approach to leadership. Successful leaders know their worth, but they remain grounded by seeking feedback from their team as well as from other leaders.

Colleagues respect a leader who is visionary and exudes charisma, but who is also approachable, genuine, and can relate to others. Having a modest approach will help you win the esteem and admiration of your employees.

Social Responsibility

Socially responsible leaders are insightful, as well as authentic leaders. Social responsibility calls for leaders to act in a moral and responsible manner, promote the greater good, and be a strong voice in their teams, organizations, and communities. A socially responsible leader takes most, if not all, opportunities to help the team and the organization. Their concern for others, whether at work or in the community, is demonstrated through the selfless contributions they make.

Leadership Implications Socially responsible leaders are purposeful and serve as champions for their team and community. You will need to uphold the moral and ethical compass in your leadership approach and often place your team's goals ahead of your own agenda. You may also strive to contribute to or make a difference in society (e.g., charity involvement/fundraising).

Reflect and Focus

Being a successful leader is not a solo activity. Real success comes from helping your team members reach professional goals and individual improvement. Always supporting others, however, can take away the time you need to spend on yourself as a leader. Try to ensure that you are not avoiding your current emotional state, goals, and functioning by focusing too heavily on others.

Reflect on how you spent your time last week. What activities and tasks did you spend your time on?

Which of those tasks were for the betterment of yourself, your family, your work, those you lead, and others? If you are over involved in any area, adjust your schedule for the next month and refocus your efforts.

Inspiring Initiative

Inspiring others to be socially responsible can create an overall feeling of meaning while contributing toward the greater good. Leverage your passion for causes you care about by reaching out to your team and organization (e.g., setting up a community support group within the organization). Brainstorm several activities that you, your team, or the organization as a whole can engage in. Ensure these activities are in line with your organization's vision and are of benefit to the employees.

Identify a plan of action to build social responsibility within your organization; identify specific roles and a time frame in which to complete the plan of action.

Interpersonal Relationships

Insightful leadership cannot exist without strong relationships. While you likely have solid technical skills, your ability to form strong relationships in your team is also important, especially to help weather difficult times. Placing an emphasis on building strong relationships and, even more than most people, model what it means to be a team player. Your leadership style will need to use people and relationships to get the job done, by gaining buy-in and commitment, building integrity, and attaining the resources your team needs to succeed.

Emotional Expression

If you have a solid understanding of what brings about your emotions, it is much easier to regulate your behavior and control the impact your emotions have on employees in the organization. Leaders with high emotional expression lead with composure and a full understanding of their impact on others.

These leaders:

- Can choose a course of action based on a "gut feeling" in time-constrained situations.
- Generate respect, admiration, and honesty from employees because they are viewed as highly self-aware.
- Generally, take time to contemplate instead of acting rashly, thereby considering their emotional response and those of others.

Leadership Implications These leaders have a thorough grasp of their emotional triggers and reactions. This in-depth understanding helps fuel a streamlined decision-making process as they incorporate their emotions into their role as a leader. Knowing your emotional triggers and reactions, enables you to use this emotional knowledge to effectively navigate through challenging or difficult situations.

Organizational Implications Emotionally expressive leaders grasp subtle emotional nuances that help them take calculated risks that help the organization meet its strategic goals. This comfort with, and knowledge of, their emotional triggers and reactions allows them to lead with authenticity and a candid approach to help them gain credibility and buy-in with employees. It allows them to manage tense and perhaps overwhelming situations with ease, and to use and recognize the full spectrum of emotions.

Be a Role Model

Through the steadfast control of your emotions, you can be innovative, successfully take risks, and gain the trust of your employees. The most prominent leaders have an aptitude for remaining composed in competitive situations and under mounting pressure and duress. Your ability to be aware of your emotions can help you serve as a model of composure and ensure that employees feel secure and content to overcome any potential challenge.

Give seminars/workshops or hire an expert to teach employees about understanding emotions and the impact of their emotions on others.

Weigh the Evidence

Leaders who are highly adept at understanding emotions, may have a tendency to be overly reliant on their emotional barometer to make decisions. It's important to incorporate objective evidence. Intuition can only carry you so far. While a deal may feel right, data may not support the intended strategy.

Be sure to seek counsel from colleagues, involve members of your team, and emphasize facts to support your proposed course of action.

The Importance of Insight

In the book, *Corporate Culture and Performance*, John Kotter and James Heskett[6] show that over a decadelong period, purposeful, value-driven companies outperform their counterparts in stock price by a factor of 12. In the absence of purpose, a company's leadership is likely to have greater difficulty in motivating employees and putting the company on the course to success. Customers are likely to have difficulty connecting with the company. With purpose, a company can create positive value that is far greater than the sum of its parts.[7]

Who Exemplifies Insightful Leadership?

While there are a number of leaders today that exemplify insightful, or purposeful leadership, perhaps one that stands out in this area is the late entrepreneur Anita Roddick, who started a chain of stores known as the Body Shop. She has been described as founding and growing "one of the most iconic and successful British brands of the 21st century, starting out of a tiny shop in Brighton."[8] Her business success included creating over 2,000 Body Shop retail outlets in 52 markets serving over 75 million customers. In fact, there are few other British brands that have enjoyed such a huge international success.

Her success has been attributed to her inspirational style of leadership and the impact that her altruistic approach to capitalism and entrepreneurship left on her customers, employees, and our society as a whole.

Roddick was considered by many to be a business and social visionary of our time. She combined the elements of entrepreneurship, strategic thinking, and ethical leadership. She also believed that "businesses have the power to do good" and really lived her vision, without exception.

"That's why the Body Shop's mission statement opens with the overriding commitment, 'to dedicate our business to the pursuit of social and environmental change.'" Roderick stated, "I want to work for a company that contributes to and is part of the community. I want something not just to invest in. I want something to believe in." As well she reported, "the business of business should not just be about money; it should be about responsibility. It should be about public good, not private greed."[9]

The socially responsible vision of the Body Shop had five core values:

1. Against animal testing
2. Support community trade
3. Activate self-esteem
4. Defend human rights
5. Protect our planet

There was no mention of "best in class" or "outstanding customer service" or any other commonly used brand values in the company vision. Insightful leaders know more than just their purpose, mission, and values. They also know how to structure their values in such a way that they become integral to employees, partners, and customers.

EQ Leader: Things to Think About

1. Do you see yourself as having a purpose or a mission?
2. How would you explain your purpose?
3. Does your personal purpose match your work purpose?
4. Think about the people you work with. How many of them have purpose or meaning in their life?
5. How could you add meaning to the lives of the people you work with?
6. What meaningful contribution do you make in your workday?
7. How do you measure if you are satisfied with the direction you are going?

Chapter 14

Pillar IV: Developing Innovation

If you want to build a ship, don't drum up people together to collect wood and don't assign them tasks and work, but rather teach them to long for the endless immensity of the sea.

—ANTOINE DE ST. ÉXUPERY

Innovation

Innovation Definition:

Foster ingenuity, imagination, and autonomous thinking:

Understands the importance of taking risks, spurring ingenuity, imagination, autonomous thinking, values knowledge, and challenges seen as learning opportunities.

What does it take to be an innovative leader? How much impact can you have as an innovative leader on the organization? In a series of studies, the McKinsey Institute looked at the gap that exists between the leaders who want to innovate and their actual ability to innovate.[1] They report that, according to their surveys, 70 percent of senior executives claim that innovation will be one of their top three drivers of growth for their companies over the next few years.

They also found that 65 percent of senior executives were somewhat or less confident about their decisions in this area.

While there are no accepted best practices to foster innovation as yet, there is near unanimous agreement among top executives that people and corporate cultures are the drivers of innovation. McKinsey identified three key people-management building blocks of an innovative organization. The first, and some would say most important, aspect of innovation is to include it in your company's strategic plan. That way it can be managed, tracked, and measured.

Second, executives can better use their existing, and perhaps unused talent for innovation. They can do this without implementing disruptive change programs. It can be done by generating the conditions that allow active innovation networks to be created and grow. Finally, they can take clear steps to nurture a culture of innovation based on trust among employees. In this culture, people would appreciate that their ideas are respected, believe that it is safe to express those ideas, and oversee risk collectively, with their managers.

In another survey, McKinsey found that 600 senior executives reported that leadership was the single best predictor of innovation. In addition, they found, "the top two motivators of behavior to promote innovation are strong leaders who encourage and protect it and top executives who spend their time actively managing and driving it."

In most organizations, there is little more than lip service paid to innovation, with rewards for short-term performance and a fear of failure stymying innovative endeavors. Three steps are recommended to overcome this inertia:

1. Define the kind of innovation that drives growth and helps meet strategic objectives.
2. Add innovation to the formal agenda at regular leadership meetings.
3. Set performance metrics and targets for innovation (both financial and behavioral).

In another study, looking at the traits of innovative leaders, Jack Zenger and Joseph Folkman interviewed and used 360-feedback with 33 individual leaders found to be high innovators.[2] Of the 10 traits identified, the most important ones included showing excellent strategic vision. This included the ability to paint a clear picture of where they wanted to go and leaving the route to get there up to the creative team. Second was having a strong customer focus. Innovation is not just for innovation's sake. Being successful at leading innovation requires you to really understand the customer—the emotional intelligence skill of empathy.

The third trait involved creating a climate of trust. Once again, this had to do with taking risks and giving people permission to fail. Collaborative relationships within the team and among others in the organization are also important. Fourth, these leaders also had a fearless loyalty toward doing what's right for the organization and for the customer. Doing the right thing for the customer took precedence over pleasing the boss. This is indicative of assertiveness as an emotional skill. Fifth, they promote a culture that takes ideas from the bottom up, as opposed to top down. They were seen as optimistic and energetic in their approach to other's ideas.

The sixth trait was their ability to be persuasive. They could get others to accept their ideas. They were described as enthusiastic. They were able to inspire others through their sense of purpose and meaning—an ability we previously described as insight.

Examples of Innovative Leaders

There have been a number of examples of innovative leaders over the past few decades: Bill Gates (Microsoft), Larry Page (Google), Elon Musk (Tesla Motors and SpaceX), Mark Zuckerberg (Facebook), Reed Hastings (Netflix), Jorgen Vig Knudstorp (Lego), Marissa Mayer (Yahoo!), Jeff Bezos (Amazon), Jeff Weiner (LinkedIn), and Jan Koum (WhatsApp), to name a few. But perhaps the most iconic is Steve Jobs (Apple).

There have been many attempts to explain the innovation success of Jobs. As pointed out by Carmine Gallo, Apple was near bankruptcy after Jobs's 12-year absence.[3] When he returned, he initiated one innovation after another and was named by CNBC as the number one most innovative and transformative leader of the past 25 years.[4]

What were the elements of his character that drove the innovation that took Apple from the verge of bankruptcy to the most successful company in the world? What can innovative leaders take from this lesson? Gallo distilled this success to a few distinct rules.

Lead with Passion and Vision

Jobs often talked about how important it was to do what you love. It was all about passion. It wasn't computers that Jobs was passionate about, but rather the potential that computers brought to people all over the world. A bold, specific vision inspires others and sets things in motion. While passion fuels the rocket, vision sets the direction. Jobs believed in hiring the best people and setting them toward the vision he shared with them.

Strive for Simplicity

When Jobs returned to Apple, he found many different, unrelated projects in progress. One of his first missions was reducing the number of projects in development. In his words, "innovation comes from saying no to 1,000 things." He believed in making things simpler. While Microsoft went about expanding the capabilities of Windows and making it more complex, Jobs set about creating an iPhone that was simpler and had fewer buttons than competing phones.

Look for Connections

A big part of innovation is connecting disparate things. Innovators know how to associate ideas from different disciplines and apply them to specific projects. Jobs was able to take different concepts and apply them to his innovations, such as using the calligraphy he learned in college on the Macintosh typeface. As Jobs stated toward the end of his life, "it's the intersection of technology and liberal arts that makes our hearts sing."

Share a Story and Sell Dreams

Being a good storyteller helps get your message across to others. Perhaps inspired by liberal arts, Jobs was a great storyteller and legions of followers would fill theatres just to hear his new product messages. Jobs knew that being a good storyteller helps get your message across to others. Having a great idea is not enough to be an innovator; you have to sell your message.

Another great attribute of Jobs was his ability to sell dreams, not products. People are generally not interested in products. They want to know how their lives will change for the better. Whether it's an iPhone or iPad, it's not about the device. It's about how easy it will be for you to use and how it will make your life easier.

Listen to Yourself

What happens when dealing with all the naysayers that innovators encounter? Well, Steve Jobs said it best with, "don't let the noise of others' opinions drown out your own inner voice. . . . And most important, have the courage to follow your heart and intuition. They somehow already know what you truly want to become."

What Is an Innovative Leader?

Our definition of an innovative leader is:

> An innovative leader focuses on taking risks, spurring colleagues' ingenuity and autonomous thought. Knowledge is valued and challenges are viewed as learning opportunities.

The basic emotional intelligence skills that contribute to innovative leadership are:

Self-Actualization
Independence
Problem Solving
Assertiveness
Flexibility
Optimism

Self-Actualization

Self-actualization is a significant factor on all four of our pillars of successful leadership. Self-actualization is strongly related to overall work success and performance. It can be summed up in three words: pursuit of meaning. While this sounds quite philosophical, as a leader it means finding purpose and enjoyment in your role and performing to your fullest potential. When you have a higher sense of accomplishment and resolve, you are more motivated, both as an individual and as an influencer for your team or organization to strive for greatness.

Self-actualized leaders are perceived as role models and as someone who is striving to learn, develop new skills, and willing to grow to fully optimize their talents. Strong self-actualized leaders permeate the entire organization, as employees may emulate their approach. This drive for self-fulfillment stimulates higher productivity and greater employee satisfaction.

Independence

Independent leaders are capable of feeling, thinking, and working on their own, a critical skill that all great leaders have in common. When well developed as a skill, you are ready and capable of holding your own ideas and making necessary decisions required for your team on your own. Independent leaders are unlikely to be swayed by popular opinion, which can help maintain an established direction for the team. Consider the following characteristics of independent leaders:

- They are comfortable providing direction and working on their own.
- They can work without emotional dependency on others, and don't require their reassurance.
- They accept responsibility for their decisions, knowing that at times people will disagree with them.

Leadership Implications Independent leaders rarely depend on others to make important decisions. These leaders are self-directed, can analyze a situation, formulate a response, and move into implementation mode without second-guessing their decisions. This skill is crucial for a leader, especially when difficult decisions need to be made and direction is limited. At the same time, they are careful not to neglect the emotions and opinions of their team, which could possibly leave them feeling alienated, and eventually disengaged.

Organizational Implications Independent leaders tend to voice their thoughts and opinions, likely adding their own perspective to the discussion and influencing the direction of the organization. They are active participants in generating ideas rather than passive receivers. Keep a close eye on how often you go off in your own direction rather than building coalitions. Teams that strive for the same values and goals build strong organizations.

Stay Connected

While being emotionally independent is important for leading a team, being completely autonomous can hurt the amount of buy-in you receive from them. Once again, here are four qualities that indicate you are too independent:

1. Ignorance: Are people feeling like I am ignoring facts in an effort to pursue my own agenda?

2. Know-it-all: Do I think I know everything, and thus my team's advice is not needed?
3. Detached: Am I hurting collaborative relationships and engagement by not including others?
4. Closed door: While I have an open-door policy, is my behavior distancing myself from my team?

Listening to Feedback

To ensure that you do not hurt any key relationships throughout the organization, balance self-directed thought with the ability to seek advice and feedback.

You do not have to be a fan of an idea to entertain the thought process of others and explore different perspectives. Doing so can help gain the support of others and perhaps even generate new possibilities.

- Examine a few of your past decisions. What did your decision-making process look like? Who did you connect with to seek advice or a differing point of view? How well did you follow along the input that was given to you?
- Next time when you are seeking advice from your team, note down the different perspectives before presenting a counterthought. Then reflect on those notes and think through the feedback and the possible impact on your decision.

Problem Solving

Solving problems is an everyday reality for leaders. However, leaders need more than just problem solving skills, they need to work with problems where emotions are involved and recognize how these emotions impact their decisiveness. This is an area of emotional intelligence that innovative leaders extensively use; they tackle problems head-on without being overwhelmed or distracted by their emotions. Their approach is likely uninterrupted and invokes a sense of steadfastness and confidence from those they lead. These leaders:

- See emotional information as playing a pivotal role but are not sidetracked by it.

- Work through the many steps to solving a problem without being emotionally distracted.
- Are likely to delve into tough or touchy problems, understanding the emotions at play.
- Rarely let emotions inhibit their decisions, but they do not take it to the extreme and ignore their feelings entirely.

Leadership Implications For almost every problem, innovative leaders show focus and a rational demeanor as they generate solutions. Their leadership approach allows them to reframe problems and approach situations in new ways, spurring the creativity of their team and allowing for process overhauls when required.

This leader still wants to appear emotionally invested in the decisions they make—they just aren't allowing their emotions to derail them from making a decision.

Organizational Implications The innovative leader's method of viewing a problem from different perspectives, without being derailed by their emotions, helps them generate a wider range of solutions than most leaders. They are likely sought out for their rational problem-solving approach, particularly when emotions are running high.

Tackling problems head-on enables them to set the tone for responsiveness and efficiency throughout the organization.

Seek Understanding First

If you find yourself quick to jump into problem-solving mode, you may start implementing solutions without fully surveying the situation.

- Begin by explaining your interpretation of a problem to at least two people, one who is connected closely to the problem and the other who is a neutral third party.
- Don't ask for solutions; have them hear your summary of the situation and ask clarifying questions if needed.
- A question to which you do not know the answer is a sign that you need a greater understanding of the problem before you begin to solve it.

Set the Emotional Stage

As a leader, you need to manage the emotional landscape of your team. Others may not be as decisive as you; don't leave people behind as you forge ahead solving problems.

- If your team needs to be innovative and consider unconventional approaches, try to evoke positive emotions within the group (e.g., recall a successful event, use humor, or hold a meeting outside of the office).
- Alternatively, to ensure others can concentrate on the details or analyze the associated costs of a problem, try to generate a slightly less positive mood that can help you with the analytical phase of problem solving.

Assertiveness

Another key emotional skill you should develop as an innovative leader is assertiveness. Picture a line between the words passive and aggressive. At the middle point of this line lies assertiveness, a place where you work with your team by finding the right language at the right time to express your feelings and thoughts. It is helpful to articulate your thoughts in a clear and confident way. You should be firm and direct when making decisions. You can guide your team toward your goals by articulating your needs and protecting their resources. As well, you should view your rights and those of your team's as sacred.

Leadership Implications Innovative leaders pull on strong emotions and convictions to state their position. This is a crucial skill to have when leading a team; it helps in gaining your team's buy-in and inspiring them toward innovative solutions. Further, a high level of assertiveness helps to gain the resources your team needs and proactively clear obstacles in the path of your team's success. While such situations require you to be an assertive leader, others may require you to be more flexible in your thinking. Becoming too rigid in defending your position may result in unproductive, stubborn, or aggressive behavior.

Flexibility

Flexibility requires that you be able to modify your thoughts, emotions, and behaviors in response to change. An innovative, flexible leader has a finely tuned ability to adapt to shifting priorities in the organization. They are a catalyst who inspires fresh ideas, and learns from unexpected events. This willingness to adapt helps them become a champion of progress and use a variety of leadership styles with direct reports. Some indicators of the flexible leader are:

- They are viewed as quick to respond to unpredictable events.
- They are reactive, and not stuck to conventional and outdated methods.
- They are able to mold their leadership style and emotional responses to changing conditions and differing needs of those on their team.

Leadership Implications An innovative, flexible leader is at ease with both minor and major transformations. They realize that they cannot control everything, which helps fuel ideas and creativity in their teams. They are not always a proponent of the status quo and are receptive to improving business processes and changing leadership styles when necessary. Nevertheless, it is important to be mindful that change is made easier when they are armed with sufficient information to make a credible decision.

Organizational Implications Innovative, flexible leaders are role models for responsiveness. Their flexibility likely helps to ensure that new insights and fresh perspectives are fostered. Different opinions are raised within their team and work relationships, and challenges to traditional procedures become the norm. They help contribute to an organization that adopts "outside the box" thinking and views change as a continual learning process. They rely on instinct and reality testing when evaluating alternative courses of action.

Remain True to Your Convictions

Watch that you are not heavily swayed or influenced by others' perspectives, as too much flexibility can pose as many challenges as too little.

- Employees respect leaders who remain true to their beliefs, even if the outcome is unexpected.
- Employees are not fond of leaders who waver, based on the opinions of others. Behave consistently so that your adaptable approach does not become counterproductive.

- Reflect on the core beliefs and values that underlie your choices and ensure that your leadership style embodies these traits.
- Be prepared to share the reason(s) why you veered from a particular course of action, so that your colleagues can understand your logic.

Establish a Culture of Innovation

Funnel your drive for innovation and creativity through the organization.

- Reward and praise your employees for their new ideas and creations. For instance, you can award a plaque of recognition to the employee who presents the most original and imaginative idea.
- Be sure to give your employees the freedom to fail. There is likely something of value within every idea that doesn't come to fruition.
- Hold your employees accountable for achieving key metrics (e.g., sales targets) but allow them the flexibility to plan how they will achieve these goals and encourage questioning of the status quo.

Optimism

Optimism, the ability to remain positive despite setbacks, is a crucial differentiator between successful leaders and others in the workplace. It permeates almost every application of emotional intelligence, from helping you persevere, to motivating and inspiring colleagues. As a leader, you need to view your work and life in a positive light.

Some characteristics of optimistic leaders are:

- They approach leadership with enthusiasm and gusto.
- They motivate colleagues to achieve success, help them set stretch goals, and reach for greater heights.
- They believe that setbacks are temporary and that they can overcome them.

Leadership Implications An optimistic leadership style helps you view most situations as malleable and controllable. By further developing a sense of optimism, when you encounter adversity, you will be able to overcome the challenge, learn from the situation, and inspire others to do the same. You will be able to set an inspiring mission and vision for the organization that produces results and productivity.

Case Example: The MHS Hackathon

The idea of a "hackathon" comes out of the software industry and has been defined as "a design sprint-like event in which computer programmers and others involved in software development, including graphic designers, interface designers, project managers, and others, often including subject-matter-experts, collaborate intensively on software projects."[5]

In our own case, we came out of one of our strategic planning retreats quite concerned about all the ways that our industry and our company could be disrupted. We had the presentation showing how Uber disrupts the taxi industry, Airbnb the hotel industry, Amazon the bookstores, digital photography Kodak, and so on. The big question was how do we avoid being a similar statistic?

We came across the idea of the hackathon and looked at modifying it for our purposes.* For example, we wanted to expand it beyond our software programming group and include everyone in the company. I will describe the process we used, which you could likely take and adapt for almost any industry. While one of our main goals was to look at how we could create products and services for the future, one of the big benefits to come out of it, as reported in staff evaluations, was the camaraderie and engagement the event created. In fact, the first event was so successful, we've launched it as an annual event. And the excitement for our second hackathon has been even greater than the first. It was also equally successful.

Before announcing the hackathon to staff we set the ground rules for the process and the event. The steps and rules were then presented to all employees. Here are the steps we presented:

1. **Pick Your Team**

   Teams can be as large or small as you wish, but four to five members is a typical sweet spot for success! Each team will need a

* The Hackathon was primarily conceived of and organized at MHS by Hazel Wheldon, Rick Walrond, and Scott Millar. We were assisted by Chetan Bagga and his team at Archetype.

team captain, and there should be no more than one programmer and one user experience (UX) member per team. Each hackathon participant can only be on one team. If you have trouble finding a team, let us know.

2. **Learn about the Hackathon**

   Attend Lunch & Learn events, review the description of our hackathon, and start brainstorming!

3. **Submit Ideas**

   Your team can submit as many ideas as you like, but you'll only be working on one for the hackathon day. Choose wisely! There will be a submission template to register your team and submit your ideas, and ideas will be reviewed and approved. Ideas are due by DATE 1.

4. **Hackathon Day**

   You'll spend a full workday developing your idea with your team on DATE 2! You'll need to produce a business plan and a PowerPoint presentation. You could also show us a prototype! You'll submit these materials at the end of the day. Food, snacks, and drinks will be provided throughout the day!

5. **Present Your Idea**

   Teams will present their ideas to the company (and our panel of hackathon judges) during a Town Hall on DATE 3. Each team will have five to 10 minutes and the slide deck from their Hackathon Day submission.

6. **Win Prizes!**

   There will be a number of smaller prizes presented based on trivia questions and draws during the hackathon day (e.g., wireless headphones), but the big winners will be the top three teams chosen by our panel of judges! The top team will receive $5,000, second place will receive $2,000 and third place will receive $1,000. And every idea has a chance of being implemented by MHS.

Four general areas of innovation were outlined as eligible. They were:

1. Process improvement: Process improvement is the proactive task of identifying, analyzing, and improving upon existing business processes within an organization for optimization and to meet new quotas or standards of quality.

2. Gamification: Gamification primarily refers to a process of making systems, services, and activities more enjoyable and motivating. Gamification commonly employs game design elements which are used in so called nongame contexts in attempts to improve user engagement, organizational productivity, flow, learning, employee recruitment and evaluation, (and) ease of use and usefulness of systems, among others.
3. Mobile Apps: Mobile apps have existed long enough for us to know what they are; we need to focus on what they can do for us, both in terms of how they can support our current products, and how we can use them to enter emerging and future markets (i.e., wearables).
4. Big data: Big data is a broad term for data sets so large or complex that traditional data processing applications are inadequate. Challenges include analysis, capture, data curation, search, sharing, storage, transfer, visualization, and information privacy. The term often refers simply to the use of predictive analytics or other certain advanced methods to extract value from data, and seldom to a particular size of data set. Accuracy in big data may lead to more confident decision making. And better decisions can mean greater operational efficiency, cost reduction, and reduced risk.

What Do Participants Produce?

Participants are expected to produce three things:

1. Business plan
2. Prototype (can be anything from hand-drawn sketches to fully interactive demo)
3. Brief presentation summarizing their projects (similar to what one would present on *Shark Tank* or to a venture capitalist)

A number of questions to be answered during the presentation are provided to guide the presentations:

What problem do you solve and for whom?

How does your idea solve the problem?

How does your idea/plan benefit MHS?

How do we implement your idea?

How is your idea/business plan innovative?

How does this improve our technology/distribution?

The day of the hackathon is an exciting day. There are T-shirts for all participants, helpers, and judges. Food is provided throughout the day. There are "consultant" stations set up where participants can get advice and assistance from senior team members in accounting, presentation skills, marketing, business plan, and so forth. Participants learn to work in cross-functional teams, develop new skills, and think more entrepreneurially.

Participation has been excellent with approximately 70 staff on teams (out of 160 staff in total, including managers) working on 15 projects. There is a lot of buildup to the event as people develop and start to research ideas. We've had many excellent ideas and have already started putting a few to market. The ideas ranged across all of the eligible areas.

One example of an idea we developed can be a game-changer in the development and assessment of higher-level job competencies. A program called AscentMode was developed that contains a database of competencies and their definitions, used for a number of senior job positions, such as sales manager. The data were collected from hundreds of ads placed by Fortune 500 companies for senior positions. Within each of the competencies, a number of test items are matched from our various talent assessments.

Competencies include, but are not limited to, Analytical Thinking, Business Acumen, Change Orientation, Communication, Integrity, Interpersonal Management, and Results Orientation. So an HR director at a large company can build their own competency model from the options provided (with industry relevant suggestions, e.g., pharma, financial services). They can, in no time, be ready to assess applicants online for the relevant skills sets needed for the job. This could provide huge savings to organizations that hire experts for competency analyses. We already have one large pharmaceutical company piloting the prototype.

Another innovative idea one of the teams came up with was based on the success of our hackathon methodology in terms of not only new products and procedures developed, but the level of staff engagement throughout the organization. They created a format, structure, forms, and materials that would allow our organizational development team to consult to other organizations so they could benefit from our experience in setting up their own hackathon.

They blueprinted a one-day consultation that would assist companies in carrying out their own hackathon and a three-day consultation where our organizational development team would come and help run the hackathon in your company. They called it Hack-A-Tron. Brilliant idea! One of our outside judges wanted to know when he could bring it to his company.

Developing the Ideas

Once projects for development were decided upon, we created an Innovation Hub. This was a specific unit of staff selected to work on some of our innovation projects. Their mandate is to take a project from prototype phase to development, and through field testing to eventually provide it to the sales and marketing teams. Our Hub was built with a combination of existing and new staff, as needed. They have no other responsibilities but to develop new projects.

Innovation takes time and commitment. There are also risks. You must be willing to accept failure. These key ingredients can help you and your team become more innovative. While there is a cost of innovation, the rewards can be huge. Innovation can make the difference between sustaining a successful organization and being disrupted.

EQ Leader: Things to Think About

1. Do you think of yourself as innovative or creative?
2. Think of ways you have innovated products or services in the past.
3. Are you able to be innovative in your work?
4. What limits are there to your ability to be innovative at work?
5. What can you do to encourage others you work with to be more innovative?
6. Can you think of opportunities you've missed by not being innovative?
7. Think about implementing an innovative work plan at work. How would you go about it?
8. How do you think people at your workplace would deal with failure of an innovative idea?

Chapter 15

What 360s Can Tell Us about Leaders and Potential Leaders

I think it's very important to have a feedback loop, where you're constantly thinking about what you've done and how you could be doing it better.

—ELON MUSK

How Can We Better Assess High Potentials or Emerging Leaders?

What more can we do to identify and develop potential future leaders? At Discovery Learning International, now a part of Multi-Health Systems, a tool was developed to identify competencies of emerging leaders. Competencies are behaviors or sets of behaviors relevant to success for, in this case, leadership. The first step in developing the model was to identify the competencies necessary for success both in business school and for long-term success as business leaders. The idea was to identify competencies that are enduring throughout a career, rather than for a specific role, and facilitating of success at all levels. By identifying and measuring these competencies, business schools, students, and companies can focus on training and developing behaviors that are most relevant to very successful individuals.

The aforementioned project began by reviewing the competency modeling and 360-degree feedback literature, including resources specifically pertaining to the success of MBA and EMBA students. A preliminary model was developed, consisting of 14 competencies.[1] From this, the goal was to create a tool that is easy to implement and interpret, and would create the foundation for a family of tools that will eventually incorporate role-specific competencies that would be valid from mailroom to boardroom (i.e., from the level of individual contributor up to senior executive). Within each competency, corresponding items that include both positive and negative inferences were developed.

In phase 1 of the survey, the data provided information on qualities seen to be essential for career success. The areas identified were ideal for inclusion in leadership curriculum development and training. Phase 2 identified and assessed deficiencies in key competencies that would require more attention in the classroom context. It was determined that the successful business students and business leaders of tomorrow will be the ones who can adapt to change, continuously update their skills, and accurately assess their strengths and weaknesses through a solid foundation of self-awareness. Some of the skills needed parallel the EQ-i 2.0 areas of Optimism, Self-Actualization, and Self-Regard.

The tool that was developed, the Emerging Leaders Profile™ (ELP), is a system that gathers the opinions of others—bosses, peers, and direct reports—and plays back the aggregate information to emerging leaders who want to improve their effectiveness. These scores are compared to the individual's own self report. The ELP analyzes raters' scores, reported on a scale of 1 to 5, for 60 observable behaviors grouped into 12 leadership competencies.

The competencies, which were identified through the aforementioned series of surveys, focus groups, and data analyses, include the following.

Learning Agility

Learning agility is the ability to diagnose the need for new skill sets and to learn them quickly; the ability to discard no longer applicable strengths, and persevere through the process of gaining new skill mastery; and learning rapidly as the pressures of change and time alter the context and demand new solutions and skill sets.

Communication Skills

Communication skills require precision and attention to the details of both oral and written communication and a facility with language and its use in conveying precise and subtle meanings. The ability to ensure the free and efficient flow of information in all directions and to choose appropriate levels of sharing includes speaking, writing, and listening.

Emotional Intelligence

Emotional intelligence is the ability to puzzle one's way through novel situations and the ability to perceive, to understand, and to manage emotion, as well as to facilitate thought with emotion when making decisions.

Resilience/Flexibility

Resilience/flexibility is the ability to recover from or adjust easily to change or misfortune. It is the ability to discard information and experience that is no longer relevant or useful and to change direction in accordance with new information.

Quest for Excellence

The quest for excellence is the ability to hold oneself to the highest standards and to frequently exceed the expectations of others, as well as to refuse to accept anything less than the highest-quality performance from oneself.

Self-Confidence

Self-confidence is possessing and displaying credible assurance and self-reliance. It is the ability to envision success in all endeavors and to communicate a sense of well-being to others.

Creativity and Innovation

Creativity and innovation is the ability to produce new ideas by thinking outside of expected parameters, as well as to solve problems through unconventional thinking and risk taking.

Moral Courage

Moral courage is a clearly articulated set of values and beliefs that informs one's decisions and is manifested in behavior that is consistent with whom one claims to be.

Accountability

Accountability is the willingness to accept full responsibility for one's actions and decisions and an aversion to excuses. It is a natural tendency to follow up on and fulfill one's commitments.

Cultural Adaptability

Cultural adaptability is the ability to perceive cultural differences between geographical regions and ethnic groups and between organizations and their component subcultures, and to adapt behavior accordingly without losing one's own identity.

Decisiveness

Decisiveness is the ability to make a resolute choice or to determine a course of action by efficiently leveraging and processing the best information available while discarding nonpertinent facts and to arrive at reasonable solutions with less than complete information.

Personal Organization and Planning

Personal organization and planning is the ability to structure and arrange information in both space and time around goals or objectives, to foresee events and needs, and to optimize the arrangement of information and time to meet those needs and prepare to respond to those events successfully.

The ELP report presents the combined data in a very simple, easy to interpret way. It reveals the evaluation of a leader, or potential leader's performance using a multi-sided circumplex. Each wedge represents one leadership competency. The report compares four to five circumplexes—one for self, one for boss(es), one for peers, one for direct reports and one for others as seen in Figure 15.1. Ratings are aggregated to assure the anonymity of respondents, except for boss and self.

Participants can easily see differences among how they are assessed by these separate raters. These new or prospective leaders quickly learn how others, who can directly impact their success (or failure), see their leadership performance. Further, they can use this report to compare their self-perception on the same competencies to the perceptions of others they work with. A benefit of the Emerging Leaders Profile is that it gives these potential leaders,

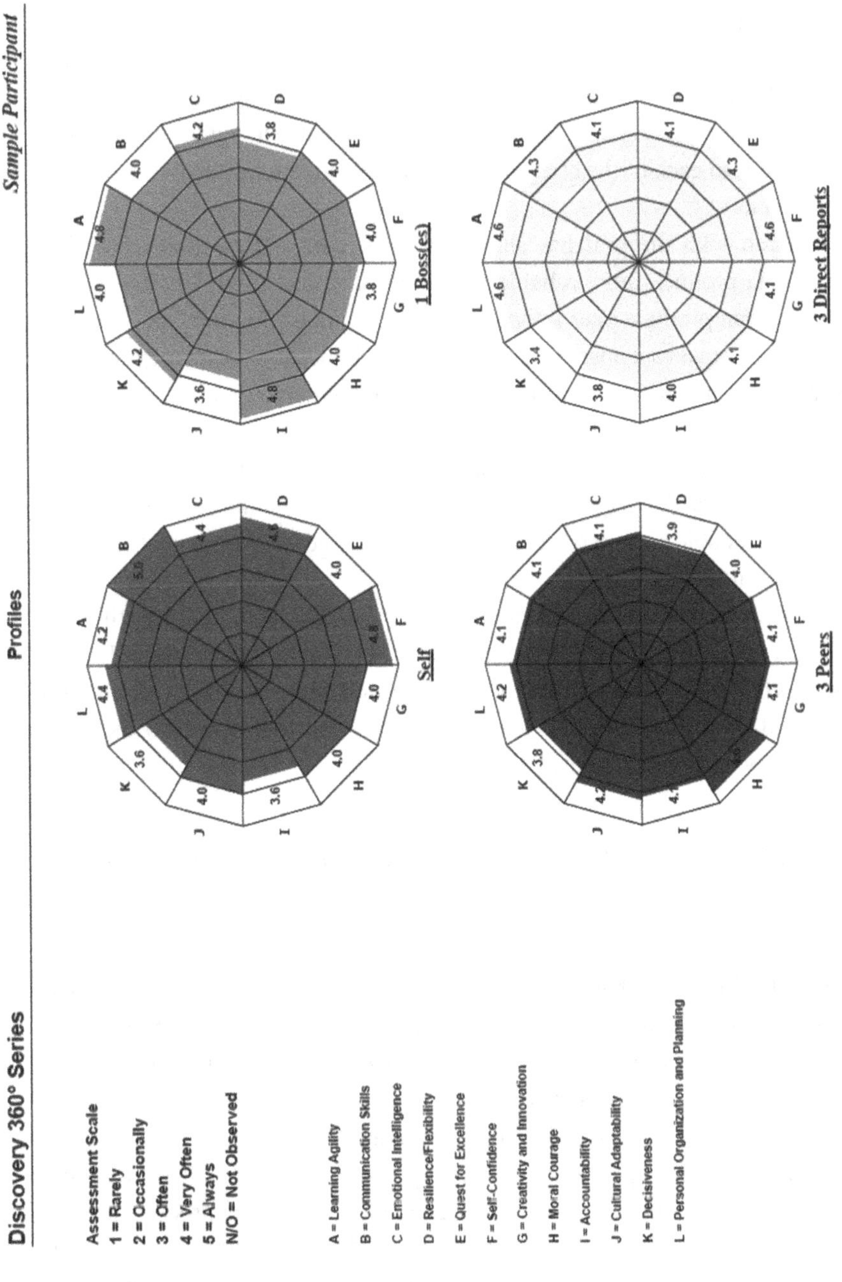

Figure 15.1 The Circumplex Model of the Emerging Leaders Profile

and those who coach them, a common model for understanding and describing leadership effectiveness.

The participant's leadership performance is also benchmarked to a common metric. This allows for the establishment of goals and the ability to monitor their efforts at adopting new behaviors where needed. Strengths and developmental needs in each of the categories can be identified for effective leadership development.

Research with the tool has shown that succinct and focused leadership assessments produce more reliable and valid data than more lengthy assessments that can produce rater fatigue. Also, the unique "do more" or "do less" response form makes it possible for each rater to indicate whether they want the person being rated to do more or less of a particular behavior as can be seen in Figure 15.2.

In addition to valuable individual feedback reports, the ELP generates composite reports that aggregate the feedback from any number of individuals creating a valuable picture of collective strengths and developmental opportunities as seen in Figure 15.3.

The ELP has been used in a number of organizations to help identify and develop high-profile leaders. Prospective research will help determine which of the scales helps predict leadership success. As well, there is a follow-up version that is used with existing leaders in organizations. This tool, as well, is used in a wide variety of organizations.

How Do Self versus Others Leadership EQ 360 Ratings Compare? Or Do Leaders Overrate Themselves?

The EQ 360 2.0 assessment, modeled on the EQ-i 2.0 self-report, was originally developed with more than 4,000 participants as part of the standardization process. From this, a sample of 3,200 participants was chosen for the EQ 360 2.0 normative sample. The original sample was evenly distributed by gender and rater type and matched to the census (North America) based on race/ethnicity.[2]

Statistical analyses revealed a lack of meaningful differences in EQ 360 2.0 scores across gender, age group, or rater type (i.e., Boss, Peer, Direct Report). Therefore, a single normative group was created. The norming process resulted in standard scores with means of 100 and standard deviations of 15 for the total emotional intelligence score, as well as composite scales, and subscales. The

Discovery 360° Series | **Individual Items** | ***Sample Participant***

Assessment Scale 1 = Rarely 2 = Occasionally 3 = Often 4 = Very Often 5 = Always N/O = Not Observed	Self	Combined Raters	Boss(es)	Direct Reports	Peers	Others	Direct Report Range 1 2 3 4 5	Peer Range 1 2 3 4 5	Do More	Do Less
Resilience/Flexibility	**4.6**	**4.0**	**3.8**	**4.1**	**3.9**	**3.9**				
16. Does not hold negative feelings and grudges for a long time.	4.0	4.1	4.0	4.3	4.0	4.0				
17. Embraces opportunities to reinvent him/herself. (+)	4.0	4.4	4.0	4.3	5.0	4.0				
18. Effectively balances his/her personal and work life. (–)	5.0	3.9	3.0	4.3	3.7	4.0				
19. Has more than one strategy for getting tasks done. (–)	5.0	3.8	4.0	3.7	3.7	4.0				
20. Acknowledges setbacks and rebounds quickly. (–)	5.0	3.7	4.0	4.0	3.3	3.7				
Quest for Excellence	**4.0**	**4.2**	**4.0**	**4.3**	**4.0**	**4.5**				
21. Takes great pride in his or her work.	4.0	4.2	4.0	4.3	4.0	4.3				
22. Expects to succeed when faced with a challenge.	4.0	4.2	4.0	4.3	4.0	4.3				
23. Wants to be the best at whatever he/she attempts.	4.0	4.2	4.0	4.3	4.0	4.3				
24. Strives for top quality in his/her standard performance.	4.0	4.2	4.0	4.3	4.0	4.3				
25. Tries to improve upon his/her previous performance. (+)	4.0	4.4	4.0	4.3	4.0	5.0				
Self-Confidence	**4.8**	**4.3**	**4.0**	**4.6**	**4.1**	**4.2**				
26. Displays a positive attitude. (+)	5.0	4.5	3.0	5.0	4.3	4.7				
27. Brings a sense of well-being to any group.	5.0	4.3	3.0	4.7	4.3	4.3				
28. Remains calm and confident when challenged by others.	5.0	4.3	4.0	4.7	4.3	4.0				
29. Sets a positive tone when working with others.	5.0	4.1	5.0	4.3	3.7	4.0				
30. Has good awareness of his/her abilities.	4.0	4.1	5.0	4.3	3.7	4.0				

Legend: Self; Boss; Peers; Direct Reports; Others

(+) Ten highest scoring

(–) Ten lowest scoring

Figure 15.2 Report Output of Emerging Leaders Profile Showing "Do More" and "Do Less" Behavior Plot

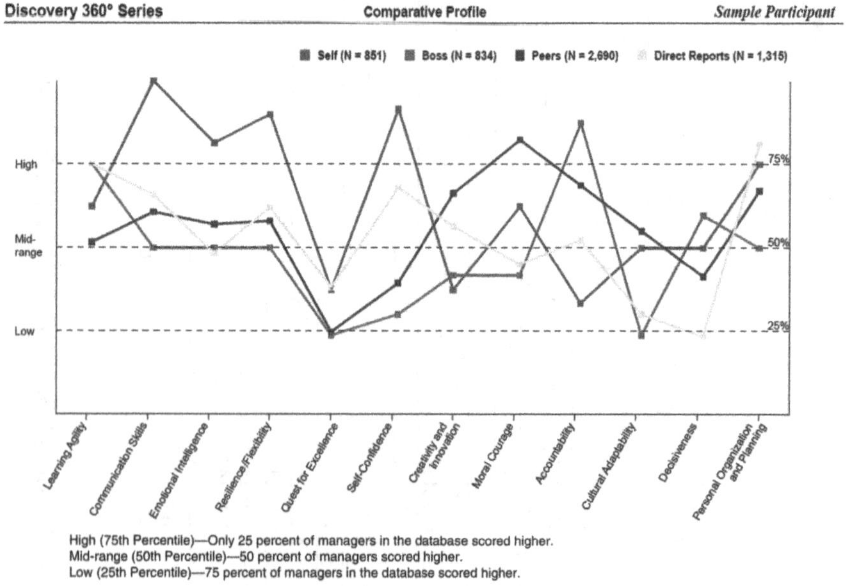

Figure 15.3 Comparative Profile of the ELP

Source: Reprinted with permission of Multi-Health Systems, © 2017.

EQ 360 2.0 and Leadership EQ 360 report were both found to meet reliability and validity criteria.

The Leadership EQ 360 report was further developed with 221 leaders from a variety of organizations throughout North America who completed the EQ-i 2.0 and the Multifactor Leadership Questionnaire. More information about the development of the Leadership EQ 360 report can be found in the manual.[3]

One of the biggest questions that gets asked about 360 leadership ratings has been about the amount of agreement that occurs between leaders and their raters. For example, do leaders have an overwhelming tendency to overrate themselves, at least when compared to subordinates, peers, and superiors?

Using Leadership EQ 360 data selected from our worldwide database we analyzed the amount of agreement among 3,238 leaders and a composite of 3,238 raters (34,924 total raters collapsed and averaged for each leader, for an average of approximately 10.78 raters for each leader). In order to determine differences between self and raters, we averaged the rater scores for each leader (excluding family and friends' ratings) as a point of comparison. We set a cutoff score of five points difference between self and others to determine whether leaders matched their raters. In other words, self and other ratings that were within five points were considered a match.

How many leaders accurately rate their emotional intelligence skills? This has been the subject of a huge debate among academics and researchers in the field for years. If you followed that literature, which is based on little actual data, you would expect to see at least 95 percent of leaders overinflating their emotional intelligence skills. However, the results of our investigation of leader self- versus other-ratings, based on the largest database of emotional intelligence 360 ratings in the world, demonstrate that overinflation is not the norm. The results are shown in Figure 15.4.

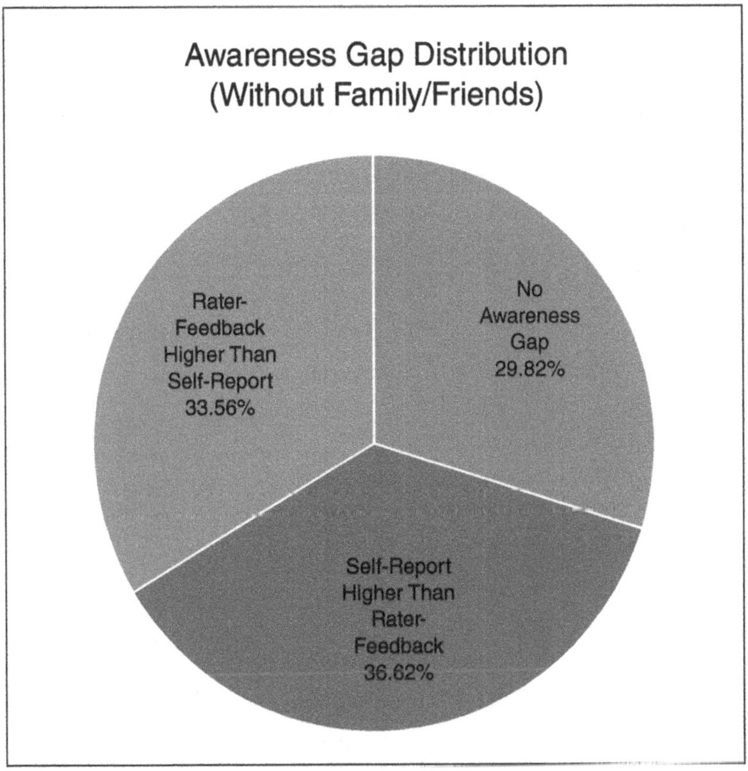

Figure 15.4 Leadership EQ 360 Data with 3,238 Leaders and 3,238 Rater Comparisons (Leaders vs. Rater Averages; based on 34,924 raters)

Source: Reprinted with permission, © Multi-Health Systems 2017.

As can be seen, approximately 30 percent of leaders are in agreement with their raters on their level of emotional intelligence. For 34 percent of leaders, their raters rated them higher than they rated themselves. That means 64 percent of leaders are either accurately rating themselves or underestimating their emotional intelligence skills. That leaves just 36 percent of leaders who rate themselves higher than their raters rate them. Once again, that's only about one-third of leaders who overinflate their emotional intelligence skills.

Subsequent analyses showed that of those that did overinflate, almost 40 percent were within 5 to 10 points, 30 percent were within 10 to 15 points, only 21 percent were between 15 and 20 points over, 10% were between 20 and 25 points over, while only .2 percent were more than 25 points over. This is shown in Figure 15.5.

One of the advantages of the MHS EQ 360 measures, unlike most other 360 assessments, is that they have validity scales (e.g., positive impression) that are used to detect faking or overinflation (or deflation) of scores by the leader being rated. In Figure 15.6, the positive impression score is plotted for each of our

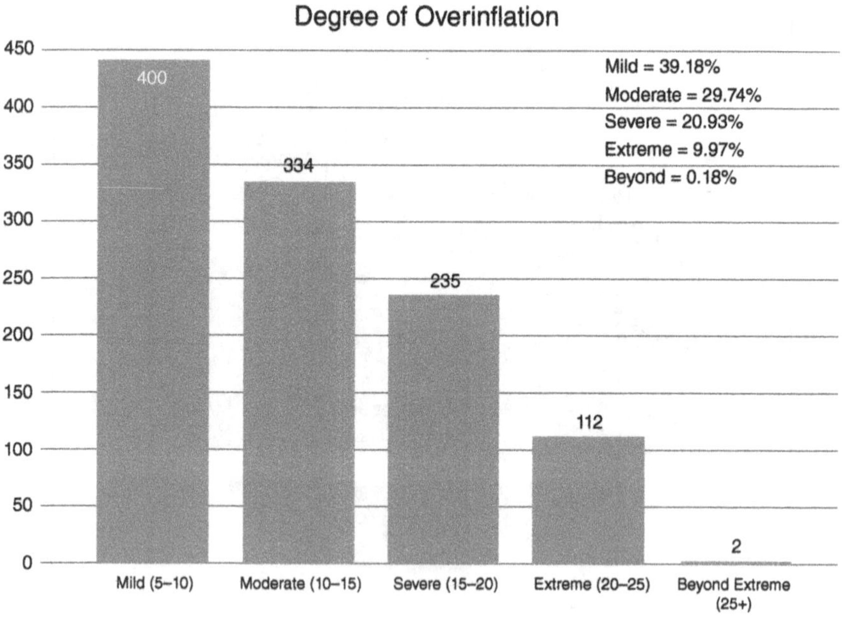

Figure 15.5 Degree of Overinflation of Self-Ratings on EQ360

Source: Reprinted with permission, © Multi-Health Systems 2017.

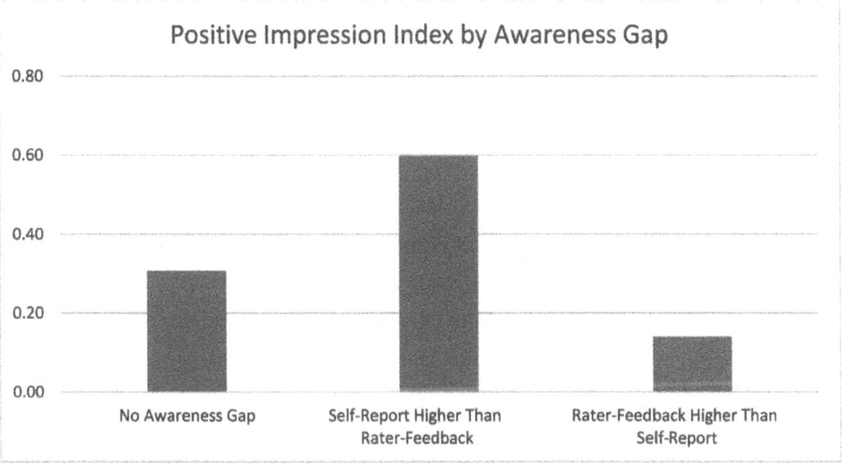

Figure 15.6 Positive Impression Index

Source: Reproduced with permission, © Multi-Health Systems 2017.

groups. You can see that the positive impression index is much higher in leaders who have overexaggerated scores.

You can see this effect even more dramatically in Figure 15.7, where we plot the positive impression scores against the degree of difference between

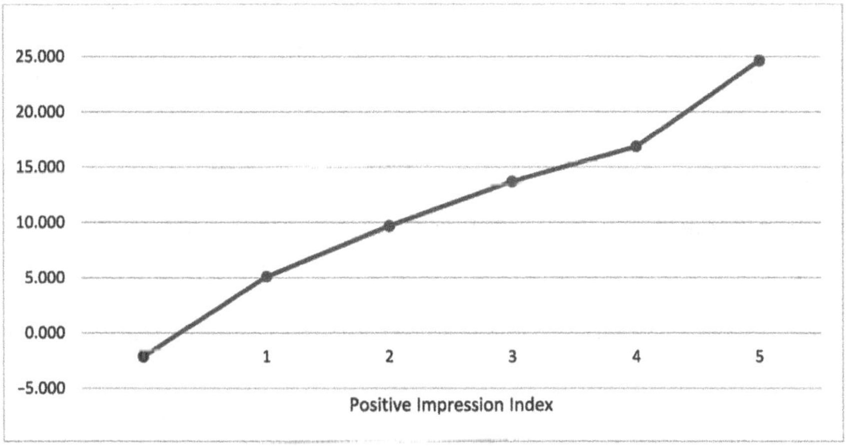

Figure 15.7 Self versus Rater Difference by Positive Impression Score

Source: Reproduced with permission, © Multi-Health Systems 2017.

leaders and their raters a clear, linear trend emerges. As the positive impression score increases, so does the difference score between the leader and their raters.

As we have shown, most leaders respond honestly to self-evaluations such as these. Furthermore, for leaders who don't respond honestly, many of them can be detected with appropriate scales and indexes that have been designed to catch over-exaggerating or self-aggrandizement. Therefore, when assessing emotional intelligence, it is crucial to use measures that contain validity scales, to ensure that the small percentage of "fakers" are easily identified.

International Trends in Leadership

How do we better understand leadership across cultures? This is becoming much more important as businesses become more internationally driven. One of the major trends today in global research of leadership behavior is the GLOBE initiative. Harry Triandis, one of the giants in cross-cultural research, calls the GLOBE research "the Manhattan Project of the study of the relationship of culture to conceptions of leadership."[4] There are a number of reasons for this assertion.

First, GLOBE is the most comprehensive study to date that *empirically* researched the relationship between culture and leader behavior in many different societies, with many different quantitative and qualitative measures and methods, and across many different organizations. This was achieved by engaging more than 170 collaborators from around the world who brought to the project an in-depth understanding of their own culture and its notion and practice of leadership.

Perhaps most important, and in the words of its principal investigator, Robert J. House, "My final conclusion is that we are in a position to make a major contribution to the organizational behavior and leadership literature. To date more than 90% of the organizational behavior literature reflects U.S.-based research and theory. Hopefully GLOBE will be able to liberate organizational behavior from the U.S. hegemony."[5]

As a first step to gauge leader effectiveness across cultures, GLOBE empirically established nine cultural dimensions that make it possible to capture the similarities and/or differences in norms, values, beliefs—and practices—among societies.[6]

Power Distance: The degree to which members of a collective expect power to be distributed equally.

Uncertainty Avoidance: The extent to which a society, organization, or group relies on social norms, rules, and procedures to alleviate unpredictability of future events.

Humane Orientation: The degree to which a collective encourages and rewards individuals for being fair, altruistic, generous, caring, and kind to others.

Collectivism I (Institutional): The degree to which organizational and societal institutional practices encourage and reward collective distribution of resources and collective action.

Collectivism II (In-Group): The degree to which individuals express pride, loyalty, and cohesiveness in their organizations or families.

Assertiveness: The degree to which individuals are assertive, confrontational, and aggressive in their relationships with others.

Gender Egalitarianism: The degree to which a collective minimizes gender inequality.

Future Orientation: The extent to which individuals engage in future-oriented behaviors such as delaying gratification, planning, and investing in the future.

Performance Orientation: The degree to which a collective encourages and rewards group members for performance improvement and excellence.

GLOBE (see Figure 15.8) placed 60 of the 62 countries into country clusters. Cultural *similarity* is greatest among societies that constitute a cluster; cultural *difference* increases the farther clusters are apart. For example, the Nordic cluster is most dissimilar from the Eastern European.

GLOBE set out to understand how leadership styles varied across countries. They surveyed and analyzed the responses of 17,300 middle managers from 61 of the 62 countries. The responses broke into 112 leader characteristics, such as modest, decisive, autonomous, and trustworthy, based on the following definition of leadership: an outstanding leader is a person in an organization or industry who is *"exceptionally skilled at motivating, influencing, or*

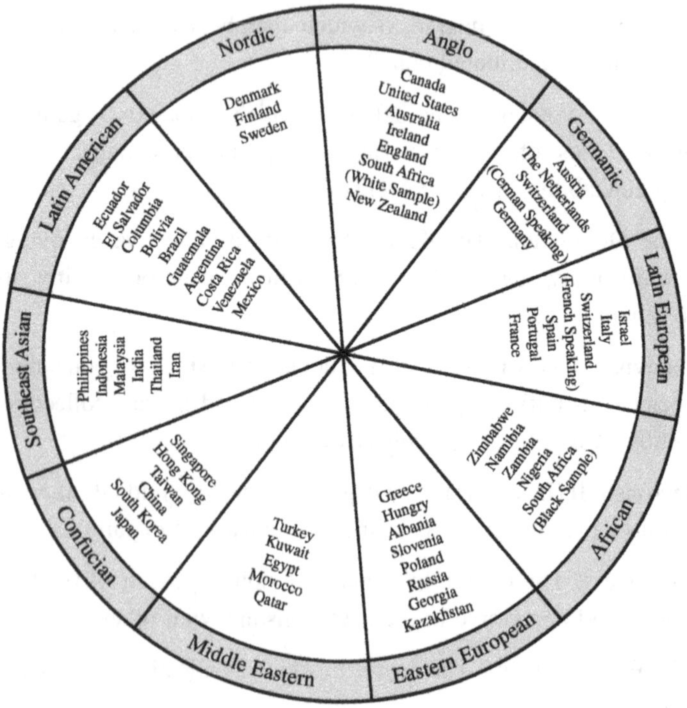

Figure 15.8 GLOBE Clustering of Countries

Source: Adapted from R. J. House, P. J. Hanges, M. Javidan, P. W. Dorfman, and V. Gupta (eds.), *Culture, Leadership, and Organizations: The GLOBE Study of 62 Societies* (Thousand Oaks, CA: Sage, 2004).

enabling you, others, or groups to contribute to the success of the organization or task."[7]

The *performance-oriented style* (called "charismatic/value-based" by GLOBE) stresses high standards, decisiveness, and innovation; seeks to inspire people around a vision; creates a passion among them to perform; and does so by firmly holding on to core values.

The *team-oriented style* instills pride, loyalty, and collaboration among organizational members; and highly values team cohesiveness and a common purpose or goals.

The *participative style* encourages input from others in decision making and implementation; and emphasizes delegation and equality.

The *humane style* stresses compassion and generosity; and it is patient, supportive, and concerned with the well-being of others.

The *autonomous style* is characterized by an independent, individualistic, and self-centric approach to leadership.

The *self-protective* (and group-protective) style emphasizes procedural, status-conscious, and "face-saving" behaviors; and focuses on the safety and security of the individual and the group.

How the Countries Ranked

The highest country groups in each leadership style were:

Performance Oriented:

Higher: Anglo, Germanic, Nordic, SE Asian, L. European, L. American

Middle: Confucian, African, E. European

Lower: Middle Eastern

Team Oriented:

Higher: SE Asian, Confucian, L. American, E. European, African, L. European, Nordic, Anglo, Middle Eastern, Germanic

Participative:

Higher: Germanic, Anglo, Nordic

Middle: L. European, L. American, African

Lower: E. European, SE Asian, Confucian, Middle Eastern

Humane:

Higher: SE Asian, Anglo, African, Confucian

Middle: Germanic, Middle Eastern, L. American, E. European

Lower: L. European, Nordic

Autonomous:

Higher: Germanic, E. European, Confucian, Nordic, SE Asian, Anglo, African, Middle Eastern, L. European, L. American

Self or Group Protective:

Higher: Middle Eastern, Confucian, SE Asian, L. American, E. European

Middle: African, L. European

Lower: Anglo, Germanic, Nordic

GLOBE's major premise (and finding) is that leader effectiveness is contextual; that is, it is embedded in the societal and organizational norms, values, and beliefs of the people being led. In other words, to be seen as effective, the time-tested adage continues to apply: "When in Rome do as the Romans do."

Emotional Intelligence and the GLOBE Theory

How does our worldwide data on emotional intelligence of leaders contribute to the GLOBE theory? We looked at our international EQ-i 2.0 Leader and Leader EQ 360 data and organized it into the GLOBE clusters of countries. First, we pulled 59,114 EQ-i 2.0 (self-report) leader profiles to see how they compare on overall emotional intelligence.

As seen in Figure 15.9, there is some variation in self-reported emotional intelligence of leaders among cultures, with Middle Eastern and Eastern European countries scoring highest and Confucian countries scoring lowest. Middle East leaders are among the highest in the Self/Group Protective style

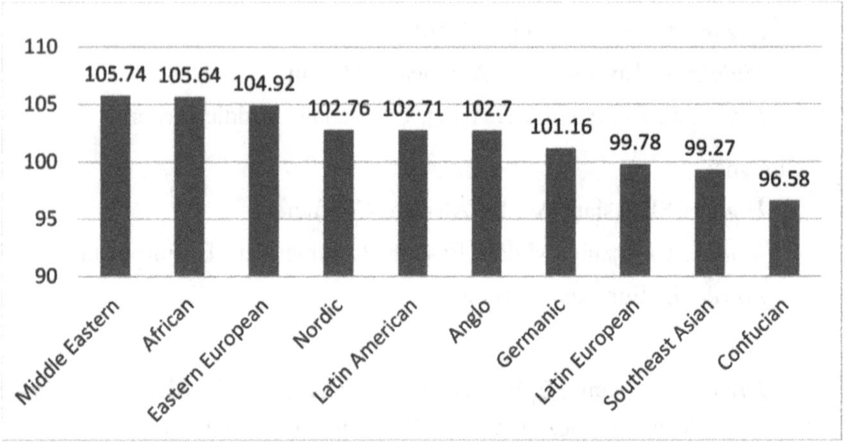

Figure 15.9 Emotional Intelligence Leader Self-Ratings by GLOBE Region

Source: Reprinted by permission, © Multi-Health Systems 2017.

and lowest in Performance Orientation style. Their emotional intelligence scores may be high as a result of "saving face" or the "status conscious" effect of trying to look good. As well, with regard to the low Performance Orientation style, it is common in many Middle East countries to have Anglo leaders (ex-patriates who are high on Performance Orientation) in management positions. Having worked with organizations in the United Arab Emirates and other Middle East countries this trend is quite apparent. Inspiration as a management technique is not yet as prevalent in these countries.

In Eastern European leaders, the high, and potentially overinflated, emotional intelligence self-rating may be influenced by the low levels of Participation Orientation style, which excludes others from participation and discourages equality. Furthermore, Eastern European leaders typically demonstrate low Humane Orientation, which is associated with low compassion and high levels of autonomy that may lead to high, perhaps overinflated, emotional intelligence self-ratings.

On the other hand, the Confucian leaders are the lowest scoring in self-reported emotional intelligence. They are high in Team Oriented, which emphasizes collaboration, but low in Participative, which excludes others from participation. They are also high in Humane—generosity, high in Autonomous—independent and self-centered; and high in Self-Protective—saving face and humility. Likely the humility contributes to the lower self-rating in emotional intelligence. In this case, being self-protective may fuel the humility in leader responses.

When working with leaders in these countries it's important to see how self-perceptions of emotional intelligence differ so that we can better understand the role that EI plays in individual careers.

How do these leaders differ based on the ratings of their coworkers? We looked at 41,555 coworkers (subordinates, peers, and supervisor) rated Leader EQ 360 scores plotted along GLOBE clusters, shown in Figure 15.10. Here we see Anglo leaders rated the highest and Nordic leaders rated the lowest in emotional intelligence. Anglos are seen, by their coworkers, as having higher levels of emotional intelligence. They are also seen as the most performance oriented of all the cultures. Nordic are lowest in Humane; and Germanic cultures, with lower rated emotional intelligence leader scores, are generally seen as more Participative and Autonomous.

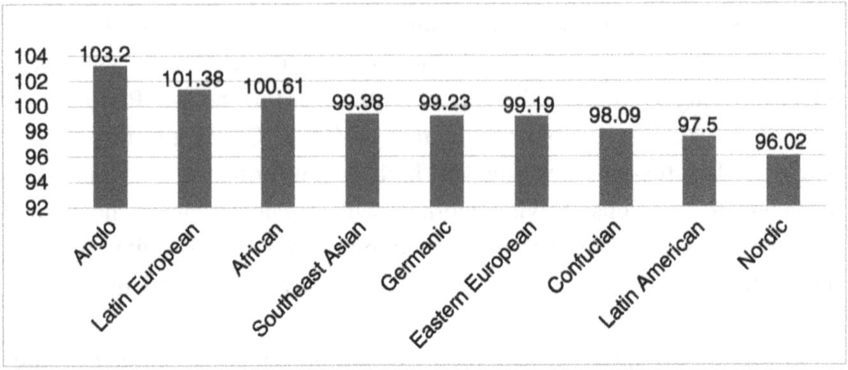

Figure 15.10 Emotional Intelligence Leader Rating Scores by GLOBE Region

Source: Reprinted by permission, © Multi-Health Systems 2017.

How do raters differ from self-ratings in the different cultural groups? We looked at 41,555 self-rater differences on the Leader EQ 360 data. Our data show that African, Southeast Asian, and Germanic leaders overrate themselves the most and Latin European raters underrate themselves the most, as seen in Figure 15.11.

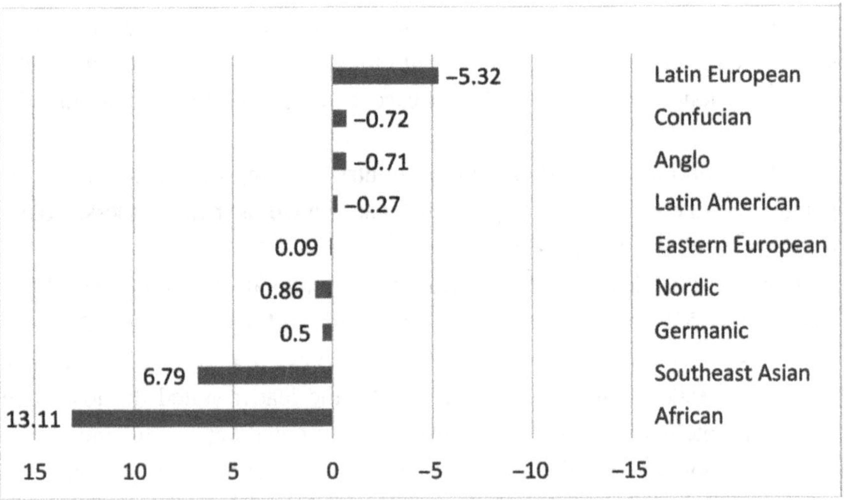

Figure 15.11 Self versus Rater Leader Emotional Intelligence Scores

Source: Reprinted with permission, © Multi-Health Systems 2017.

African leaders see themselves as having much higher levels of emotional intelligence than their coworkers attribute to them. Interestingly, they are highest on Humane culture style. The Humane style stresses compassion and generosity. These people are patient, supportive, and concerned with the well-being of others. In trying to explain this result, it was suggested to me by some South Africans that as a result of many years of Apartheid, the sudden freedom and rise to power, has led to a feeling of overconfidence. This overconfidence may lead them to overrate themselves.

Germanic leaders tend to agree with the levels of emotional intelligence that their coworkers attribute to them. This may be because Germanic leaders are the most participative *and* autonomous of the cultures. They encourage decision making and delegation of authority to others and perhaps because of their participative nature, there is a high level of agreement between how their raters see them and how they see themselves. Also, because of their high level of delegating to others, their subordinates are likely not shy to accurately rate them, even though their leader's scores are quite average.

Latin European leaders, on the other hand, underestimate their levels of emotional intelligence. They are higher in Performance Orientation (inspiring others), high in Autonomous (independent), and lower in Humane (patient and supportive). It may be that their high performance orientation raises their expectations of where their emotional intelligence should be. They may feel that they have not yet achieved their aspirations in terms of where they feel they should be.

We see that most cultures display agreement between self versus rater differences, which again attests to the validity of self-report data. However, we see that countries with a lack of agreement tend to be highly self-centered and that may be influencing these overinflated ratings.

Leadership Orientations and Emotional Intelligence

When we examine Performance-oriented cultures, as in Figure 15.12, we find that the high performance culture leaders are rated with higher EQ scores on all of the composites, especially in interpersonal skills. This orientation requires strong interpersonal skills as it involves inspiring others and getting them to be passionate about their work.

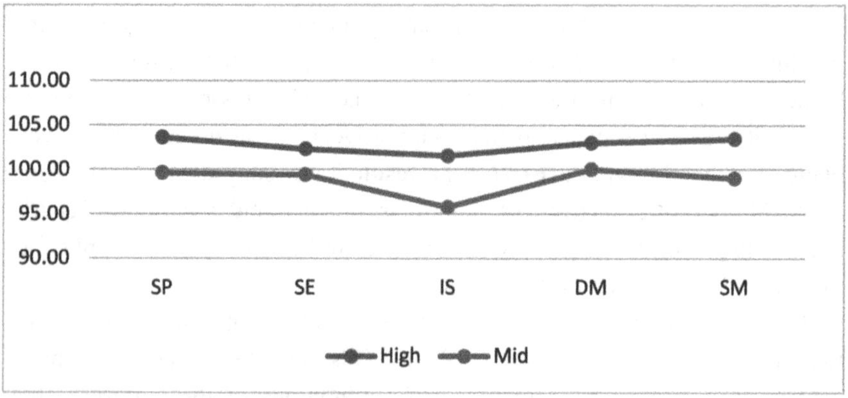

Figure 15.12 Emotional Intelligence Leader Rated Composite Scores in Performance Cultures

Source: Reprinted with permission, © Multi-Health Systems 2017.

When we examine Participative-oriented cultures, as in Figure 15.13, we find that the high participate cultures have higher EQ scores on self-expression, interpersonal skills, decision-making, and stress management composites. This style encourages decision making in others as well as requesting their input on issues.

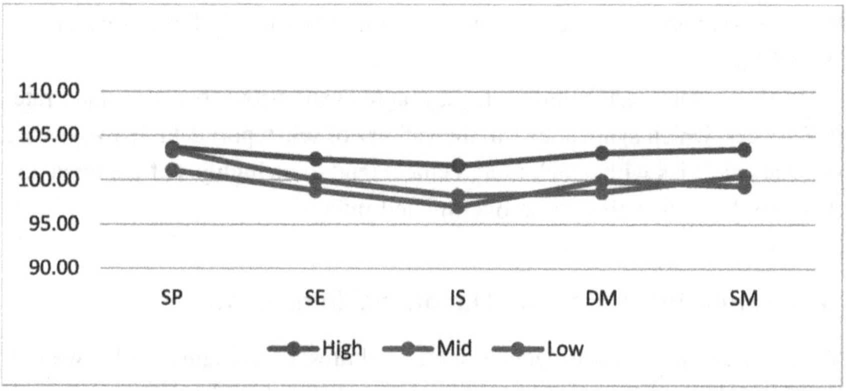

Figure 15.13 Emotional Intelligence Leader Rated Composite Scores in Participative Cultures

Source: Reprinted with permission, © Multi-Health Systems 2017.

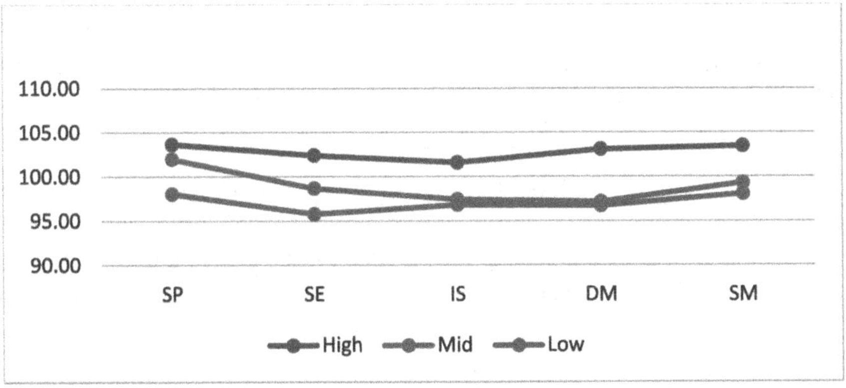

Figure 15.14 Emotional Intelligence Leader Rated Composite Scores in Humane Cultures

Source: Reprinted with permission, © Multi-Health Systems 2017.

When we examine Humane-oriented cultures, as in Figure 15.14, we find that the high humane cultures have higher EQ scores on most of the composites, especially in decision-making skills. This style encourages patience, support, and compassion. It is not surprising that most of the composites are higher in this style.

When we examine Self-and Group-Protective-oriented, as in Figure 15.15, we find that the high-level protective cultures have lower EQ scores on most of

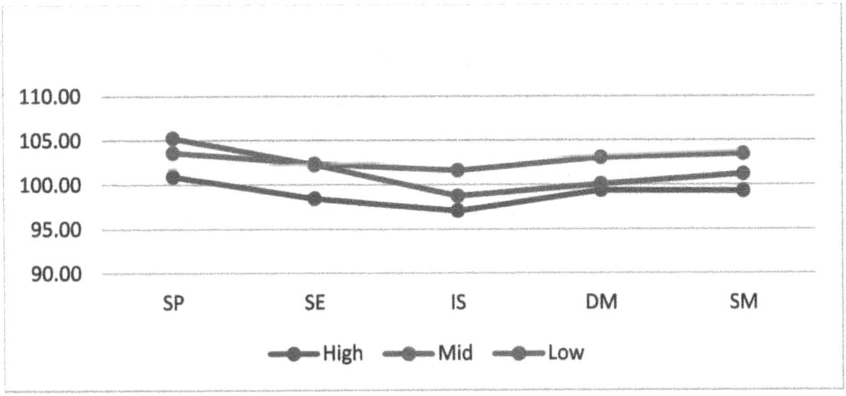

Figure 15.15 Emotional Intelligence Leader Rated Composite Scores in Protective Cultures

Source: Reprinted with permission, © Multi-Health Systems 2017.

the composites, especially in interpersonal skills. This group is very procedure-oriented, status conscious, and face-saving. It should not be surprising that leaders with this orientation would have lower emotional intelligence.

EQ Leader: Some Summary Points

1. The Emerging Leadership Profile (ELP) is a useful tool for honing in on the specific behaviors that new leaders need to develop and it does this by collecting multiple sources of feedback. How do you see yourself in each of these areas?
2. Although the validity of self-report emotional intelligence has been questioned, our analyses show that this is a much smaller problem that once thought. Do you think you would overrate your own emotional intelligence?
3. When understanding the role that emotional intelligence and other competencies play in leadership it is crucial to remember "When in Rome do as the Romans." How comfortable are you with different cultures? Do you have a multicultural workplace? Do you notice differences in people's behavioral styles when they have backgrounds that differ from yours?
4. Our data show interesting differences that emerge across cultures and across leadership styles and these findings are important to note for anybody in organizational behavior research and for practitioners looking to best tailor their approach with conducting business in a global economy. Has your work given you an opportunity to deal with people from different cultures? What has been your experience? How have you adapted?

Chapter 16

Entrepreneurial Leadership and EQ

Before you are a leader, success is all about growing yourself. When you become a leader, success is all about growing others.

—JACK WELCH

The EQ Leader: Entrepreneurial CEOs

What do we know about entrepreneurial leaders and their emotional intelligence? There have been relatively few studies that have looked at this aspect of leadership, especially in relation to performance. How do we gauge performance of entrepreneurs? Well in this case, one of the measures that matters is profitability. After all, if a company isn't profitable it's not likely to exist for long.

In a study we published in *The Leadership and Organization Development Journal*, we assessed the emotional intelligence of entrepreneurial CEOs. We were interested in a number of questions that related to leadership, emotional intelligence, and business success.

We recruited a sample of 186 executives (159 males and 27 females) belonging to one of two executive mentoring associations, the Young Presidents' Organization (YPO) and the Innovators' Alliance (IA), who voluntarily participated in our study. Participants ranged in age from 27 to 59 years, with an average age of 41.37. To gain membership into these associations (at the time of the study), an individual must hold the title of CEO, Owner, President, or Managing Director of his or her company, and that organization must generate a minimum of $2 million annually. The minimum number of full-time employees in these organizations was 10; however, many of those included in the sample had 50 or more employees. The type of industry in which each firm operated varied substantially, ranging from information technology to professional services to manufacturing.

Members of the two leadership organizations were enlisted to complete the EQ-i as part of a series of emotional intelligence presentations that I gave to CEOs. Participants were also asked to respond to a questionnaire examining their perceptions of common business challenges they were experiencing. The same group was also evaluated on organizational performance, which was measured by an organization's profitability. All participants were aware that their results would be analyzed at the group level for research and teaching purposes.

How does the emotional intelligence of business leaders compare to the general population? There has actually been some speculation that business CEOs have lower emotional intelligence than the average person. Some "experts" in emotional intelligence have claimed that as someone rises up the corporate ladder, their emotional intelligence decreases.

Well, our evidence-based research on CEOs paints a somewhat different picture. The CEOs in our study scored significantly higher in 8 of 15 EQ-i scales than the general public as shown in Figure 16.1. The average person (based on the scores of thousands of people in our standardization sample, which was stratified based on North American census data) scores 100 on our scale (standard deviation of 15). The CEOs scored significantly higher in Self-Regard, Self-Actualization, Assertiveness, and Independence. These subscales reflect skills that facilitate self-awareness and self-expression effectiveness. The ability to put together assumptions, theories, and beliefs with confidence, as well as remaining self-directed, likely enhances the level of influence for those holding leadership positions.

In addition, CEOs scored higher in Problem Solving, Flexibility, Optimism, and Stress Tolerance. These subscales constitute the Decision Making and Stress Management composites, suggesting that executives can succeed leading their companies through the continual adjustment of emotions and

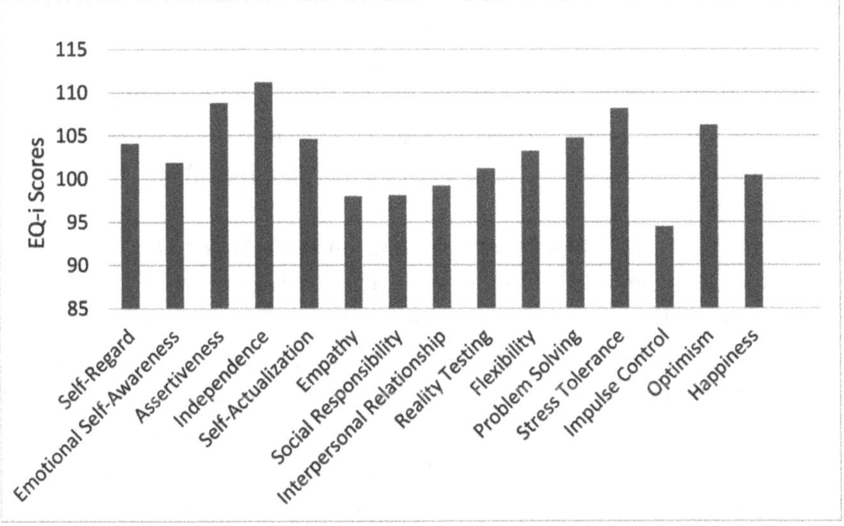

Figure 16.1 EQ-i Scores of CEOs

Source:

thoughts, and the ability to assess problems and offer solutions. These findings support Shaul Fox and Yair Amichai-Hamburger,[1] who found that to empower an organization, a leader must maintain a positive and calm attitude when facing adversity, as well as when setting a corporate vision.

We might have expected that these leaders score higher than the general public on all the emotional intelligence scales. However, this was not the case. There were some scales where this group scored lower than the average. These CEOs scored significantly lower than the general population on the subscales of Social Responsibility and Impulse Control. A lower than average score from the executive sample on the Social Responsibility scale may not be that surprising when considering all of the different responsibilities that an executive performs. A leader often faces difficult decisions (e.g., layoffs, restructuring, mergers) that are relevant for the organization's continued prosperity; however, the same decision may be detrimental to smaller groups or individuals. In order to make these tough decisions, an executive may at times have to lower his or her social consciousness. However, leaders who score higher in social responsibility may stand out from the crowd.

In addition, these leaders scored lower than the average person in impulse control. This score taps into the construct of impatience, as well as impulsivity. The constantly changing demands of the marketplace coupled with executives' desire for organizational success may impact the leaders' level of patience. Entrepreneurs tend to have lower impulse control as they get bored with routine tasks or jobs.

Another area we examined was the relationship between various business challenges and emotional intelligence. The challenges we thought most relevant to CEOs of growing organizations were: hiring employees, managing others, retaining employees, training employees, raising capital, managing growth, marketing, innovation, and coping with technological change. All of these challenges were identified as requiring effort and focus for this group.

To what degree does emotional intelligence play a role in managing these business challenges? Our first finding here was that the CEO overall emotional intelligence score was positively related to the degree to which a challenge was perceived as easy with respect to managing growth, managing others, training employees, and retaining employees. Not surprisingly, emotional intelligence showed significant relationships with those challenges that center on interpersonal activities as opposed to more task-oriented challenges such as raising capital and coping with technological change. In other words, those with higher emotional intelligence scores perceive these interpersonal activities as less challenging.

The results support the theoretical and empirical components of the Interpersonal Relationship composite scale. Given that the relationship between the emotional and social perceptions of business challenges is derived from social interactions, it is only natural that the strongest and most significant relationships exist between this global construct of emotional intelligence and social challenges. That is, leaders with enhanced interpersonal skills better manage those aspects of the business that involve dealing with people.

An interesting pattern of correlations was found between the composite scales of Self-Perception and Stress Management and the business challenges of: managing others, training employees, and retaining employees. These findings suggest that top executives are aware of key emotional information (their own and the people they lead) and use this information in their interactions with others, as well as when delivering their message to the organization. By doing so, executives are better able to increase staff motivation and dedication. Decision making was also positively related to managing growth, coping with technological change, managing people, and training employees. How leaders manage change, consequently, may have to do with their capacity to use emotions when making decisions as opposed to simply relying on analytic frameworks.

At the subscale level, we found that Flexibility had the highest positive association with perceived business challenges, thereby underscoring the role that emotional change can have when coping with organizational change. In other words, individuals with greater flexibility were more likely to perceive ease in dealing with business challenges.

Optimism, the capability to maintain a positive attitude even under trying conditions, was positively related with perceived ease of managing growth, managing others, and training employees. These leaders benefit from viewing their subordinates in a more encouraging way in order to tap into any unrealized skill sets. Lastly, both Self-Regard and Self-Actualization, which comprise the Self-Perception composite scale, were positively related to managing others, training employees, and retaining employees, thereby indicating that intrinsic motivation and self-assuredness can likely moderate interpersonal challenges that arise within the workplace.

Another analysis we did with this group was quite unique. We separated the "top CEOs" from the rest of the group based on what we thought to be the most important measure of success for this group—profitability. So we compared the most profitable CEOs to the least profitable based on their financially reported data. We did a complex statistical analysis to see if there were any EQ factors that differentiated these groups. One hypothesis we had was that being really good at managing stress would predict profitability. Or, perhaps the more successful CEO's would be happier than their less profitable counterparts.

Well, we didn't quite predict that correctly. Surprisingly, the EQ-i subscale of Empathy was shown to best differentiate between high and low profitability CEOs. The more empathic CEOs were more profitable. This finding lends support to the assertion put forward by Neil Ashkanasy and Barry Tse[2] that effective leaders regularly display empathic behavior to demonstrate their understanding of how others feel, which fortifies working relationships and unifies teams.

Another distinguishing predictor of profitability was Self-Regard, which is defined as the ability to respect and accept oneself as basically good with general feelings of security, inner strength, and self-assuredness. We found that leaders with higher levels of self-regard had more profitable companies. This lends credence to David De Cremer and Daan van Knippenberg[3] who suggested that leader self-confidence affects perceptions of leadership effectiveness, therefore, executives who project a strong sense of identity will more likely be able to motivate their workforce to perform at higher levels, ultimately resulting in greater profits.

Reality Testing and Problem Solving, both underlying the Decision Making composite scale, were also related to profitability. Hence, leaders who can realistically and accurately interpret external events and who are effective problem solvers tend to be capable of realizing higher profits.

How well was the EQ-i, on its own, able to predict profitable from less profitable CEOs? We were able to develop a formula with a high classification accuracy rate to discriminate the executives in the top profitability group from the other executives. We correctly identified 87 percent of the sample using this formula based on the EQ-i pattern of scores. In other words, the classification model used is capable of predicting the profitability grouping 87 percent of the time, simply based on the leader's emotional intelligence (EQ-i) score.

Because of this and other studies we've carried out with leaders, we created a special version of the EQ-i 2.0 that looks specifically at leadership skills. We can compare any leader's (or potential leader's) scores to other organizational leaders and break their scores into the four pillars of Authenticity, Coaching, Insight, and Innovation. A tailored coaching program can then be developed based on the results. This leadership report is currently being used by hundreds of organizations around the world, including profit, nonprofit, military, and government.

Succeeding in a Small Enterprise: Success Running a Dentist Office

A dental, medical, or any other health professional office is a business and requires entrepreneurial skills to set up and run effectively. Healthcare practices are often limited in size by the number of contact hours per day that a practitioner can manage. However, there are still a variety of measures of success.

Dana Ackley, a psychologist and EQ Leader coach, who has worked with organizations and dentists, paints the following picture of two dentists, equally skilled, in the same professional building.[4]

> Dr. Griffin goes home on time each day and rarely works weekends, whereas Dr. Bartlett is almost always late for dinner and spends a lot of weekend time at the office. Dr. Griffin's staff have been together for years while Dr. Bartlett has constant staff turnover. Referring dentists hear great feedback about Dr. Griffin from his patients, but they hear more complaints from Dr. Bartlett's patients. Dr. Griffin's practice appears more professional with a nicer office, newer equipment, and staff retreats.
>
> Interestingly, none of these differences are likely due to their IQ or their grade ranking in dental school. While Dr. Bartlett stood near to the top of his class in dental school, he focusses much of his time on technical aspects of dentistry and very little of it on the social side of practice—e.g., networking with referral sources, building patient rapport.

Dana points out that higher-EQ dentists:

- Attract enough of the right kind of patients
- Develop better working relationships with patients
- Organize the practice team into a more effective workforce

Together with his dentist colleagues, Irwin Becker and Richard Green, Ackley carried out a study looking at the role emotional intelligence plays in a successful dental practice.[5] Their study, done in conjunction with the Pankey Institute, a world renowned training center for dentists, included 144 dentists who had trained at the center. They administered the EQ-i along with a Survey of Progress (SOP) to these dentists. The SOP evaluates the dentists' actual practice following their training at the institute. The areas evaluated include (1) technical diagnostic skills taught at the institute; (2) behavioral steps of relationship building (such as initial patient interviews, co-discovery, and team development); and (3) business practices that benefit both patient and dentist.

They found a direct relationship between emotional intelligence scores and the dentists' practice results, such that dentists with greater emotional intelligence tended to have more successful practices. They identified the most important emotional intelligence skills related to dental practice results: emotional self-awareness, reality testing, assertiveness, and self-actualization.

These emotional skills can play out in the day-to-day experience of the dentist. For example, emotional self-awareness helps the practitioner become aware, at the end of the day when she is tired, that she may not be as understanding when dealing with a patient's discomfort. Reality testing enables the dentist to realistically be aware of conflicts with his staff that need to be dealt with. The assertive dentist is better able to develop a nonthreatening doctor/patient relationship with her patients (which is not easy, given that many people feel threatened before they walk into the reception area). Self-actualization enables the dentist to pursue continuing education, learn, and improve oneself, yet still live a balanced lifestyle. Dentists higher in emotional intelligence not only do better in their practice but can better influence their patients in having good dental health.

What Does It Take to Be an Entrepreneur?

Wouldn't it be good to know if someone is likely to be successful as an entrepreneur? Better still, wouldn't it be useful to know which skills can be developed to become a more successful entrepreneur? Those were the ideas behind the development of the *Entrepreneur Edge*™.[6]

These authors have researched entrepreneurship and identified four key success factors for success. These include having the right Mind-Set, Self-Management, Dealing with Others, and Business Orientation. Regarding Mind-Set, successful entrepreneurs tend to act on their own hunches and pursue calculated risks. They are likely to be optimistic and confident, and usually prefer to set their own goals.

The second area is Self-Management. Most successful entrepreneurs are action oriented and energized by multiple tasks and challenges. They tend to follow their own paths, often using stress as a motivator. The third area is Dealing with Others. Entrepreneurs must deal with many different types of people, initiate relationships, and network to their advantage. They tend to be excited to engage others in their ideas. Finally, they tend to have a Business

Orientation. Much of the entrepreneur's business perspective is driven by new ideas. While they tend to be drawn to big-picture thinking, successful entrepreneurs act on their ideas.

These four areas then break down into 17 specific entrepreneur competencies:

I. Mind-Set
   1. Independent minded
   2. Risk tolerant
   3. Knowledge seeker
   4. Innovator
   5. Individual achiever
   6. Optimistic

II. Self-Management
   7. Action-oriented
   8. Analytical
   9. Multitasker
   10. Stress motivated
   11. Self-directed

III. Dealing with Others
   12. Initiator
   13. Networker
   14. Explorer

IV. Business Orientation
   15. Opportunistic
   16. Strategic
   17. Proactive

The Entrepreneur Edge can be used with MBA students considering their future direction, young entrepreneurs just starting out, people thinking of starting a business, people looking at a career transition, people investing in a business wanting to evaluate the leadership or even retirees looking to start a business. It's also part of a project we're involved with looking at *intra-preneurship* in some Fortune 500 companies—identifying people with entrepreneurial spirit within companies that can help them innovate and develop new products and processes. In Chapter 14 I presented information on our (MHS) annual hackathon, a process that we adapted and can now be used in any organization that wants to not only be innovative, but increase their staff engagement.

Musician Entrepreneurs

The music industry has changed a great deal over the years and in order to succeed today artists require more than musical talent. Not only are record sales (I realize there is a new generation unaware of what "records" are) decreasing (with live concert sales increasing as a trade-off), but there are also fewer record labels and talent management companies available for an artist to seek help from. In the past, many performers would rely on being "discovered" by an executive from a record label after being seen in a live performance. Those days are gone. As a result, artists have had to take on the role of an entrepreneur (on top of their normal role as a musician), which includes marketing and promoting themselves.

In order to survive, artists need to be creative, marketing themselves through live venues, social media, and other novel ways. Managing a career in music today has many similarities to running a small business. It's my belief that artists require emotional intelligence as well as a set of entrepreneurial skills to make it in the music industry today.

Over the past few years I've been able to further explore this. I've been working with some experienced professionals in the business side of the music industry who set up a nonprofit program designed to help working musical artists. Canada's Music Incubator's (CMI) Artist Entrepreneur program at Coalition Music is a nonprofit initiative devoted to providing coaching and professional development for emerging artists in the music industry. Their goal is to help artists build the skills they need to thrive as small business owners, as well as provide ongoing support beyond an initial 10-week incubation period. The focus of the program includes mentoring, collaborating, and networking.

As part of my work with this group we have used a number of assessments to gauge the skills and competencies of these aspiring young artists. The assessments are used as part of their coaching process, but also as part of our research to help determine success factors in the industry.

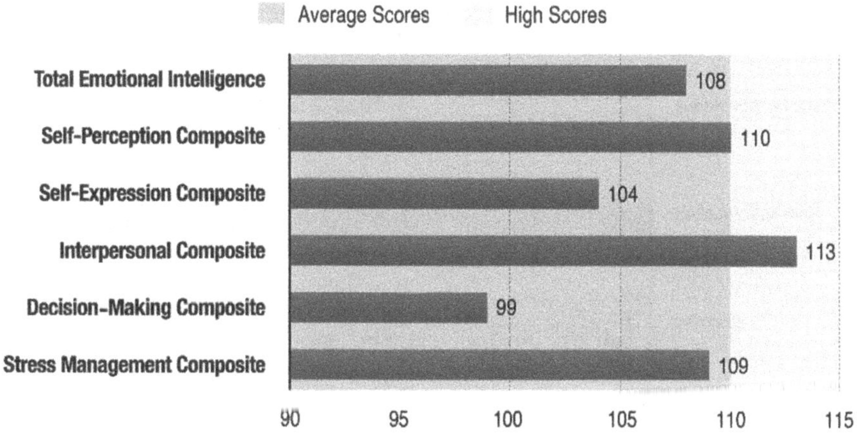

Figure 16.2 Total Emotional Intelligence and Composite Scale Scores for Musical Artists

Source: Reprinted with permission, © Multi-Health Systems, 2016.

All of the participants are administered the EQ-i 2.0 and the Entrepreneur Edge, among other tools upon entering the program. In Figure 16.2 you can see their composite scores in emotional intelligence with the EQ-i 2.0.

In our work with these artists we have already begun to find some trends. For example, as seen in Figure 16.2, this group is particularly strong in their Interpersonal composite (consisting of Interpersonal Relationships, Empathy, and Social Responsibility). The Interpersonal composite describes an individual's ability to connect with others in a meaningful way. This ability is especially important for musicians who make concerts more enjoyable by connecting with the audience. This ability also facilitates getting along with fellow musicians, booking agents, managers, and others.

When we look more specifically at their emotional intelligence strengths we find that their highest scores are in Social Responsibility, Self-Actualization, and Empathy as shown in Figure 16.3.

The high Social Responsibility score suggests that these artists are constructive members of society who act in support of the common good. As artists, many are involved in social causes and they tend to be very socially conscious. Many of them gain strength and inspiration from their concerns about the world around them and reflect this in their music.

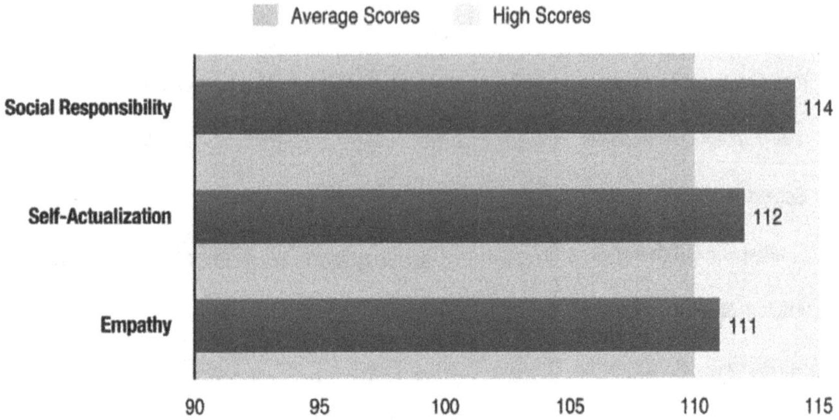

Figure 16.3 Highest Emotional Intelligence Scores for Musical Artists
Source: Reprinted with permission, © Multi-Health Systems, 2016.

A high Self-Actualization score suggests that these artists find meaning and purpose in their careers. They will often set challenging goals for themselves and motivate themselves to reach these goals. The artists continually find ways to ensure that their talents are being optimally leveraged, and seek advice from mentors for ideas when needed.

Their high Empathy score indicates that this group shows the ability to recognize, understand and appreciate the way others feel. Music manager Irving Azoff, probably one of the most successful talent managers in the business, whose clients include Christina Aguilera, Journey, the Eagles, Dan Fogelberg, Joe Walsh, Van Halen, Thirty Seconds to Mars, Steely Dan, Bon Jovi, and many others, talked about this in an interview in a *Billboard Magazine* video.[7] He said that the most important thing for an artist's success was to know how to read and interact with a live audience.

Empathy is particularly important in the ability to connect with others, and helps the artists read an audience to determine how their performance is being received. It helps discern whether or not the audience connects with a particular song, or even more generally, with how they present themselves as an artist.

Empathy is also important in dealing with fellow band members and other musicians. Not long ago I had an opportunity to meet Max Weinberg, the highly successful drummer in Bruce Springsteen's E-Street Band. We talked about my research and he told me about how he started drumming at six years

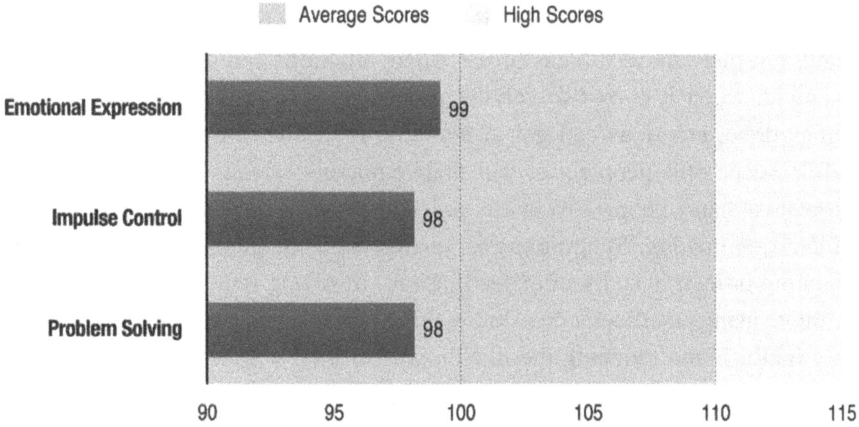

Figure 16.4 Lowest Emotional Intelligence Scores for Musical Artists

Source: Reprinted with permission, © Multi-Health Systems, 2016.

of age. It was after seeing Ron Tutt (Elvis Presley's drummer) perform on TV that he was hooked. Max had his first performance in front of an audience at age seven. But one of the key elements of his success (how he beat out 63 drummers who originally auditioned for Springsteen) was his ability to focus, listen, and watch. He knew his job was to support the other musicians, not to overshadow. It takes a lot of self-awareness (knowing your strengths), impulse control (keeping from showboating), empathy (reading others), and interpersonal skill (working with others) to pull this off.

The challenges in emotional skills for our musical artist sample can be seen in Figure 16.4. These include Emotional Expression, Impulse Control, and Problem Solving.

The lower scores suggest that, while the group may be aware of their feelings, they may have difficulty expressing or articulating some emotions. Although they may express themselves through their music, they are coached on better using emotional expression in relationships and performances.

Their impulse control was within the average range, suggesting that the artists are generally able to resist or delay impulses to act. However, under times of stress or pressure, they may be more impulsive than normal. This was a rich area for coaching.

The Problem Solving scale measures how effectively an individual uses their emotions in the process of solving problems. The group average suggests that the artists can use their emotions effectively to focus on the problem at hand, but there may be areas of life where emotions can get in the way. For example, when it comes to solving problems, making decisions, or getting things done, emotions can get in the way, more than helping the situation. While successful people can use their emotions effectively to focus on a problem at hand, people low in this skill sometimes let emotions get in the way of decision making. Suggestions for change have included working on better planning processes and setting deadlines for resolving issues. These strategies promote using an efficient decision-making process, using emotion to enhance (not inhibit), and reducing the likelihood that they will delay addressing the tough decisions.

The Entrepreneur Edge provides the mentors of the CMI program with an overview of entrepreneurial skills which the artist currently uses, along with those in need of development. It looks at broad areas, such as Mind-Set, Self-Management, Dealing with Others, and Business Orientation, along with a number of more specific, actionable competencies.

As seen by Figure 16.5, this group shows the most strength in their ability to deal with others. This group will likely have few issues in introducing themselves to others, networking with others, and seeking the advice of others in order to overcome challenges. This pairs well with the findings in the EQ-i 2.0.

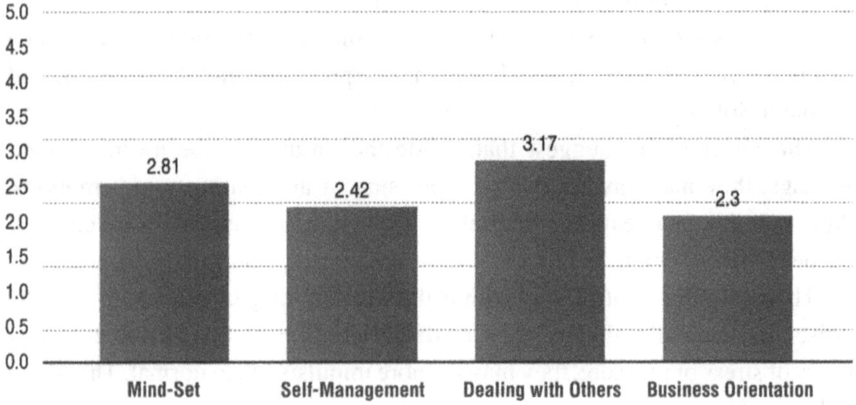

Figure 16.5 Key Entrepreneur's Success Scores for Musician Artists

Source: Reprinted with permission, © Multi-Health Systems, 2016.

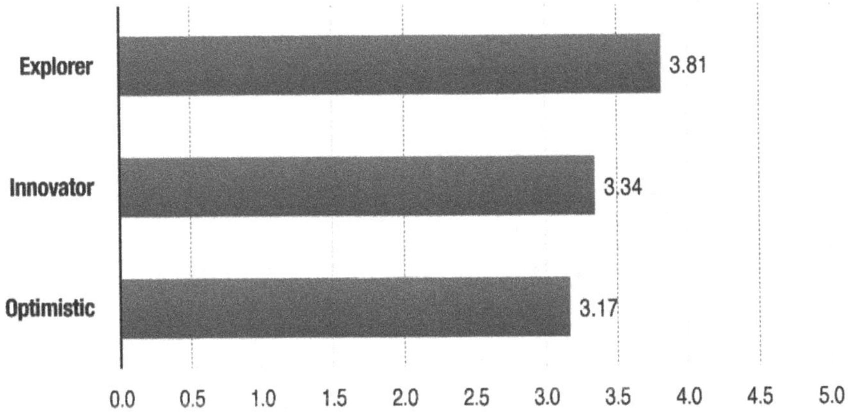

Figure 16.6 Entrepreneurial Strengths of Musician Artists

Source: Reprinted with permission, © Multi-Health Systems, 2016.

The specific entrepreneurial strengths can be seen in Figure 16.6. These include strengths in the Explorer area—creative problem solving; Innovation—looking at new ways of doing things; and Optimism—identifying the opportunities ahead.

An individual with a high Explorer score involves others in creative problem solving and shares knowledge with others. Continuing to harness these skills will help the artist maintain close bonds with their mentors and other artists. It is interesting to note that this coincides with the finding that this group possesses strong interpersonal emotional intelligence competencies.

Artists with high Innovator scores take pride in suggesting alternatives and new solutions, and show a preference toward rethinking existing assumptions. Apart from the benefit that innovative creativity can bring to an artist's music, this creativity can be used to develop different solutions to new challenges that the artist will encounter in his or her career.

Individuals with a high Optimistic score can quickly identify the positive, even in challenging situations. Maintaining this optimistic outlook can help the artist overcome setbacks in their career, especially as they seek alternate outcomes to current challenges. When this score is considered together with their Innovator score, it suggests that they may see success as an indicator that they can trust their instinct toward innovation, making them more willing to take creative risks.

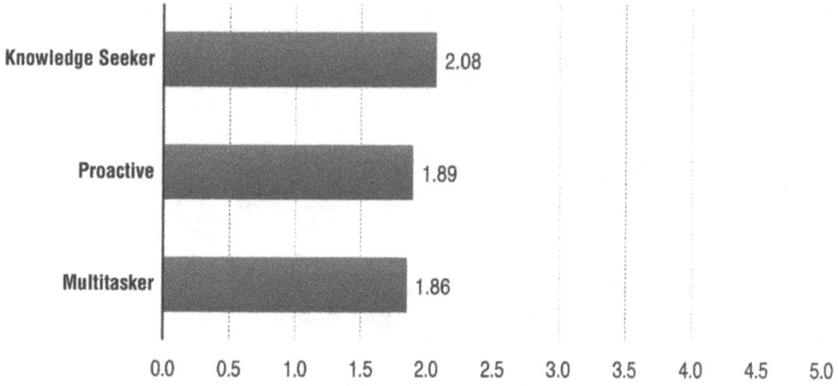

Figure 16.7 Entrepreneurial Challenges of Musician Artists

Source: Reprinted with permission, © Multi-Health Systems, 2016.

The lower scores for this group are shown in Figure 16.7.

A person with a high score in Knowledge Seeking seeks the knowledge and advice of industry experts. They are also future-looking and attracted to emerging technologies that have the potential to change the industry. As this group of artists are students of the CMI program, it's likely that they value the knowledge and advice of industry experts. However, as this is one of the group's lower scores, they may be too focused on the present and not enough on upcoming changes in the industry.

Individuals with high Proactive scores consider the need for change an important issue, and seek to develop new skills. They are likely to monitor and measure the results of their efforts to evaluate progress and demonstrate the value of change. As this is one of the group's lower scores, they may be focusing on improving their existing skills (such as their vocal talent), rather than developing new skills (such as the ability to market themselves). Thus, they may be missing opportunities created as the result of changes in the music industry.

People with high Multitasker scores can work effectively across disciplines (such as both music and finances). In addition, they are more likely to seek multiple ventures simultaneously. As this is one of the group's lower scores, they are likely focusing too much on the music discipline while neglecting other competencies required for a successful career as an artist. Alternatively, they may even be focusing too much on one project or genre. Multitasking, in this case, involves paying attention to a number of different areas—from business-oriented activities (booking gigs, managing bandmates, publicity, legal) to perfecting your music (ensuring your music is the right genre, writing new music, arranging the music, rehearsals).

Succeeding as a musician is probably more difficult today than at any other time in the entertainment industry. There's no clear path to success and there are fewer venues promoting live performances. The role of the recording labels has significantly shifted with the demise of traditional albums. Of course, there are challenges in many careers in today's fast-moving world. Our research has shown that understanding one's emotional intelligence and entrepreneurial preferences can be a useful endeavor for anybody looking to understand how to leverage their unique strengths and focus their development in our fast-paced world.

EQ Leader: Things to Think About

1. Do you see yourself as an entrepreneur?
2. Does your current work allow you to be entrepreneurial?
3. What do you see as your top skills enabling you be entrepreneurial?
4. To what degree do you like taking work-related risks?
5. Do you see your interpersonal skills as one of your strengths?
6. Do you feel you have the confidence needed to succeed as an entrepreneur?
7. If you work in a traditional company, do you have opportunities to be more intrapreneurial?
8. If not, are there ways you can get your workplace to think more innovatively?

Chapter 17

Some New Things We're Learning about Leadership

Do not follow where the path may lead. Go instead where there is no path and leave a trail.

—RALPH WALDO EMERSON

This Chapter

I wanted to include a number of topics in this chapter, not all of which are related to each other. They contain areas I am following and trends in the field of leadership. The first covers some of the work related to the neuroscience of leadership. It is becoming popular to use work from neuropsychology and apply it to leadership. At MHS we've been leading the way with some of our research on executive functioning. We'll look at how it can apply to leadership.

Then I cover the topic of change. It seems that you can't really talk about leadership without dealing with change. Change is everywhere today, and, of course, we all react to change in different ways. I'll present some of the work that originated at Discovery Learning International (now part of MHS) and the Center for Creative Leadership that companies around the world have found useful in helping manage change in their organizations.

It seems that everywhere you look there is something about Millenials or Gen Zers. There is still some debate about the usefulness of the various generational distinctions and whether they even exist. Well, I won't deal with the speculation, just the data. We have the largest database of emotional intelligence test scores in the world, and we'll explore what our data say about these generational differences. There's nothing like evidence-based information.

A concept that gets talked about a lot is the idea of servant leadership. That is, the importance of starting out as a follower, and being a good follower, before you make it to leader. One of the groups that I've had the privilege to work with is the U.S. Navy SEALs, and I'll present some data from that group.

Perhaps the highest seat of power in organizations today is the board of directors. I have had the opportunity, through my teaching at The Directors College, to work with and test many individuals who sit on boards. It's pretty clear that the emotional intelligence level of the board can play a major factor in its success. I'll be presenting some new data on this group and look at gender differences of board members.

While I've presented a number of stories and anecdotes about leaders throughout the book, most books about leadership focus on the kinds of people we might expect to see as leaders. I like taking the theory of emotional intelligence and trying to see how it helps understand the more unusual, or out-of-the-box type of leader. In this section, I'll present a case study of someone whose background is probably unlike any leader that you've ever seen.

Finally, I'll look at some of what we know about improving leadership through emotional intelligence training. I'll highlight a study that looks at worldwide trends in leadership training and development and, specifically, emotional intelligence training in organizations. Then I'll present some research that demonstrates that emotionally intelligent leadership in organizations can be developed.

Neuroscience and Leadership

It's becoming quite popular in the business literature to start borrowing concepts from the neuroscience literature and applying them to leadership. At MHS, we are in the unique position of having done extensive research in neuroscience from both the clinical perspective, as well as having looked at it from the organizational/business angle.

Some of the concepts making their way from neuroscience to the executive suite comes from research on *executive functioning* of the brain. Neuropsychologists investigate brain-behavior relationships by using informal and standardized methods to understand an individual's functioning across a wide variety of areas, including cognitive, language, emotional, social, and motor activities. Technologies such as magnetic resonance imaging (MRI), functional MRI (fMRI), positron emission tomography (PET), computed tomography (CT), and diffusion tensor imaging (DTI) have been used to help localize brain-behavior relationships.

As well, neuropsychological tests play an important role in quantifying the cognitive abilities necessary for effective thinking, executive function, problem solving, learning, and behavior and in measuring behavioral symptoms associated with executive function. At MHS, we publish one of the most widely used measures of executive functioning in the clinical and education marketplace, the *Comprehensive Executive Functioning Inventory* (*CEFI*).[1] We've assessed and analyzed tens of thousands of individuals' abilities in this area.

Executive function has become an overall term for cognitive processes such as planning, working memory, attention, problem solving, reasoning, inhibition, mental flexibility, multitasking, initiation, and monitoring of actions. These cognitive processes are largely carried out by prefrontal areas of the frontal lobe. These prefrontal areas include the dorsal lateral prefrontal cortex, the anterior cingulate cortex and the orbital frontal cortex. The dorsal lateral prefrontal cortex is thought to be involved with processing of information, such as integrating different dimensions of cognition and behavior. The anterior cingulate cortex is believed to be involved in emotional drivers, experience, and integration. Finally, the orbital frontal cortex is considered to play a key role in impulse control, maintenance of set (ability to follow rules), monitoring ongoing behavior, and socially appropriate behavior. The orbital frontal cortex also has a role in representing the value of reward based on sensory stimuli and evaluating subjective emotional experience.[2]

In the research literature there is still not a single, agreed-upon definition of executive function, nor is there consensus on what it encompasses. Although various definitions have been proposed, there is a central theme that executive function includes exertion of control over automatic responses in order to regulate autonomous, goal-directed behavior. Inhibiting automatic responses

Scale	Definition
Executive Function (Overall)	Overall executive function is made up of nine different areas that include Attention, Emotion Regulation, Flexibility, Inhibitory Control, Initiation, Organization, Planning, Self-Monitoring, and Working Memory).
Attention	Describes an individual's ability to avoid distractions, concentrate on tasks, and sustain attention.
Emotion Regulation	Indicates the individual's ability to control and manage emotions, including staying calm when handling small problems and reacting with the right level of emotion.
Flexibility	Reflects an individual's ability to adjust behavior to meet circumstances, including coming up with different ways to solve problems, changing behavior when needed, and being able to come up with new ways to reach a goal.
Inhibitory Control	Describes the individual's ability to control behavior or impulses, including thinking about consequences before acting, maintaining self-control, and thinking before speaking.
Initiation	Indicates an individual's ability to begin tasks or projects on his/her own including starting tasks easily, being motivated, and taking the initiative when needed.
Organization	Reflects the individual's ability to manage personal effects, work, or multiple tasks, including organizing tasks and thoughts well, managing time effectively, and working neatly.
Planning	Describes an individual's ability to develop and implement strategies to accomplish tasks, including planning ahead and making good decisions.
Self-Monitoring	Indicates the individual's ability to evaluate his/her own behavior in order to determine when a different approach is necessary, including noticing and fixing mistakes, knowing when help is required, and understanding when a task is completed.
Working Memory	Reflects an individual's ability to keep information in mind that is important for knowing what to do and how to do it, including remembering important things, instructions, and steps.

Figure 17.1 Definitions for Executive Functioning Scales

Source: Reprinted with permission, © MHS 2017.

and controlling voluntary behavior is said to be accomplished by a set of overlapping cognitive abilities associated with the prefrontal cortex and interconnected subcortical system.[3]

As a result of our research at MHS, we have identified a number of functions that make up our model of executive functioning in adults.[4] These are shown in Figure 17.1.

We've taken these factors from our clinical work and modified them for the organizational context. We've made changes to the items and scales to be applicable for leadership in organizations. We've begun to pilot the new inventory with hundreds of leaders and nonleaders from a variety of organizations. All leaders in our sample managed at least one direct report.

The data conformed to a two-factor model. One factor is referred to as Managing Myself and Others; the second factor is Managing the Organization. We'll be subjecting this tool to more research studies looking at how the various scales may influence successful functioning at the executive level in organizations.

The Managing Myself/Others factor includes the following scales:

- Attention
- Emotion Regulation
- Flexibility
- Growth Mind-Set
- Inhibitory Control
- Initiation
- Interpersonal
- Organization
- Self-Monitoring
- Self-Planning

The Managing the Organization factor includes the following scales:

- Analytical and Systems Thinking
- Foresight
- Organizational Planning
- Strategic Visioning
- We hope in due time to be able to flesh out these areas in more detail and determine which functions are most important for successful leadership.

How Do We Manage Change?

One thing we can be certain about in today's business environment is that things are not going to stay the same. Change is a part of any organization, anywhere in the world today. Even though most leaders know change is inevitable, there has been little done to better understand or plan for the inevitable. In a report by Christopher Musselwhite of Discovery Learning International (now part of Multi-Health Systems), a project is described that helps us better understand change. In addition, an instrument was developed to help leaders deal with change in their organizations.[5]

The report explores the research around how people react to change in different ways. Although we can all experience a similar situation that requires change, we tend to respond to these situations in our own unique style. Our preference for dealing with change, whether reacting to it or initiating it, can be described and measured along a continuum that ranges from a preference for gradual incremental change to significant and wholesale change. These preferences are different and can sometimes vary by occupational groups or even industries. Understanding these preferences can, in part, explain conflict that occurs between individuals during the change implementation process. It also helps us understand noticeable differences between professions, organizational functions, and entire industries.

By understanding these change preferences, it is possible to better match change strategies to: individuals, situations, and desired outcomes. Musselwhite created the *Change Style Preference* model, which helps reframe existing beliefs and ideas about what constitutes good and bad, successful and unsuccessful change. He presents the benefits as follows:

> This ultimately produces more effective organizations, happier workers, and a more flexible work force. When people can understand the connection between the need for change, the change strategy, and their own comfort level with the change, they are much more willing to bend. A new dialogue can be created which has the capacity to unfreeze and redefine our mental models about desirable organizational change, whatever our personal preferences may be.

Musselwhite created the *Change Style Indicator* (CSI), which is a 22-item self-assessment tool that measures an individual's preference for creating and responding to change. The indicator helps people find where they fit on a continuous scale that includes three preferences.

On one end of the continuum are *conservers*. They are characterized as people who prefer a gradual but continuous approach to change. Conservers prefer the current circumstances to the unknown. The goal of the conserver is to better use the organization's resources, while preserving existing structure. When this approach is applied over time, the outcome can be significant change, which does not threaten or disrupt the stability of the organization.

At the other end of the continuum are *originators*. Originators are characterized as people who prefer a quicker and more radical approach to change. If conservers represent the Total Quality Management (TQM) approach to change, then originators are the reengineering champions. When this approach is applied effectively, the outcome can be very significant change, which occurs systemically and quickly. With the originator approach to change, existing organizational structure will be challenged and systemic change can occur. Musselwhite's research has shown that conservers and originators each account for about *25 percent* of the general population.

Pragmatists fall between conservers and originators on the *Change Style Preference* model and account for the remaining 50 percent of the general population. Pragmatists may appear reasonable, practical, agreeable, and flexible. However, to conservers and originators pragmatists may appear noncommittal or indecisive. Pragmatists tend to solve problems in ways that emphasize practical, workable outcomes and focus more on results than preserving or challenging organizational structure. Pragmatists are perceived to be more team-oriented than either conservers or originators.

Participants who take the *Change Style Inventory* receive their scores on a graph like Figure 17.2.

The *Change Style Inventory* has been used successfully since 1996 in a variety of programs and settings. In addition to extensive use in North America, the instrument has been used with success by Motorola University in management development programs in China and India. It has been used with engineers in South Korea, by bankers in England, by manufacturing executives and business students in Italy, and by high school students in Indonesia. Applications have ranged from management and leadership assessment and development to organizational work redesign efforts. The tool and its

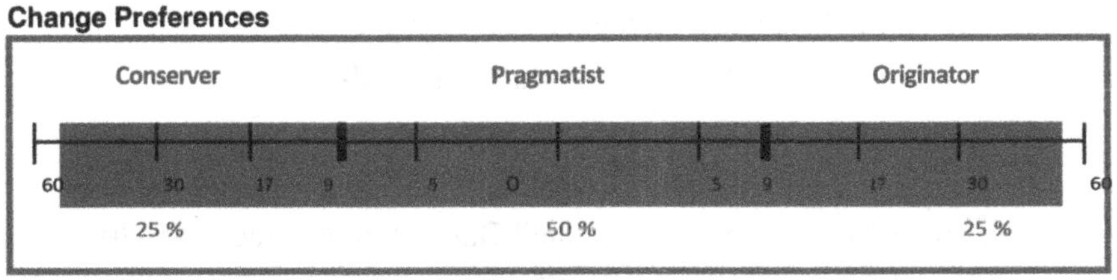

Figure 17.2 Change Preference Inventory Graph

implementation have helped many individuals and organizations better manage the change process.

How Gen Zers Will Impact the Workplace

Generation Z (ages 17–26, born between 1990 and 2000) is catching the attention of marketers, media, and the entertainment industry. But what makes this new generation different? As the newest cohort begins to enter the workforce, it's time to evaluate how they stack up to previous generations and how leaders may need to prepare for the changing capabilities of their workforce.

It seems like every generation complains about what the newest cohort brings to the table in terms of work skills, and this group is no different in that respect. Employers also tend to be critical about the newest group's behaviors and attitudes to work. These recurring themes have transcended from the GI generation, to Mature, to Baby Boomer, to Gen X, Y Millennials, and now Z. Although each generation seems to have adjusted to their own work patterns.

This time, however, things may actually be somewhat different. The Gen Z cohort *is* different from their parents and grandparents. We looked at a sample of 259,000 working people ages 15–75 selected from our worldwide data of approximately 2 million people tested for their emotional intelligence skills with the EQ-i 2.0. As previously stated, emotional intelligence is a set of emotional and social skills that influence the way we perceive and express ourselves, develop and maintain social relationships, cope with challenges, and use emotional information in an effective and meaningful way. The generational comparisons can be seen in Figure 17.3.

Our data shows that Gen Zers:

- Score significantly lower in independence:
  - 5.1 points lower than Generation Y (ages 27–38)
  - 7.5 points lower than Generation X (ages 39–50)
  - 8.2 points lower less than Baby Boomers (ages 51–70)
- Struggle with emotional problem solving, scoring an average of 6.6 points lower than Generation Y and X, and Baby Boomers (ages 51–70)
- Are indecisive, with an average 5.5 points lower decision-making score than previous generations

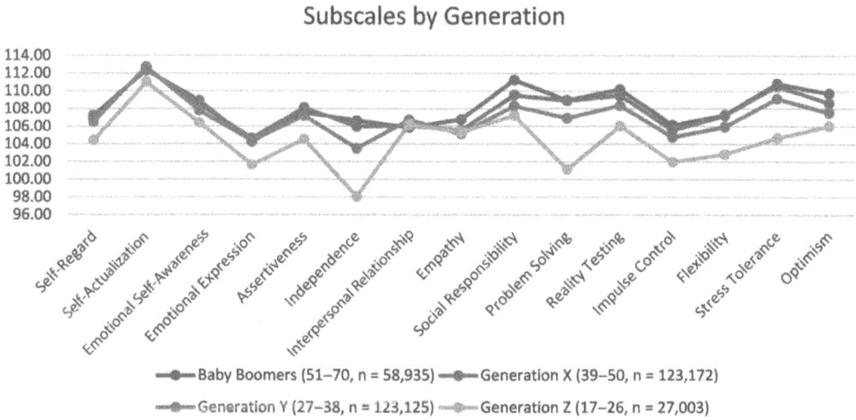

Figure 17.3 Age Cohort Emotional Intelligence Scores (EQ-i 2.0®)

Source: Graph provided by Multi-Health Systems 2017 ®.

- Don't deal as well with stress, almost 5 points lower than previous generations
- Yet are not significantly less happy than other generations, despite their overall lower emotional intelligence

The lowest score of Gen Zers is in independence. This group wants to check things out with others more than their predecessors. Even though they have more information available than ever before—all at the tips of their fingers via smartphone; they still depend more on others before taking action. They're less sure of themselves and want to confirm that they are making the right moves. They will want to check with peers, social media, and websites before acting, more than other groups tend to. They also have a greater need for approval before they are ready to carry out tasks.

This may be partially due to another skill they score low on–emotional problem solving. This isn't math or science logical problem solving; it involves the influence of emotions when solving real-life problems. Good problem solving requires the appropriate use of emotions—in other words, not too much or too little. However, this group seems to let emotions get in the way of sound decision making.

Finally, stress tolerance differentiates this group from preceding generations. When things start to get out of control or emotions run high, don't look to the Gen Zer to manage the situation. This group would rather avoid the stress, not deal with it at all, or, if they choose to not avoid the situation, they may not adequately manage the situation.

While this may seem like a bit of an overgeneralization, this is the pattern we find when looking at a large group of cohorts. Of course, there are exceptions in every group, but these are signs to look for when selecting, hiring, or training this group. Also, not all the news is bad. This cohort has been found to have a number of positive attributes as well. They are digitally aware, socially conscious, eager to learn, and driven by purpose or meaningful work. So, if you employ this group it will be important to stress the meaningfulness and contribution of the work they perform.

How do some of the challenges of Gen Zers play out in everyday life? This group is more dependent on others. They have a greater need for approval. So whether it's moving out on their own, purchasing health insurance, getting a car, switching jobs, they are more likely to depend on significant others, family, or friends before making that final move. This indecision may influence their performance at work if they are unable to take initiative without first seeking approval.

Gen Z also struggles with "emotional problem solving." What does this mean exactly, and what can companies do to help their younger employees cope with this problem? Emotional problem solving refers to being able to come up with solutions to problems without using too much or too little emotion. Whatever problem we're attempting to solve, whether it's which job to take or which car to buy, there's always an emotional component involved. When emotion gets in the way of solving problems, we tend to go off course, and it can lead to poor decision making.

When you use too much emotion in a situation, such as anxiety, you can be sidetracked and make poor decisions. If you use too little emotion, you can make a very logical decision, but one that you may not ultimately feel good about.

Leaders can help guide Gen Zers in how they go about coming up with solutions to problems. Generally, this group welcomes coaching and additional training. Coaching should ensure that they have an opportunity to generate a number of solutions to problems they are working on, and that they receive some guidance and direction when it comes to selecting and implementing solutions. Teach them to come to you with solutions, not problems. Then go through the potential solutions with them, evaluating the potential consequences together.

This group wants more guidance than other cohorts and welcomes multifaceted learning opportunities. So use face-to-face time as well as online training solutions. Do not just use digital solutions with this group; they highly value in-person time.

Gen Z is less efficient at decision making. How does this affect them in the workplace? Being less efficient in decision making means that when they make decisions they can be distracted by their emotions or other factors. It's important to be clear about tasks you want accomplished. You don't need to tell them how to do it, but indicate the kinds of solutions you are looking for. You want to ensure they see the problem as it is; they don't jump too quickly (or take too long) in coming up with solutions. And you don't want them to be overwhelmed with the size or nature of the job.

Being direct and having clear expectations will help keep this group on task. They are fast learners and can be very creative. Also, it's important to reinforce the importance of the work they are doing. This group values meaningful work.

The distance between Gen Z and previous generations seems to go up with age. How much of these trends can be attributed to youth/inexperience? Some of the trends we see in emotional intelligence are age related. That is, we get better at certain skills with experience. We learn to be more patient, take more things in stride without overreacting, and concern ourselves more with the needs of others. We also get better at managing ourselves and our emotions. So you would expect to see certain increases occur with age or maturity.

However, there seem to be some larger than expected gaps with this group. The gaps in the areas identified: independence, problem solving, and stress tolerance, are greater than what you would expect from age differences alone. Other differences, in component of emotional intelligence scores, that we see in this group compared with the other groups, are more in line with the expectations of natural growth.

How Does the Servant Leader Model Relate to Emotional Intelligence?

What is servant leadership, and how does it relate to emotional intelligence? The idea of servant leadership dates back to ancient philosophy. The following quote is attributed to fourth-century BCE Indian teacher, philosopher, economist, jurist, and royal adviser, Chanakya. He wrote, in the fourth century BCE, in his book *Arthashastra* (ancient Indian treatise on statecraft):

> the king [leader] shall consider as good, not what pleases himself but what pleases his subjects [followers]
>
> the king [leader] is a paid servant and enjoys the resources of the state together with the people.

While servant leadership is a timeless concept, the phrase "servant leadership" was coined by Robert K. Greenleaf in "The Servant as Leader," an essay that he first published in 1970 and revised in 1991.[6]

In that essay, Greenleaf wrote:

> The servant-leader is servant first. . . . It begins with the natural feeling that one wants to serve, to serve first. Then conscious choice brings one to aspire to lead. That person is sharply different from one who is leader first, perhaps because of the need to assuage an unusual power drive or to acquire material possessions. . . . The leader-first and the servant-first are two extreme types. Between them there are shadings and blends that are part of the infinite variety of human nature.

In terms of leadership styles, servant leadership can be most likely associated with the participative leadership style. There have been many studies of the servant leadership model, but only a few looking at the relationship between emotional intelligence and servant leadership.

In a paper drawing a parallel between servant leadership and the history of leadership in the United States Navy SEALs, LCDR (Ret) Chris Auger, a former active duty Navy SEAL and executive officer at the Center for SEAL and SWCC (Special Warfare Combatant Crewman), included the connection with emotional intelligence. He describes how the servant leader model is embedded in Navy SEAL training, "The entire program is shaped around pushing the individual beyond their perceived level of performance and then introducing them to the power of the Team. Throughout the training each candidate is expected to follow and lead various physical and intellectual blocks of training. This further reinforces the servant follower-leader mindset."[7]

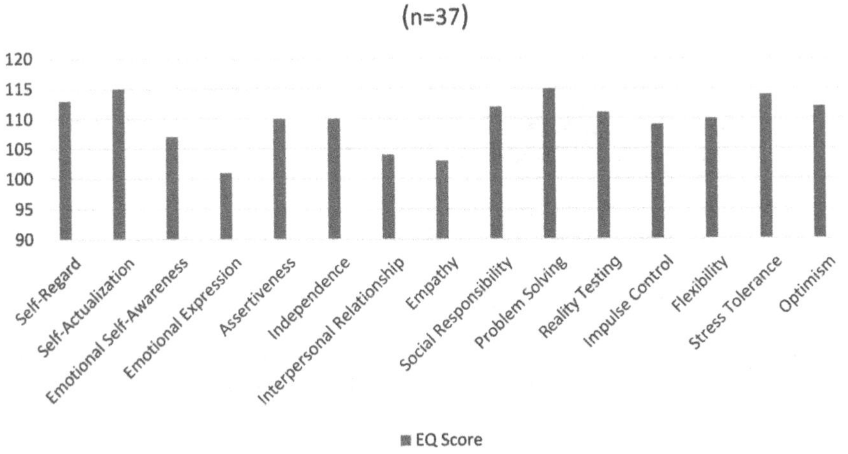

Figure 17.4 EQ-i Scores of Sample of Navy SEALs

Source: Reprinted permission of © Multi-Health Systems 2017.

Auger points out how Naval Special Warfare discovered, through the use of the EQ-i 2.0 group profile, that their top EQ behaviors were self-actualization, problem solving, stress tolerance, self-regard, and social responsibility as seen in Figure 17.4. They also discovered that their lowest EQ behaviors were emotional expression, empathy, and interpersonal relationships.

In knowing the top three strengths and bottom three, an organization can understand whether behaviors are being overused or underused. The example from the SEALs is that having low empathy when going into a combat situation is necessary for the survival of you and your teammates. However, after the shooting has stopped, it is important to dial up the empathy to lead through the situation which in many cases involves noncombatants and civilians. Similar examples of "dialing-up" empathy can be found in how police officers respond to volatile situations.

I had the privilege of working with Chris and the Navy SEALs using the EQ-i 2.0 in both Virginia Beach and San Diego. As emotional intelligence relates to servant leadership, I found that assessing social responsibility helps reinforce the service component of leadership. It enables leaders and aspiring leaders to evaluate the concern one has for others. Auger describes how the SEAL training process allows for career maturation as subject matter experts eventually take on leadership positions. Throughout the process, the leader and follower mentalities

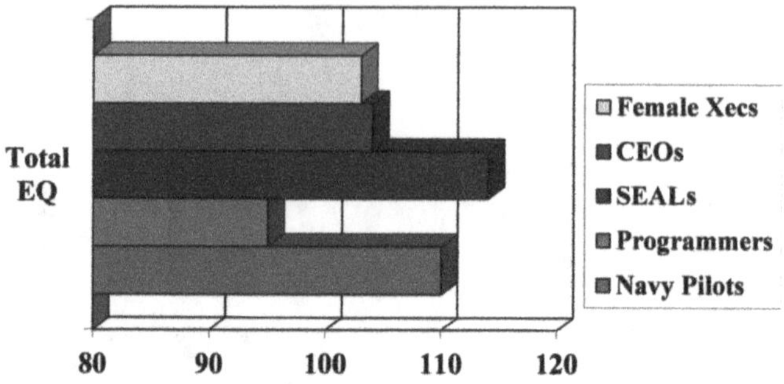

Figure 17.5 Comparison of EQ-i Scores for Samples of Female Executives, Corporate CEOs, Navy SEALs, Computer Programmers, and Navy Pilots

Source: Reprinted with permission, © Multi-Health Systems 2016.

are maintained. One of the strengths of the operational unit is that everyone knows how to step in and step out of their follower and leader roles. The ability to transfer in, and out of, leader and follower roles is becoming increasingly important with the rise of remote work and leaderless teams.

Interestingly, in Figure 17.5 I've compared some samples of emotional intelligence scores from groups I've tested. The Navy SEAL group is my highest-scoring group to date, surpassing navy pilots (many of whom were Top Gun trained), corporate CEOs, and a group of high-level female C-suite executives. The computer programmers were added to round out the group.

Using the EQ 360, Jane Waddell took a direct look at the relationship between emotional intelligence and servant leadership.[8] Her study used data from 44 professional leaders to examine the relationship of emotional intelligence to servant leadership attribution. The Servant Leadership Inventory[9] was used to measure the seven virtues of a servant leader according to Patterson's model. The leader's emotional intelligence was measured by the followers' ratings on the EQ-360.

Waddell found that there was a positive relationship between servant leadership attribution and the leader's emotional intelligence, as rated by followers. She reported that 56.7 percent of the variance in servant leadership attribution was accounted for by only one of the EQ-360's subscales, the followers' perception of the leader's reality testing. Reality testing is described as the ability to accurately size up a situation. In this instance, it allows the servant leader to accurately assess the follower's highest priority needs.

Working one's way up from follower to leader can help set in place a level of reality testing that enables leaders to be more aware of not just followers' needs, but those of customers and partners. Many people who have experienced working at the front lines of an organization have direct experience of the concerns and wishes of customers.

Leading from the Top: Effective Boards of Directors

Boards of directors have enormous responsibility in managing the major for-profit and nonprofit organizations around the world. What does it take to make a successful board of directors? One of the best reports looking at what differentiates great boards from the rest was done by Jeffery Sonnenfeld and published in *Harvard Business Review*.[10] He looked at traditional measures of a board's performance—board members' attendance at board meetings, equity involvement of board members, board member skills (technical, e.g., finance), board members' ages, presence of past CEOs, independence of board members from the organization, board size, committees, and other factors. None of these factors differentiated high-functioning boards from the poorly functioning. Companies such as Enron, WorldCom, and Tyco had great boards based on some of these criteria, but it made no difference in the end. The companies failed dramatically.

The bottom line, according to Sonnenfeld, is the human element, the social component—the people. He concludes, "What distinguishes exemplary boards is that they are robust, effective social systems."

What are those social systems? This is something I've had the opportunity to investigate. I've been on the teaching faculty for a number of years at The Directors College, which is the original university-accredited corporate director education program in Canada. It was founded in 2003 and is a joint venture between The Conference Board of Canada and the DeGroote School of Business at McMaster University. The approach at The Directors College is unique. It's an immersive, residential program that allows participants to put the lessons learned in the classroom into practice on the board. The mission of the college is to advance transformative governance for the benefit of business and society—this is at the heart of their Gold Standard in Governance Education.

As part of the course, participants take the EQ-i 2.0 to learn more about their strengths and challenges and to apply their self-awareness in their working

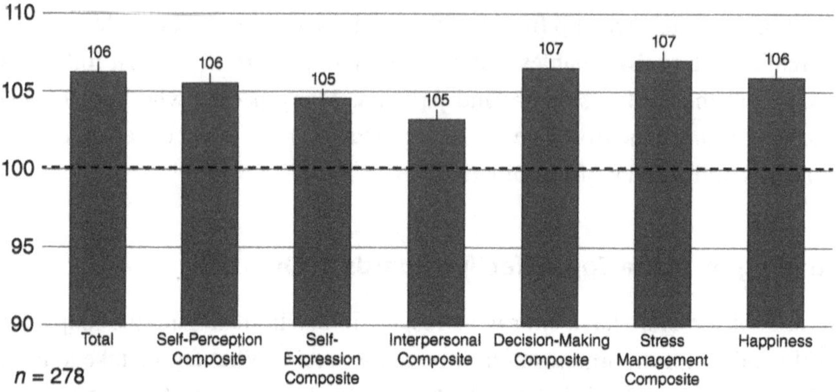

Figure 17.6 Composite EQ-i 2.0 Scores from Participants of The Directors College

Source: Reprinted with permission, © MHS 2017.

groups. The composite scores of a large number of participants (n = 278) are presented in Figure 17.6.

Their highest composites are in Stress Management and Decision Making. Most of these participants have many years' experience working in organizations and have worked their way up the ladder to the senior management level. Their current, or next step, is sitting on a board of a for-profit or nonprofit organization. They have dealt with stress throughout their career and at this stage are more balanced in dealing with difficult situations. Also, they have been at a decision-making level for a significant amount of time and therefore manage the decision-making process well.

The top three strengths for this group can be seen in Figure 17.7.

The top strength of this group is in Stress Tolerance. As previously mentioned, these seasoned executives have had many years' experience in management and tend not to get too stressed by work events. Their second strength is in Self-Actualization. Most of these people are at a stage in their career where they want to learn and give back. For example, they chose (and paid) to take this course that will teach them a great deal about serving on a board. They see themselves as contributing their knowledge and skills at a new level.

The emotional intelligence challenges for this group can be seen in Figure 17.8.

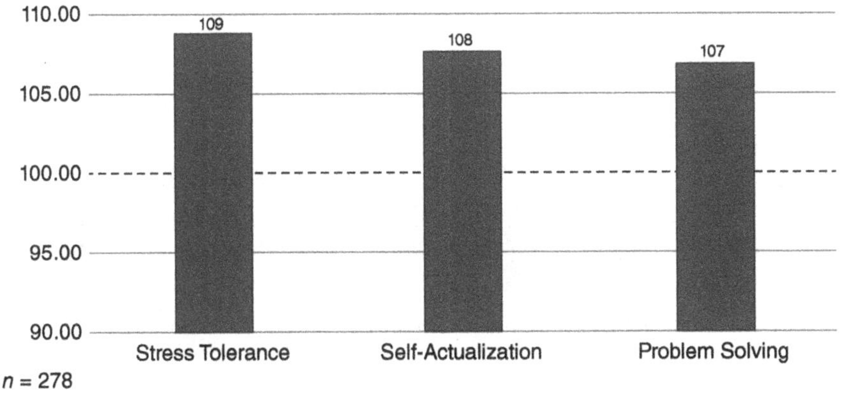

Figure 17.7 Top EQ-i 2.0 Scores of Participants at The Directors College

Source: Reprinted with permission, © MHS 2017.

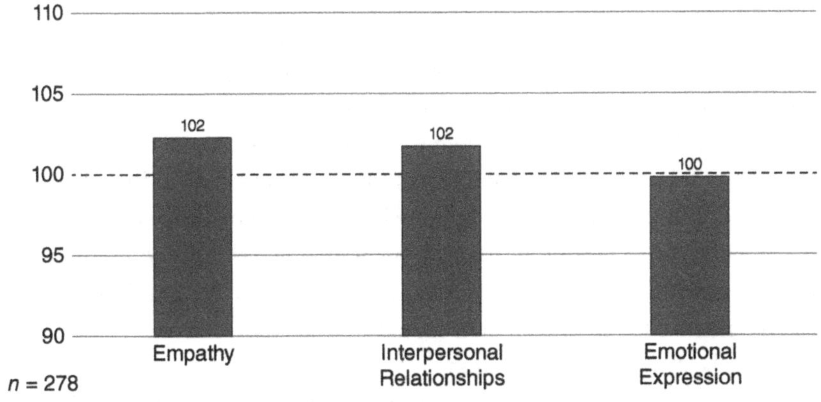

Figure 17.8 Top Three Challenges from EQ-i 2.0 Scores of Participants from The Directors College

Source: Reprinted with permission, © MHS 2017.

Their top three challenges for these directors are Empathy, Interpersonal Relationship, and Emotional Expression. This is not too surprising considering many of the participants of this course are highly technically skilled professionals. They include accountants, lawyers, and engineers. These are generally very business-oriented types and not naturally empathic or sociable. They tend

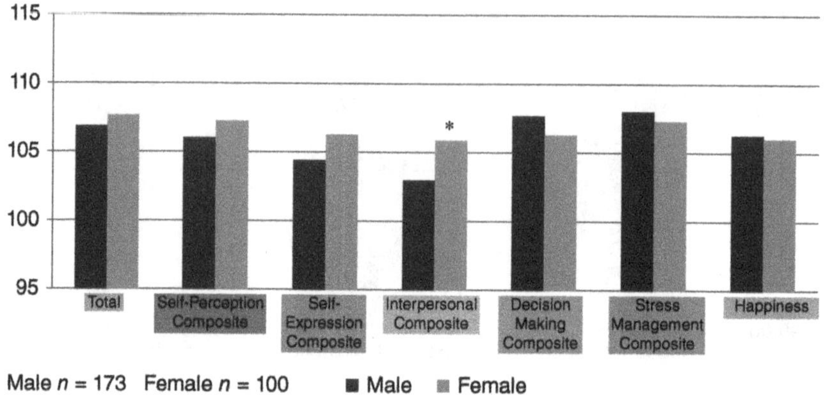

Figure 17.9 EQ-i 2.0 Composite Score Differences between Male and Female Board Members

Source: Reprinted with permission, © MHS 2017.

to not be very emotionally expressive. As senior managers, they like to keep their thoughts and feelings close to the chest.

Part of what they learn in the course is to be more open socially, to network, and be more transparent emotionally. As a director, it's helpful for other board members and the senior staff to know where you are coming from, why you feel the way you do about an issue, as well as how strongly you feel. Board members need to trust each other and be willing to have candid discussions. Disagreements should be open and focused on the merit of one's case guided by what's best for the organization.

One of my interests has been differences between male and female board members. I've had the opportunity to get a reasonably sized sample of male and female directors. In Figure 17.9, you can see the significantly different composite scores.

Although at first glance there appears to be large differences between males and females, there was only one composite with a significant difference. Female board members scored higher than males in the Interpersonal composite; males didn't score higher than females in any of the composites.

The specific EQ-i 2.0 scales that differentiated the sexes can be seen in Figure 17.10.

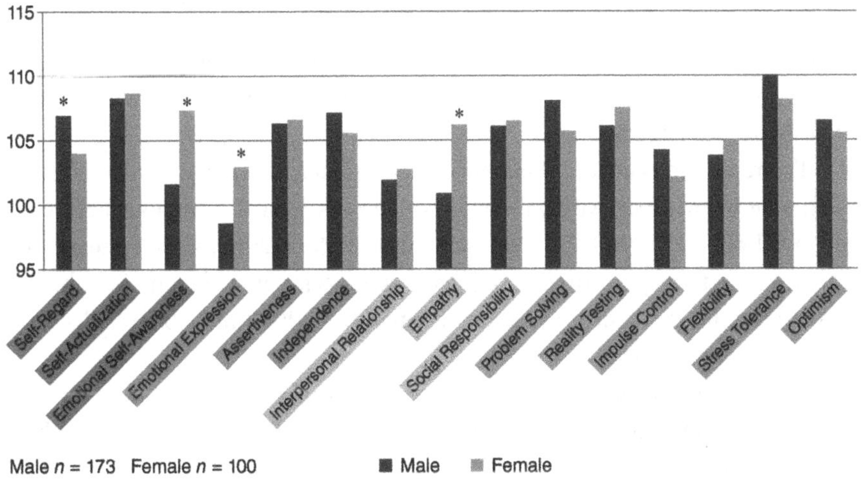

Figure 17.10 EQ-i 2.0 Scale Score Differences between Male and Female Board Members

Source: Reprinted with permission, © MHS 2017.

These differences, showing men having higher self-regard, and women having significantly higher scores in emotional self-awareness, emotional expression, and empathy, are slightly different from our general norms and professional norms data, which include hundreds of thousands of cases. In the general population, there are no overall differences in total EQ-i 2.0 scores, but women score higher than men in emotional self-awareness, emotional expression, and empathy. Men, on the other hand, score higher in independence, problem solving, and stress tolerance.[11]

In this sample of directors, women have basically closed the gap in the areas men traditionally score higher in—independence, stress tolerance, and problems solving. It seems the women who make it to this level—senior executives moving on to boards, bring some extra skills with them to the boardroom. Unfortunately, the number of women getting to the boardroom is still much lower than men.

What difference does it make having females on the board of directors? The *New York Times* reported on a study by Credit Suisse looking at gender differences of board members.[12] They examined almost 2,400 global corporations from 2005 to 2011, including the years directly preceding and following the financial crisis, and found that large-cap companies with at least one woman on their boards outperformed comparable companies with all-male boards by 26 percent.

The report continued, "Some might assume that there was a cost to this as well, that boards with women must have been excessively cautious before the financial crisis of 2008. . . . Not so. From 2005 to 2007, Credit Suisse also found, the stock performance of companies with women on their boards essentially matched performance of companies with all-male boards. Nothing lost, but much gained."

It could be that women with higher scores in emotional self-awareness, emotional expression, and empathy can act as a stabilizing force, especially in times of crisis.

What Can We Learn from Unusual Leaders?

Over the course of time, I've had the opportunity to meet hundreds of leaders. I have interviewed, worked with, psychologically tested, coached, learned from, taught, and interacted in many ways with many different types of leaders. In general, most leaders I've met would not surprise you. They have many of the attributes you would expect. Most have good, or excellent, educations. For the most part, they tend to have good childhood backgrounds and histories, perhaps some experiencing bumps in the road—parents divorced, loss of a parent or sibling, growing up on the wrong side of the tracks, lower middle class upbringing, or an immigrant family. Their personalities are generally what you would expect, with some individual variances—confident, passionate, intelligent, extraverted, focused, honest, engaged, social, dominant, decisive, conscientious, proud, authoritative, and so on.

Most leadership theories and books focus on the prototypical kind of leader that you would expect to see leading an organization. But what makes the study of leadership interesting is when you try to explain leaders that don't fit in the box. If we can look at the unusual, outside the box kind of leaders, and understand their success, we may be better at understanding leadership in general.

Allow me to tell you a story about one outside the box leader, Lia Grimanis. I get hundreds of e-mails and phone calls from people I don't know. Many are trying to sell me something, others are looking for employment, and some just want answers to questions. Regardless, like many busy people, I can't answer all the requests I get. Some informational requests, for example, I delegate to others.

One day I got a request from someone that struck me as a bit unusual. The nature of the request, asking for information about emotional intelligence, was not unusual. But something that struck me was on the signature line of the note—**2 Time Guinness World Record Holder. See Lia pull a jet airplane.**

Of course, I was intrigued. I then got in touch with Lia Grimanis. We soon met, and I got to hear her story. Lia is the founder and CEO of a charity. She was listed in Canada's *Financial Post Magazine* as one of Canada's 100 Most Powerful Women. She won Chatelaine's (*Canadian Magazine*) Woman of the Year Award. She also appeared on the NBC *Today Show*. And, yes, she's pulled not one, but two airplanes. Grimanis now holds two Guinness World Records: "Heaviest Vehicle Pulled 100 feet by a Woman" (18,000 pounds) and "Heaviest Vehicle Pulled in High Heels" (15,000 pounds).

Prior to her forming and leading a charity, Lia worked in the business world. She spent 18 years managing complex projects in the technology sector. She was a high-earning, successful sales professional for technology solutions with a large software company. Her last corporate position was a regional head of Financial Services, Americas, for the global technology firm, TIBCO Software.

Most of this story seems conventional. However, there is a twist to Lia's story. Lia spent some of her adolescence as a homeless person. She left an abusive family home in her late teens and ended up couch surfing and living in a shelter for the homeless. She never completed high school. The shelter was her primary support. She struggled to survive on the streets of Toronto. She was suicidal, experienced depression and other mental health challenges (possible autism spectrum disorder), but she managed to keep hope alive.

During her time in the homeless shelter, she made two promises to herself—to become successful and to fulfill her big dreams. One of those dreams was owning a motorcycle, which she has since accomplished. Another was to play the harp, which she saw as an elitist instrument, something unusual for someone growing up in poverty (she had a stipend of a dollar a day at the homeless shelter). She has since earned a scholarship at the Royal Conservatory for Music.

Lia shared a few of her other accomplishments with me. She was the first Canadian to complete the Fjordrally (a 1,000 km motorcycle rally on the ice and snow in subarctic Norway), she's fed sharks underwater without a cage, hung out in a pit of live alligators, learned to joust in full armor, wing walked, learned to pilot a helicopter, driven a tank in east Germany, scaled an 80-foot tree, built a treehouse, learned falconry, and proposed to her partner while parahawking. Oh, and she also mentioned that she was flying a helicopter before she ever owned a vehicle to drive.

Lia's charity is called *Up With Women* and is dedicated to helping recently homeless at-risk women rebuild their careers. She does this in an unconventional way: through partnering clients with highly skilled business coaches and professionals for biweekly career coaching, group development, and highly focused workshops. She targets a very challenged group of women and some are physically challenged. Others have fled domestic abuse or have immigrated as refugees. Some are single moms, straight out of family shelters.

How has her success rate been? Within the first three months of starting in the program, 80 percent of their clients (first cohort of 20 women) were employed. Confidence, in terms of score out of 10, had gone up from 5.3 to 7.9 on average. Over the course of the year, they have seen these achievements also translate into small-business start-ups by 50 percent of their program participants.

Lia believes emotional intelligence can be a big part of the success story for her clients. We've partnered with Lia and her program to measure the emotional intelligence at the beginning of their clients' journey, in an effort to help coaches focus on areas of strength and challenge. We hope to posttest a sample of these women to document changes in these areas, and validate these against real-world gains.

What about Lia's own story? How did she become a successful leader? Lia took the EQ-i 2.0, and her results are seen in Figure 17.11.

Lia's strengths are in Emotional Expression, Independence, and Self-Actualization. Her challenges are in Empathy, Interpersonal Relationship, and Reality Testing. One of the first things you notice about Lia is that she is very expressive. She captures your attention immediately and has been very successful presenting her story and representing her passion in presentations, one-on-one meetings, and in media interviews. She's also very independent. Surviving trauma, poverty, and homelessness at an early age contributes to

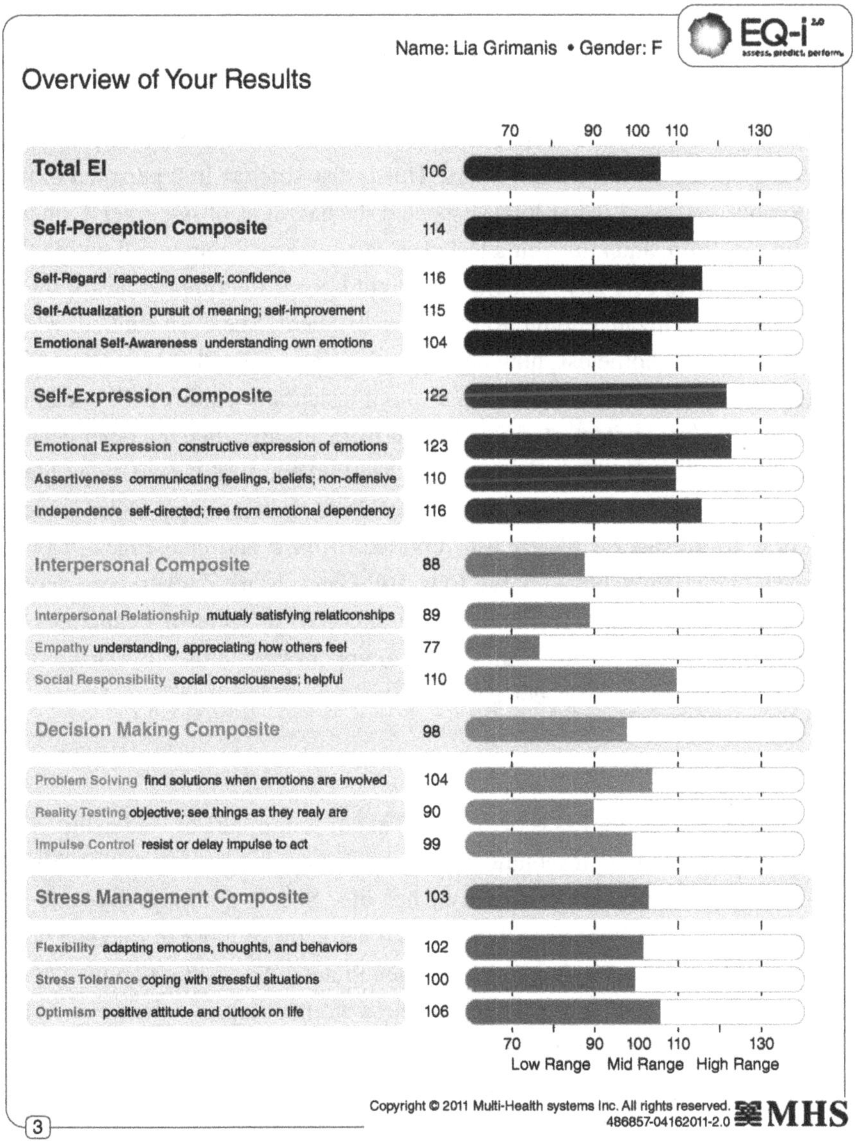

Figure 17.11 Lia Grimanis's EQ-i 2.0 Profile

that. Having to fend for herself for so much of her life, she has learned to follow her heart and make things work. Her Self-Actualization score represents her discovering her life's work and her passion for the direction she's headed.

Lia's lower scores can be instructive as well. Her low Empathy is something Lia has grappled with for many years. This is also true for Interpersonal Skills and Reality Testing. Lia has long suspected she has signs of Asperger's, on the autistic spectrum, and after being tested as an adult was found to fall within the autism spectrum. She has deliberately taught herself to compensate for these skills that she is aware enough to know are deficient. She even studied, while on the streets and homeless, how other people interacted with one another. She watched people socializing, looking through restaurant windows. She learned about making eye contact, stopping herself from talking when the other person wanted to speak, and many other social graces that many of us take for granted.

Lia has been successful despite some of these shortcomings. Other leaders we know to be successful are also reported to have had challenges in their interpersonal relationships—Steve Jobs, Bill Gates, Mark Zuckerberg, among others. How is it that some leaders can succeed, in spite of challenges in interpersonal skills? Clearly, they have compensated, either by struggling more, suffering more, or sheer persistence.

Using the Four Pillars

What does stand out for Lia is her strength in our four pillars of leadership. She is very authentic in her presentation, and her life story is as real as can be. She's had to overcome serious struggles in her life. She is a strong advocate of coaching and not only has coaching helped her achieve more in life, she now uses a coaching model to help other women in need. She is high on insight as she has a purpose, which is to help homeless women improve their lives. She communicates this purpose very effectively. Finally, as far as innovation, she has demonstrated many innovations in her methods of helping people. And, of course, pulling an airplane is one that sticks in my mind.

Investing in Improving Leaders' Emotional Intelligence

There have been many studies and many examples of programs that have been designed to improve a leader's emotional intelligence. Unfortunately, some of the work in this area has been done with Fortune 100 companies that prefer we do not share their data, largely for competitive reasons. However, there is research we can share, as well as information about the program designed by our own MHS Organizational Development (OD) group that organizations are taking and using in-house for their leader development.

First, let's look at the state-of-the-art in organizational leadership training of emotional intelligence. The Human Capital Institute, together with Multi-Health Systems, undertook a study looking at these practices in organizations around the world.[13] We surveyed 784 respondents representing more than 500 organizations worldwide. These included 73 percent who were leaders within the organizations and 27 percent of whom were individual contributors or line workers. The majority of respondents were in human resources/recruiting (56 percent), and 19 percent were in executive management. Organization size ranged from less than 100 employees to more than 20,000. Industries included government, health care, financial services, real estate, automotive, IT/software, chemical/energy/utilities, retail, construction, pharma, food and beverage, telecom, defense, and more.

One of the key findings was that more than half of survey respondents think the current leadership development efforts at their organizations are less than effective. While there was some disagreement between staff and leaders over priorities for leadership training (Chapter 12's "Coaching" section pointed out that staff rated coaching as a higher priority than managers did), communication, interpersonal skills, and self-awareness were seen as important by everyone. Leaders believed the most important skills they need were adaptability, problem solving, and interpersonal skills. Staff believed the most important leadership skills were coaching, empathy, and interpersonal skills.

The survey looked at the investment organizations made in leadership training. It found that organizations that spend more than 31 percent of their annual training and development budgets on leadership development were 12 percent more likely to report increased revenue. Looking at different types of training that was being provided, they found that 60 percent of those who use emotional intelligence assessments said they were effective or very effective. Equally efficient methods of development included executive coaching, job rotations, and global assignments.

Many organizations, however, are not yet tapping into the potential of emotional intelligence. In fact, 29 percent of survey respondents report that emotional intelligence is not a focus for their organization. That's unfortunate

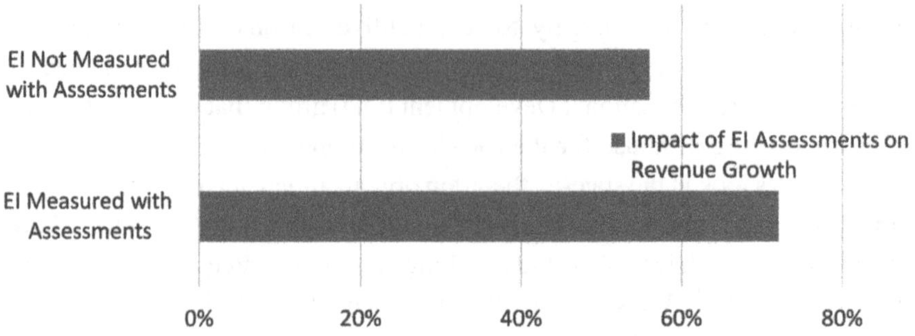

Figure 17.12 Impact of Emotional Intelligence Assessments on Revenue Growth

Source: Adapted and reprinted with permission of HCI.

because it was also reported that organizations that value and widely use emotional intelligence were 3.2 times more effective at leadership development. In other words, there is a 31 percent gap in leadership development effectiveness between organizations where emotional intelligence is valued, versus those in which it is not.

Organizations that integrate emotional intelligence in at least two different ways are 25 percent more likely to have extremely effective leadership development. In contrast, only 15 percent of organizations that do not widely implement emotional intelligence report effective leadership development. Incorporating emotional intelligence as part of leadership coaching supports higher performance. When organizations incorporate emotional intelligence in leadership coaching, they are 36 percent more likely to report effective emotional intelligence training performance.

Finally, the report looked at the bottom line, revenue effects of measuring emotional intelligence through the use of assessments, as seen in Figure 17.12. Using assessments to track or measure emotional intelligence was found to help support positive revenue growth rates. While many factors impact revenue growth, organizations that measure emotional intelligence are 16 percent more likely to report positive revenue growth.

A Study Increasing Leaders' Emotional Intelligence

While it's difficult to validate the effectiveness of leadership programs, and whether they make any measurable differences in an organization, there are some examples of emotional intelligence training programs making a difference. One such program was reported on by Mark Slaski and Susan Cartwright.[14]

The aim of this study was to investigate whether emotional intelligence could be developed in managers, and if so, whether increased emotional intelligence has a beneficial impact on health, well-being, and performance.

In their study, they looked at 120 managers from a large U.K. retail chain who volunteered for the research. These managers were assigned to either a training or a control group. The training group, of 60 managers, attended a developmental emotional intelligence training program for one day per week over a four week period. The control group of 60 managers received no training at all.

In addition to demographic questionnaires, all managers completed the EQ-i, a general health questionnaire, a psychological outcomes questionnaire, and a stress index. To measure any performance changes, their immediate supervisors completed a performance management tool that evaluated 16 performance factors used by the organization. Qualitative performance data was also collected from their direct managers. These assessments were completed prior to the program starting and six months after completion. A six-month time frame was chosen in order to give participants enough time to practice the exercises given and consolidate their skill development.

At the end of six months, the training participant's EQ-i scores significantly increased. During the same period, the control group's average EQ-i score dropped slightly. Interestingly, for the control group, morale, and quality of life scores were significantly poorer over time and distress had significantly increased, suggesting that this study took place in an organizational climate of increasing stress and falling morale. The training group, however, had increased morale, quality of life, and lower stress, all at significant levels.

There was no significant difference in the performance review indicator that was used. The authors claim that this may have been due to the nature of the tool, which failed to capture some of the more emotion-laden management competencies. However, the qualitative measure indicated that there was improvement seen by the managers' supervisors for many of the training participants.

This study helps document some of what I believe and have seen in organizations for years. Improving emotional intelligence can have many benefits that go beyond the workplace. Leaders with high emotional intelligence tend to be happier, less stressed, and generally have a better quality of life. When I present this information in organizations around the world, one of the questions I get asked is why we don't teach these skills earlier. Why do we wait until people are already so deep into their careers? Well the good news is that we developed an emotional intelligence program for use in colleges and universities.[15] The EQ-i has been adapted for use by college-aged students, and there is a workbook and resource materials for instructors. The program is widely used in colleges and universities throughout North America and is starting to be adopted internationally.

Emotional Intelligence Training in Organizations

There are now thousands of trainers around the world that have been certified to use the EQ-i 2.0 in organizations and higher education. As well, the Organizational Development (OD) group at MHS has put together leadership programs that are already being used in a number of organizations. *The Leading Strategically with Emotional Intelligence* program is a two-day experiential training program for established leaders looking to increase their skills in leading others. This program can be run in organizations with eight or more participants. To learn more about these and other programs you can visit mhs.com or send me an email at EQLeader@mhs.com.

It is my hope that this book has provided you with new information that you can use in your quest to become a better leader. The goals of this book have been (a) to help you better understand what emotional intelligence is, (b) to show you how emotional intelligence is a crucial part of the Four-Pillar Model, (c) to demonstrate how emotional intelligence encompasses behaviors that facilitate leadership effectiveness for both individuals and the organization, and, finally, (d) to convince you that developing emotional intelligence is possible. If I have succeeded in at least some of these goals I feel gratified. Thank you for coming along with me on this journey.

Notes

Chapter 1 Leadership: What Do We Really Know About Leadership?

1. Bill Gates, Nathan Myhrvold, and Peter Rinearson, *The Road Ahead* (New York: Viking Press, 1995).
2. Walter Isaacson, *Steve Jobs* (New York: Simon & Schuster, 2011).
3. Rudolph W. Giuliani and Ken Kurson, *Leadership* (New York: Hyperion, 2002).
4. Jack Welch and Suzy Welch, *Winning* (New York: HarperBusiness, 2005).
5. Carly Fiorina, *Tough Choices: A Memoir* (New York: Portfolio, 2007).
6. Michael Dell, *Direct from Dell—Strategies That Revolutionized an Industry* (New York: HarperCollins, 2000).
7. Richard Branson, *Losing My Virginity: How I Survived, Had Fun, and Made a Fortune Doing Business My Way* (New York: Crown Business, 2011).
8. John C. Maxwell, *The 21 Irrefutable Laws of Leadership: Follow Them and People Will Follow You*, rev. and updated ed. (Nashville, TN: Thomas Nelson, 2007).

9. David Cottrell, *Monday Morning Leadership: 8 Mentoring Sessions You Can't Afford to Miss* (Dallas, TX: Cornerstone Leadership Institute, 2002).

10. Michael Useem, *The Leadership Moment: Nine True Stories of Triumph and Disaster and Their Lessons for Us All*, rev. ed. (New York: Crown Business, 1999).

11. Peter Northouse, *Leadership: Theory and Practice*, 7th ed. (Thousand Oaks, CA: SAGE Publications, 2015).

12. Simon Sinek, *Start with Why: How Great Leaders Inspire Everyone to Take Action*, reprint ed. (New York: Portfolio, 2011).

13. Jim Kouzes and Barry Posner. *The Leadership Challenge: How to Make Extraordinary Things Happen in Organizations*, 5th ed. (San Francisco: Jossey-Bass, 2012).

14. Jim Collins, *Good to Great: Why Some Companies Make the Leap . . . And Others Don't* (New York: HarperBusiness, 2001).

15. Ibid.

16. Ibid.

17. Steven J. Stein and Howard E. Book, *The EQ Edge: Emotional Intelligence and Your Success* (San Francisco: Jossey-Bass, 2000, 2011).

18. Steven J. Stein, *Make Your Workplace Great: The 7 Keys to an Emotionally Intelligent Organization* (Mississauga, ON: Jossey-Bass, 2007).

19. Jeff Schwartz, Josh Bersin, and Bill Pelster, *Global Human Capital Trends 2014: Engaging the 21st-Century Workforce* (Westlake, TX: Deloitte University Press, 2014).

20. Lee Iacocca, "Driving Force: Henry Ford," *Time* (December 7, 1998).

21. Bill Gates, "Remarks by Bill Gates," Microsoft.com, www.microsoft.com/billgates/speeches; Corey Grice and Sandeep Junnarkar, "Gates, Buffett a Bit Bearish," *CNET News*, July 2, 1998.

22. David Gelernter, "Bill Gates: Software Strongman," *Time* (December 7, 1998): 540–553.

Chapter 2 What Have We Learned About Leadership?

1. Robert B. Kaiser, Robert Hogan, and S. Bartholomew Craig, "Leadership and the Fate of Organizations," *American Psychologist* 63, no. 2 (February–March 2008): 96–110.
2. R. G. Lord, C. L. DeVader, and G. Alliger, "A Meta-Analysis of the Relation between Personality Traits and Leader Perceptions," *Journal of Applied Psychology* 71 (1986): 402–410.
3. S. J. Stein and J. Deonarine, *Can Emotional Intelligence Help Determine the Next US President?* (Toronto, ON: Multi-Health Systems, 2016).
4. L. R. Sayles, *The Working Leader: The Triumph of High Performance over Conventional Management Principles* (New York: McGraw-Hill, 1993).
5. N. Dixon, *On the Psychology of Military Incompetence* (New York: Basic Books, 1976).
6. B. M. Bass and B. J. Avolio, *Full Range Leadership Development: Manual for the Multifactor Leadership Questionnaire* (Palo Alto, CA: Mind Garden Inc., 1997).

Chapter 3 Leadership: Why Emotional Intelligence?

1. A. Binet, "Les Premiers Mots de la Thèse Idéaliste," *Revue Philosophique* 61 (1906): 599–618; C. Binet-Sanglé, "Racine," *Chronique Medical XII* (1905): 12–13; A. Binet and T. Simon, "Conclusions," *L'Année Psychologique* 16 (1910): 361–371; K. L. Johnston, "M. Binet's Method for the Measurement of Intelligence," *Report of the British Association for the Advancement of Science* 80 (1910): 806–808; Edmund B. Huey, "The Binet Scale for Measuring Intelligence and Retardation," *Journal of Educational Psychology* 1, no. 8 (September 1910): 435–444.
2. H. H. Goddard, "The Binet and Simon Tests of Intellectual Capacity," *Training School Bulletin* 5 (1908): 3–6; H. H. Goddard, "Two Thousand Normal Children Measured by the Binet Measuring Scale of Intelligence," *Pedagogical Seminary* 18 (1911): 232–259.

3. L. M. Terman, "The Binet-Simon Scale for Measuring Intelligence: Impressions Gained by its Application," *Psychological Clinic* 5 (1911): 199–206; Lewis M. Termanand H. G. Childs, "A Tentative Revision and Extension of the Binet-Simon Measuring Scale of Intelligence. Part III. Summary and Criticisms," *Journal of Educational Psychology* 3, no. 5 (May 1912): 277–289.
4. Richard K. Wagner, "Intelligence, Training, and Employment," *American Psychologist* 52, no. 10 (Oct. 1997): 1059–1069. This review article points out that the average observed validity coefficient or correlation between cognitive ability test scores and job performance is between .20 and .30, which amounts to between 4 and 9 percent of the variance. That leaves somewhere between 91 and 96 percent of job performance due to other factors.
5. Robert J. Sternberg, Richard K. Wagner, Wendy M. Williams, and Joseph A. Horvath, "Testing Common Sense," *American Psychologist* 50, no. 11 (November 1995): 912–927.
6. C. Darwin, *The Expression of the Emotions in Man and Animals* (Chicago: University of Chicago Press, 1965 [originally published in 1872]).
7. A. R. Damasio, *Descartes' Error: Emotion, Reason, and the Human Brain* (New York: Grosset/Putnam, 1994).
8. Roderick Gilkey, Ricardo Caceda, and Clinton Kilts, "When Emotional Reasoning Trumps IQ," *Harvard Business Review*, September 2010.
9. P. Salovey and J. D. Mayer, "Emotional Intelligence," *Imagination, Cognition and Personality* 9 (1990): 185–211.
10. Jim McGee, Tom Fiedler, and James Savage, "Gary Hart and the 'Monkey Business,'" *The Miami Herald*, May 10, 1987.
11. Matt Bai, "How Gary Hart's Downfall Forever Changed American Politics," *The New York Times Magazine*, September 18, 2014.
12. Salovey and Mayer, "Emotional Intelligence."
13. D. Goleman, *Emotional Intelligence: Why It Can Matter More Than IQ* (New York: Bantam Books, 1995, 2005).

14. J. D. Mayer, P. Salovey, and D. Caruso, *Mayer-Salovey-Caruso Emotional Intelligence Tests (MSCEIT) User's Manual* (Toronto: Multi-Health Systems, 2002).

15. David Roseteand Joseph Ciarrochi, "Emotional Intelligence and Its Relationship to Workplace Performance Outcomes of Leadership Effectiveness," *Leadership & Organization Development Journal* 26, no. 5 (2005): 388–399.

16. S. Côté, P. N. Lopes, and P. Salovey, "Emotional Intelligence and Vision Formulation and Articulation" (manuscript in preparation, 2003).

17. S. J. S. Giles, "The Role of Supervisory Emotional Intelligence in Direct Report Organizational Commitment" (unpublished master's thesis, University of New South Wales, Sydney, Australia, 2001).

18. W. Lee Turner, *Exploring the Correlation between Cognitive and Emotional Intelligences with Leadership Performance in the Public Sector* (doctoral dissertation, School of Business and Technology Management, Northcentral University: Dissertation Abstracts International Section A: Humanities and Social Sciences, 2016).

19. Reuven Bar-On, "The Development of a Concept of Psychological Well-Being" (unpublished doctoral dissertation, Psychology, Rhodes University, South Africa, 1985); R. Bar-On, "The Era of the EQ: Defining and Assessing Emotional Intelligence" *104th Annual Convention of the American Psychological Association* (Toronto, 1996); R. Bar-On, *Bar-On Emotional Quotient Inventory (EQ-i) Technical Manual* (Toronto: Multi-Health Systems, 1997).

20. MHS Staff, *Emotional Quotient Inventory 2.0 (EQ-i 2.0)* (Toronto: Multi-Health Systems, 2011).

21. American Psychological Association, *Standards for Educational and Psychological Testing* (Washington, DC: American Psychological Association, 1985).

22. Equal Employment Opportunity Commission, *Adoption by Four Agencies of Uniform Guidelines on Employee Selection Procedures* (Washington, DC: Equal Employment Opportunity Commission, Civil Service Commission, Department of Labor, and Department of Justice,

1978); Society for Industrial and Organizational Psychology, *Principles for the Validation and Use of Personnel Selection Procedures*, 3rd ed. (College Park, MD: Society for Industrial and Organizational Psychology, 1987); Joint Committee on Testing Practices, *Code of Fair Testing Practices in Education* (Washington, DC: Joint Committee on Testing Practices, 2004); American Psychological Association, *Ethical Principles of Psychologists and Code of Conduct* (Washington, DC: American Psychological Association, 2002).

23. Ezra W. Zuckerman and John T. Jost, "It's Academic," *Stanford GSB Reporter* (April 24, 2000): 14–15; Ezra W. Zuckerman and John T. Jost, "What Makes You Think You're So Popular? Self Evaluation Maintenance and the Subjective Side of the 'Friendship Paradox,'" *Social Psychology Quarterly* (August 29, 2009): 207–223.
24. Starke R. Hathaway and J. C. McKinley, *MMPI* (Minneapolis: University of Minnesota, 1939); J. C. McKinley and S. R. Hathaway, "A Multiphasic Personality Schedule (Minnesota): II. A Differential Study of Hypochondriasis," *Journal of Psychology* 10 (1940): 255–268.
25. Dana L. Joseph, Jing Jin, Daniel A. Newman, and Ernest H. O'Boyle, "Why Does Self-Reported Emotional Intelligence Predict Job Performance? A Meta-Analytic Investigation of Mixed EI," *Journal of Applied Psychology* 100, no. 2 (March 2015): 298–342.
26. Dana L. Joseph and Daniel A. Newman, "Emotional Intelligence: An Integrative Meta-Analysis and Cascading Model," *Journal of Applied Psychology* 95, no. 1 (2010): 54–78.
27. World Economic Forum, *The Future of Jobs: Employment, Skills and Workforce Strategy for the Fourth Industrial Revolution* (Geneva, Switzerland: World Economic Forum, January 2016).
28. Career Builders Survey, *Seventy-One Percent of Employers Say They Value Emotional Intelligence over IQ, According to CareerBuilder Survey* (Chicago: CareerBuilder, 2011).

Chapter 4 Emotional Contagion

1. Sigal Barsade, "Faster than a Speeding Text: 'Emotional Contagion' at Work: How Others' Feelings Are Influencing Our Business Decisions,"

Psychology Today, October 15, 2014; S. G. Barsade, "The Ripple Effect: Emotional Contagion and Its Influence on Group Behavior," *Administrative Science Quarterly* 47 (2002): 644–675.

2. Barsade, "The Ripple Effect."
3. Sigal Barsade and Olivia A. O'Neill, "Manage Your Emotional Culture," *Harvard Business Review* (January–February 2016).
4. Ibid.
5. Philip Elmer-DeWitt, "Fortune Magazine Names Apple's Steve Jobs CEO of the Decade," *Fortune*, November 5, 2009.
6. Brent Schlender and Rick Tetzeli, *Becoming Steve Jobs: The Evolution of a Reckless Upstart into a Visionary Leader* (New York: Random House, 2015); Walter Isaacson, *Steve Jobs* (New York: Simon & Schuster, 2011).
7. John Brownlee, "Steve Jobs More Beloved by Employees Than Any Other CEO in Big Tech," *Cult of Mac*, December 3, 2010: 1.
8. Walter Isaacson, "The Real Leadership Lessons of Steve Jobs," *Harvard Business Review*, April, 2012.
9. Ibid.
10. Kurt Badenhausen, "Apple Dominates List of the World's Most Valuable Brands," *Forbes*, November 6, 2013.
11. Patricia Sellers, "The 50 Most Powerful Women in American Business," *Fortune*, October 12, 1998.
12. Paolo Del Nibletto, "Top 10 Terrible Tech CEOs of All Time," *Computer Dealer News*, June 21, 2013.
13. Craig Johnson, "The Rise and Fall of Carly Fiorina: An Ethical Case Study," *Journal of Leadership & Organizational Studies* 15, no. 2 (November 2008): 188–196.
14. Kimberly Elsbach, Ileana Stigliani, and Amy Stroud, "The Building of Employee Distrust: A Case Study of Hewlett-Packard from 1995 to 2010," *Organizational Dynamics* 41, no. 3 (July–September 2012): 254–263.
15. Ibid.

16. P. Burrows, *Backfire: Carly Fiorina's High-Stakes Battle for the Soul of Hewlett-Packard* (Hoboken, NJ: John Wiley & Sons, 2003); M. S. Malone, *Bill and Dave: How Hewlett and Packard Built the World's Greatest Company* (New York: Portfolio, 2007).

17. Neil McAllister, "Tech's All-Time Top 25 Flops: These Pivotal Moments Are the History You Don't Want to Repeat," *InfoWorld*, January 21, 2008.

18. Jeffrey Sonnenfeld, "Why I Still Think Fiorina Was a Terrible CEO," *Politico Magazine*, September 20, 2015.

19. Ibid.

20. Chao Miao, Ronald H. Humphrey, and Shanshan Qian, "Leader Emotional Intelligence and Subordinate Job Satisfaction: A Meta-Analysis of Main, Mediator, and Moderator Effects," *Personality and Individual Differences* 102 (2016): 13–24.

21. J. M. George, "Emotions and Leadership: The Role of Emotional Intelligence," *Human Relations* 53 (2000): 1027–1055.

Chapter 5 Self-Perception: Know Thyself

1. Wilder Penfield, *Mystery of the Mind: A Critical Study of Conciousness and the Human Brain* (Princeton, NJ: Princeton University Press, 2015).

2. Frederick S. Barrett, Kevin J. Grimm, Richard W. Robins, Tim Wildschut, Constantine Sedikides, and Pet Janata, "Music-Evoked Nostalgia: Affect, Memory, and Personality," *Emotion* (2010): 390–403.

3. A. Keller, K. Litzelman, L. E. Wisk, T. Maddox, E. R. Cheng, P. D. Creswell, and W. P. Witt, "Does the Perception That Stress Affects Health Matter? The Association with Health and Mortality," *Health Psychology* 31, no. 5 (2012): 677–84.

4. Ibid.

5. Robert Hogan, "Rethinking Self-Awareness: Freud versus Socrates," Coach Federation, August 31, 2016, coachfederation.org.

6. Virginia K. Bratton, Nancy G. Dodd, and F. William Brown, "The Impact of Emotional Intelligence on Accuracy of Self-Awareness and Leadership

Performance," *Leadership & Organization Development Journal* (2011): 127–149.

7. Jonathan Bryson, "A Theoretical Framework of Self-Awareness Based on Perceived and Actual Interpersonal Competence" (paper presented at the American Psychological Association Convention, Denver, CO, August 2016).
8. Prajya R. Vidyarthi, Smriti Anand, and Robert C. Liden, "Do Emotionally Perceptive Leaders Motivate Higher Employee Performance? The Moderating Role of Task Interdependence and Power Distance," *The Leadership Quarterly* (2014): 232–244.

Chapter 6 Self-Expression: Communication through Words and Actions

1. Charles Darwin, *The Expression of Emotions in Man and Animals* (Chicago: University of Chicago Press, 1965 [originally published in 1872]).
2. K. M. Kendrick, A. P. da Costa, A. E. Leigh, M. R. Hinton, and J. W. Peirce, "Sheep Don't Forget a Face," *Nature* 414 (2001): 165–166.
3. Kristi Lewis, "When Leaders Display Emotion: How Followers Respond to Negative Emotional Expression of Male and Female Leaders," *Journal of Organizational Behavior* 21, no. 2 (March 2000): 221–234.
4. Brian Walsh, "Oil Spill: Goodbye, Mr. Hayward," *Time*, July 25, 2010.
5. Juan M. Mader and Brent Smith, "The Effects of Leaders' Negative Emotions on Evaluations of Leadership in a Crisis Situation: The Role of Anger and Sadness," *The Leadership Quarterly* 20, no. 2 (April 2009): 103–114.
6. Reinhard Pekrun, Andrew Elliot, and Markus Maier, "Achievement Goals and Achievement Emotions: Testing a Model of Their Joint Relations with Academic Performance" *Journal of Educational Psychology* 101, no. 1 (2009): 115–135.
7. Daniel R. Ames and Francis R. Flynn, "What Breaks a Leader: The Curvilinear Relation Between Assertiveness and Leadership," *Journal of Personality and Social Psychology* 92, no. 2 (2007): 307–324.

8. P. W. Dorfman, P. J. Hanges, and F. C. Brodbeck, "Leadership and Culture Variation: The Identification of Culturally Endorsed Leadership Profiles," in *Culture, Leadership, and Organizations: The GLOBE Study of 62 Societies* ed. R. J. House, P. J. Hanges, M. Javidan, P. W. Dorfman, and V. Gupta (Thousand Oaks, CA: Sage, 2004), 669–719.

9. William A. Gentry, Alexander Patterson, Sarah A. Stawiski, David C. Gilmore, and Taylor E. Sparks, "A 30-Country Multilevel Test of Cultural Convergence or Divergence of Three Managerial Skillsets," *Consulting Psychology Journal: Practice and Research* 65, no. 1 (2013): 17–39.

10. R. J. House, P. J. Hanges, M. Javidan, P. W. Dorfman, and V. Gupta (eds.), *Culture, Leadership, and Organizations: The GLOBE Study of 62 Societies* (Thousand Oaks, CA: Sage, 2004).

11. G. H. Hofstede and M. H. Bond, "The Confucius Connection: From Cultural Roots to Economic Growth," *Organizational Dynamics* 16 (1988): 5–27.

Chapter 7 Interpersonal: Creating the Bonds of Trust

1. Gary Yukl and Leslie Kanuk, "Leadership Behavior and Effectiveness of Beauty Salon Managers," *Personnel Psychology* 32 (1979): 663–675.

2. W. Christopher Musselwhite and Tammie Plouffe, *Influence Style Indicator: Facilitator Guide* (Toronto: Multi-Health Systems, 2011).

3. *Inc.* Staff, "John Mackey of Whole Foods on Hiring Leaders," *Inc.*, July 1, 2009.

4. Mike Krzyzewski, Donald T. Phillips, and Grant Hill, *Leading with the Heart: Coach K's Successful Strategies for Basketball, Business, and Life* (New York: Warner Business Books, 2001).

5. Stéphane Côté, Paulo N. Lopes, Peter Salovey, and Christopher T. H. Miners, "Emotional Intelligence and Leadership Emergence in Small Groups," *The Leadership Quarterly* 21, no. 3 (June 2010): 496–508.

6. Kristin Byron, "Male and Female Managers' Ability to 'Read' Emotions: Relationships with Supervisors' Performance Ratings and Subordinates'

Satisfaction Ratings," *Journal of Occupational and Organizational Psychology* 80, no. 4 (2007): 713–733.

7. William A. Gentry, Todd J. Weber, and Golnaz Sadri, "Empathy in the Workplace: A Tool for Effective Leadership" *Society of Industrial Organizational Psychology Conference* (New York: Center for Creative Leadership White Paper, 2007).
8. R. J. House, P. J. Hanges, M. Javidan, P. W. Dorfman, and V. Gupta (eds.), *Culture, Leadership, and Organizations: The GLOBE Study of 62 Societies* (Thousand Oaks, CA: Sage, 2004).
9. Christine Ma-Kellams and Jennifer Lerner, "Trust Your Gut or Think Carefully? Examining Whether an Intuitive, Versus a Systematic, Mode of Thought Produces Greater Empathic Accuracy" *Journal of Personality and Social Psychology* 111, no. 5 (2016): 674–685.
10. Bob Liodice, "10 Companies with Social Responsibility at the Core," *Advertising Age*, April 19, 2010.
11. Annebel H. B. De Hoogh and Deanne N. Den Hartog, "Ethical and Despotic Leadership, Relationships with Leaders' Social Responsibility, Top Management Team Effectiveness and Subordinates' Optimism: A Multi-Method Study," *The Leadership Quarterly* 19 (2008): 297–311.
12. S. J. Stein and H. B. Book, *The EQ Edge: Emotional Intelligence and Your Success* (Toronto: Jossey-Bass [Wiley], 2000, 2011).
13. Stephen Brammer, Andrew Millington, and Bruce Rayton, "The Contribution of Corporate Social Responsibility to Organizational Commitment," *The International Journal of Human Resource Management* 18, no. 10 (2007): 1701–1719.
14. Neil Howe and Reena Nadler, *Why Generations Matter* (Great Falls, VA: LifeCourse Associations, 2012), https://www.lifecourse.com/assets/files/Why%20Generations%20Matter%20LifeCourse%20Associates%20Feb%202012.pdf.
15. Economist Intelligence Unit, *Corporate Citizenship: Profiting from a Sustainable Business*, November 2008, http://graphics.eiu.com/upload/Corporate_Citizens.pdf#page=1&zoom=auto,-175,765.

16. Jacquelyn Smith, "The Companies with the Best CSR Reputations," *Forbes*, October 2, 2013.

Chapter 8 Making Better Decisions: Emotionally

1. Erika Andersen, "It Seemed Like a Good Idea at the Time: 7 of the Worst Business Decisions Ever Made," *Forbes*, October 4, 2013.
2. Spencer Leigh, "Mike Smith: Record Producer Who Had a String of No 1 Hits But Turned Down the Beatles," *Independent*, December 30, 2011.
3. Norbert Schwarz and Gerald L. Clore, "Mood, Misattribution, and Judgments of Well-Being: Informative and Directive Functions of Affective States," *Journal of Personality and Social Psychology* 45, no. 3 (September 1983): 513–523.
4. Donald A. Redelmeier and Simon D. Baxter, "Rainy Weather and Medical School Admission Interviews," *Canadian Medical Association Journal* 181, no. 12 (December 2009): 933.
5. Ana Swanson, "Why Gut Feelings May Really Help You Make Risky Decisions," *Washington Post* (November 16, 2016).
6. Narayanan Kandasamy, Sarah N. Garfinkel, Lionel Page, Ben Hardy, Hugo D. Critchley, Mark Gurnell, and John M. Coates, "Interoceptive Ability Predicts Survival on a London Trading Floor," *Scientific Reports* 6 (2016): 1–6.
7. Joseph A. Mikels, Sam J. Maglio, Andrew E. Reed, and Lee J. Kaplowitz, "Should I Go with My Gut? Investigating the Benefits of Emotion-Focused Decision Making," *Emotion* 11, no. 4 (2011): 743–753.
8. R. Nisbett and L. Ross, *Human Inference: Strategies and Shortcomings of Social Judgment* (Englewood Cliffs, NJ: Prentice Hall, 1980).
9. Rebecca K. Ratnera and Kenneth C. Herbstb, "When Good Decisions Have Bad Outcomes: The Impact of Affect on Switching Behavior," *Organizational Behavior and Human Decision Processes* 96 (2005): 23–37.
10. Eric J. Johnson, John Hershey, Jacqueline Meszaros, and Howard Kunreuther, "Framing, Probability, Distortions, and Insurance Decisions," *Journal of Risk and Uncertainty* 7 (1993): 35–51.

11. Christopher K. Hsee and Yuval Rottenstreich, "Music, Pandas, and Muggers: On the Affective Psychology of Value," *Journal of Experimental Psychology: General* 133, no. 1 (2004): 23–30.
12. Veronika Denes-Raj and Seymour Epstein, "Conflict Between Intuitive and Rational Processing: When People Behave Against Their Better Judgment," *Journal of Personality and Social Psychology* 66, no. 5 (1994): 819–829.
13. David Schkade, Cass R. Sunstein, and Daniel Kahneman, "Deliberating about Dollars: The Severity Shift," *Society for Judgment and Decision Making Annual Meeting Schedule* (2000).
14. Timothy Wilson and Sara Hodges, "Attitudes as Temporary Constructs," In *The Construction of Social Judgments*, ed. L. L. Martin and A. Tesser (Hillsdale, NJ: Erlbaum, 1992), 37–65; T. D. Wilson, D. Kraft, and D. J. Lisle, "The Disruptive Effects of Self-Reflection: Implications for Survey Research," *Advances in Consumer Research* 17 (1990): 212–216.
15. Anthony Damasio, *Descartes' Error: Emotion, Reason, and the Human Brain* (New York: Penguin Books, 2005).
16. Daniel Kahneman, *Thinking, Fast and Slow* (New York: Farrar, Straus and Giroux, 2013).
17. Roderick Gilkey Ricardo Caceda, and Clinton Kilts, "When Emotional Reasoning Trumps IQ," *Harvard Business Review*, September 2010.

Chapter 9 Stress Management and Leadership

1. Dina Gerdeman, "How Rigid Leaders Kill Their Companies," *Forbes*, September 26, 2016, 1–2.
2. Charles O'Reilly and Michael Tushman, *Lead and Disrupt: How to Solve the Innovator's Dilemma* (Stanford, CA: Stanford Business Books, 2016).
3. IBM, *Chronological History of IBM*, IBM Archives, www-03.ibm.com/ibm/history/history/history_intro.html.
4. Virginia M. (Ginni) Rometty, *About IBM* (December 31, 2015), www.ibm.com/ibm/ca/en/?lnk=fab-caen.

5. Gary Yukl and Rubina Mahsud, "Why Flexible and Adaptive Leadership Is Essential," *Consulting Psychology Journal: Practice and Research* 62, no. 2 (2010): 81–93.

6. M. N. Ruderman, K. Hannum, J. B. Leslie, and J. L. Steed, "Leadership Skills and Emotional Intelligence," Applying Emotional Intelligence to Business Solutions & Success Conference (Toronto: Multi-Health Systems, 2001).

7. Cheryl L. Meredith, *The Relationship of Emotional Intelligence and Transformational Leadership Behavior in Non-Profit Executive Leaders*, 11-A. Vol. 68. Dissertation Abstracts International Section A: Humanities and Social Sciences, 2008.

Chapter 10 The Four Pillars of Successful Leadership: Developing the Model

1. Neal M. Ashkanasy and Barry Tse, "Transformational Leadership as Management of Emotion: A Conceptual Review," in *Emotions in the Workplace: Research, Theory, and Practice*, ed. Neal M. Ashkanasy, Charmine E. Härtel, and Wilfred J. Zerbe (Westport, CT: Quorum Books/Greenwood Publishing Group, 2000), 221–235; Julian Barling, Frank Slater, and E. Kevin Kelloway, "Transformational Leadership and Emotional Intelligence: An Exploratory Study," *Leadership & Organization Development Journal* 21, no. 3 (2000): 157–161.

2. James M. Burns, *Leadership* (Oxford, England: Harper & Row, 1978).

3. Bernard M. Bass, and Bruce J. Avolio (eds.), *Improving Organizational Effectiveness through Transformational Leadership* (Thousand Oaks, CA: Sage Publications, 1994).

4. Barling, Slater, and Kelloway, "Transformational Leadership and Emotional Intelligence."

5. Bernard M. Bass and Bruce J. Avolio, *Multifactor Leadership Questionnaire Manual* (Menlo Park, CA: Mind Garden, 1995).

6. MHS Staff, *EQ-i 2.0 Leadership Report Interpretive Guide* (Toronto: Multi-Health Systems, 2013).

7. Timothy A. Judge and Ronald F. Piccolo, "Transformational and Transactional Leadership: A Meta-Analytic Test of Their Relative Validity," *Journal of Applied Psychology* 89, no. 5 (2004): 755–768.
8. Anders Skogstad, Ståle Einarsen, Torbjørn Torsheim, Merethe Schanke Aasland, and Hilde Hetland, "The Destructiveness of Laissez-Faire Leadership Behavior," *Journal of Occupational Health Psychology* 12, no. 1 (2007): 80–92.
9. Steven J. Stein, Peter Papadogiannis, Jeremy A. Yip, and Gill Sitarenios, "Emotional Intelligence of Leaders: A Profile of Top Executives," *Leadership & Organization Development Journal* 30, no. 1 (2009): 87–101.
10. Jennifer M. George, "Emotions and Leadership: The Role of Emotional Intelligence," *Human Relations* 53, no. 8 (2000): 1027–1055.
11. Abraham Carmeli, "The Relationship between Emotional Intelligence and Work Attitudes, Behavior and Outcomes: An Examination among Senior Managers," *Journal of Managerial Psychology* 18, no. 8 (2003): 788–813.
12. Victor Dulewicz and Malcolm Higgs, "Leadership at the Top: The Need for Emotional Intelligence in Organizations," *The International Journal of Organizational Analysis* 11, no. 3 (2003): 193–210.
13. Jon Aarum Andersen, "Are Power Motivated Leaders More Effective? A Review of McClelland's Theory," in *Current Topics in Management* Vol. 4, ed. M. Afzalur Rahim, Robert T. Golembiewski, and Kenneth D. Mackenzie (Stamford, CT: JAI Press, 1999), 41–59.
14. Cynthia Marie Martin, *A Meta-Analytic Investigation of the Relationship between Emotional Intelligence and Leadership Effectiveness* (dissertation, East Carolina University), ProQuest Dissertation Abstracts International Section A: Humanities and Social Sciences, Vol. 69(2-A) 2008, 530; Ashleigh D. Farrar, *The Role of Emotional Intelligence in Leadership Effectiveness: A Meta-Analysis* (unpublished masters thesis, University of Tennessee at Chattanooga, 2009).
15. Peter D. Harms and Marcus Credé, "Emotional Intelligence and Transformational and Transactional Leadership: A Meta-Analysis," *Journal of Leadership & Organizational Studies* 17, no. 1 (2010): 5–17.

Chapter 11 Pillar I: Developing Authenticity

1. Bill George, *Authentic Leadership: Rediscovering the Secrets to Creating Lasting Value* (San Francisco: Jossey-Bass, 2004).
2. Kevin Kruse, "What Is Authentic Leadership?" *Forbes*, May 12, 2013.
3. Mark Bonchek, "Purpose Is Good. Shared Purpose Is Better," *Harvard Business Review* (March 2013): 1.
4. Conrad Black, "Conrad Black: Jordan Peterson Speaks for Those of Us that Refuse to Follow the 'Great Liberal Death Wish,'" *National Post*, December 2, 2016.
5. Carmine Gallo, "What Starbucks CEO Howard Schultz Taught Me about Communication and Success," *Forbes*, December 19, 2013: 1.
6. Andy Dehnart, "Reality TV Is Dominating Broadcast and Cable Ratings This Summer," July 13, 2016, https://www.realityblurred.com/realitytv/2016/07/reality-summer-ratings-domination.
7. Shakiel Mahjouri, "'The Amazing Race Canada' Is Country's Most Watched Show, Reality and Drama Dominate Ratings," January 4, 2017, http://etcanada.com/news/192721/the-amazing-race-canada-is-countrys-most-watched-show-reality-and-drama-dominate-ratings.
8. Taffy Brodesser-Akner, "Living in Andy Cohen's America," *New York Times*, January 12, 2017.
9. Brian Stelter, "Debate Breaks Record as Most-Watched in U.S. History," September 27, 2016, http://money.cnn.com/2016/09/27/media/debate-ratings-record-viewership/; Wikipedia, "List of Most Watched Television Broadcasts in the United States," January 13, 2017, https://en.wikipedia.org/wiki/List_of_most_watched_television_broadcasts_in_the_United_States#cite_note-5.

Chapter 12 Pillar II: Developing Leader Coaches

1. Jenna Filipkowski and Mark Ruth, *Building a Coaching Culture for Increased Employee Engagement* (Cincinnati, OH: Human Capital Institute, 2015).

2. Human Capital Institute and International Coach Federation, *Building a Coaching Culture with Managers and Leaders* (Cincinnati, OH: Human Capital Institute, 2015).
3. Aubrey K. Wiete, *Leadership and Emotional Intelligence: The Keys to Driving ROI and Organizational Performance* (Toronto: Human Capital Institute and Multi-Health Systems, 2013).
4. William Arruda, "Coaching Skills Every Leader Needs to Master," *Forbes*, October 27, 2015, 1–2.
5. Forbes Coaches Council, "10 Coaching Skills Every Leader Should Master," *Forbes*, May 12, 2016, 1–2.
6. Ibid.
7. Sheryl Sandberg, *Lean In: Women, Work, and the Will to Lead* (New York: Knopf, 2013).
8. Farnaz Namin-Hedayati, "Leadership Qualities of Sheryl Sandberg," March 26, 2014, www.centerforworklife.com/leadership-qualities-sheryl-sandberg-2.
9. Right Management, "Learn the Art of Leadership from Sheryl Sandberg," March 4, 2015, www.right.com/wps/wcm/connect/right-us-en/home/thoughtwire/categories/career-work/learn-the-art-of-leadership-from-sheryl-sandberg.
10. Namin-Hedayati, "Leadership Qualities of Sheryl Sandberg."
11. Susan Adams, "10 Things Sheryl Sandberg Gets Exactly Right in 'Lean In,'" March 2013, http://churchillleadershipgroup.com/10-things-sheryl-sandberg-gets-exactly-right-in-lean-in.
12. Jessica Chivers, "Sheryl Sandberg's 'Lean In' Digested Chapter by Chapter," March 18, 2013, http://jessicachivers.com/2013/03/18/sherylsandberg.

Chapter 13 Pillar III: Developing Insight

1. Viktor Frankl, *Man's Search for Meaning* (Boston: Beacon Press, 1959, 2006).
2. Nick Craig and Scott Snook, "From Purpose to Impact," *Harvard Business Review*, May 2014, 1.

3. Mark Bonchek, "Purpose Is Good. Shared Purpose Is Better," *Harvard Business Review*, March 2013, 1.
4. Craig and Snook, "From Purpose to Impact."
5. Jeff Boss, "3 Brilliant Ways to Communicate Purpose," *Forbes*, July 6, 2016, 1.
6. John Kotter and James Heskett, *Corporate Culture and Performance* (New York: The Free Press, 2011).
7. Sherry Hakimi, "Why Purpose-Driven Companies Are Often More Successful," *Fast Company*, July 21, 2015, 1.
8. Bob Buckley, "Women in Leadership: Anita Roddick," June 22, 2014. https://getpocket.com/a/read/1121107913.
9. *Living Our Values: The Body Shop International PLC Values Report 2009* (London: The Body Shop, 2009).

Chapter 14 Pillar IV: Developing Innovation

1. Joanna Barsh, Marla M. Capozzi, and Jonathan Davidson, "Leadership and Innovation," *McKinsey Quarterly*, January 2008, 1.
2. Jack Zenger and Joseph Folkman, "Research: 10 Traits of Innovative Leaders," *Harvard Business Review*, December 15, 2014, 1.
3. Carmine Gallo, "The 7 Innovation Secrets of Steve Jobs," *Forbes*, May 2, 2014, 1.
4. Tyler Mathisen, "The List: CNBC First 25: Rebels, Icons and Leaders," April 29, 2014, www.cnbc.com/2014/04/29/thefirst25.html.
5. Steven Leckart, "The Hackathon Is On: Pitching and Programming the Next Killer App," *Wired*, March 2012.

Chapter 15 What 360s Can Tell Us about Leaders and Potential Leaders

1. Chris Platamone and Matthew Larson, *Developing a 360 Degree Feedback Instrument for MBA/EMBA Students* (Palm Desert, CA: UC Riverside–Palm Desert, 2009).

2. MHS Staff, *EQ-i 2.0 and EQ 360 2.0 User Manual* (Toronto: Multi-Health Systems, 2011).
3. MHS Staff, *Leadership EQ 360 Assessment: Report Supplement* (Toronto: Multi-Health Systems, 2011).
4. H. C. Triandis, foreword to *Culture, Leadership, and Organizations: The GLOBE Study of 62 Societies*, edited by R. J. House, P. J. Hanges, M. Javidan, P. W. Dorfman, and V. Gupta (Thousand Oaks, CA: Sage, 2004); R. J. House, P. J. Hanges, M. Javidan, P. W. Dorfman, and V. Gupta (eds.), *Culture, Leadership, and Organizations: The GLOBE Study of 62 Societies* (Thousand Oaks, CA: Sage, 2004).
5. House et al., Culture, *Leadership, and Organizations.*
6. Michael H. Hoppe, "Culture and Leader Effectiveness: The GLOBE Study," September 18, 2007.
7. Ibid.

Chapter 16 Entrepreneurial Leadership and EQ

1. S. Fox and Y. Amichai-Hamburger, "The Power of Emotional Appeals in Promoting Organizational Change Programs," *Academy of Management Executive* 15 (2001): 84–96.
2. N. M. Ashkanasy and B. Tse, "Transformational Leadership as Management of Emotion," in *Emotions in the Workplace: Research, Theory, and Practice* ed. N. M. Ashkanasy, W. J. Zerbe, and C. E. J. Härtel (Westport, CT: Quorum Books, 2000), 221–235.
3. D. De Cremer and D. van Knippenberg, "Leader Self-Sacrifice and Leadership Effectiveness: The Moderating Role of Leader Self-Confidence," *Organizational Behavior and Human Decision Processes* 95 (2004): 140–155.
4. Dana Ackley, "Emotional Intelligence: Keys to Success in Today's Dentistry," *Dentistry Today* 20 (2001): 56–59.
5. I. M. Becker, D. C. Ackley, and R. A. Green, "New Study: The Value of Emotional Intelligence in Dentistry," *Dentistry Today* 22 (2003): 106–111.

6. Roger R. Pearman, R. Daniel Parks, Barry Phillips, and Marcus C. King, *Your Entrepreneur Edge* (Toronto: Multi-Health Systems, 2013).

7. Irving Azoff, interview by Bille Werde, Irving Azoff Touring Conference Keynote Q&A, November 9, 2012.

Chapter 17 Some New Things We're Learning about Leadership

1. Jack Naglieri and Sam Goldstein, *Comprehensive Executive Functioning Inventory: Adult Manual* (Toronto: Multi-Health Systems, 2017).

2. Ibid.

3. Donald T. Stuss, "Biological and Psychological Development of Executive Functions," *Brain and Cognition* 20, no. 1 (September 1992): 8–23.

4. Naglieri and Goldstein, *Comprehensive Executive Functioning Inventory—Adult Manual.*

5. Christopher W. Musselwhite, *Change Style Indicator: Research and Development Report* (Toronto: Multi-Health Systems, 2000).

6. R. Greenleaf, *The Servant as Leader*, rev. ed. (Indianapolis, IN: Robert K. Greenleaf Center, 1991).

7. Chris Auger, "The Nature of Global Leadership Is Being Reshaped" (unpublished manuscript, Virginia Beach, 2016).

8. Jane T. Waddell, "Exploratory Study of the Relationship between Servant Leadership Attribution and the Leader's Emotional Intelligence," Dissertation Abstracts International Section A: Humanities and Social Sciences, 2010, 4072.

9. Justin A. Longbotham and Gail J. Irving, "Team Effectiveness and Six Essential Servant Leadership Themes: A Regression Model Based on Items in the Organizational Leadership Assessment," *International Journal of Leadership Studies* 2, no. 2 (2007): 98–113.

10. Jeffrey A. Sonnenfeld, "What Makes Great Boards Great," *Harvard Business Review*, September 2002, 1.

11. Steven J. Stein and Howard E. Book, *The EQ Edge: Emotional Intelligence and Your Success* (Toronto: Jossey-Bass, 2000, 2011).

12. Therese Huston, "Are Women Better Decision Makers?" *New York Times*, October 17, 2014, 1.

13. Human Capital Institute and Multi-Health Systems, *Leadership and Emotional Intelligence: The Keys to Driving ROI and Organizational Performance* (Cincinnati, OH: Human Capital Institute, 2013).

14. Mark Cartwright and Susan Slaski, "Emotional Intelligence Training and Its Implications for Stress, Health and Performance," *Stress and Health* 19 (2003): 233–239.

15. Steven J. Stein, Howard E. Book, and Korrel Kanoy, *The Student EQ Edge: Emotional Intelligence and Your Academic and Personal Success* (San Francisco: John Wiley & Sons, 2013).

Acknowledgments

I am indebted to many people who have influenced me in the development of this book. I am grateful to all of those who have taken the EQ-i, EQ-i 2.0, EQ360, and MSCEIT, contributing to our knowledge base of emotional intelligence and leadership. I hope that the experience has been enlightening and rewarding for you.

The term *emotional intelligence* as it is widely used today is due to the work of Peter Salovey and John (Jack) Mayer. They also developed the first ability model of emotional intelligence. The concept of EQ and the model behind the EQ-i 2.0 was originated by Reuven Bar-On.

I want to thank all of the great people who work at MHS who enabled me to have the time and resources to pull this book together under tight deadlines. Thanks to Hazel Wheldon who leads our teams and ensures that everything at MHS runs smoothly. I want to thank my assistants Justin Deonarine and Donna Penticost and all our research and development people who contributed—including, but not limited to—Blaine Mackie (for his great editing and helping to fix so many details), Jonathan Stermac, and Lindsay Ayearst.

I want to thank for their contributions Navy SEAL LCDR (Ret.) Chris Auger and Lia Grimanis. I am grateful to Chris Bart and Michael Hartmann of The Directors College for the opportunity they provided to share information and collect data. I also want to thank Eric Lawrence and Rob Lanni, music artist managers and directors of Coalition Music, who have taught me a lot about the music business.

A special thanks to Elizabeth Gildea and Shannon Vargo at John Wiley & Sons for contacting me and encouraging me to write this book. They caught me at just the right time and frame of mind and I appreciated their support along the way. Thanks, too, to Lauren Freestone at Wiley, for her editing skills.

I am indebted to my wife Rodeen for her support and patience while I spent time on these extracurricular activities.

About the Author

Steven J. Stein, PhD, is a clinical psychologist and founder and CEO of Multi-Health Systems (MHS), one of the world's leading and most innovative test publishing companies. He has authored (and coauthored) several books on emotional intelligence, including *The EQ Edge: Emotional Intelligence and Your Success* (coauthored with Dr. Howard Book), *Make Your Workplace Great: The Seven Keys to an Emotionally Intelligent Organization*, *Emotional Intelligence For Dummies*, and *The Student EQ Edge: Emotional Intelligence and Your Academic and Personal Success* (coauthored with Drs. Howard Book and Korrel Kanoy).

He has shared information on emotional intelligence with audiences throughout the United States, Canada, Mexico, Europe, Asia, Africa, and the Middle East, and he has appeared on hundreds of TV, radio, webinars, blogs, and print media productions.

Previous clients have included: the Canadian Forces, U.S. Air Force, U.S. Army, U.S. Navy, special units of the Pentagon, U.S. FBI Academy, American Express ©, Coca-Cola © (Mexico), Air Canada ©, Canadian Imperial Bank of Commerce (CIBC), Emirates Airlines, Canyon Ranch®, The Toronto Maple Leafs ©, and many others.

Dr. Stein is the psychologist and casting screener for many reality TV shows, including *Big Brother Canada ©, The Amazing Race Canada ©, MasterChef Canada ©, Intervention Canada ©, The Real Housewives of Toronto ©, Bachelor Canada®, Game of Homes®, Panic Button ©, Scare Tactics®, Fool's Gold*, and many others.

As one of the first psychologists to study emotional intelligence, Dr. Stein is passionate about finding ways to employ EI skills to every part of life, including the workplace, leadership, politics, sports, entertainment, and more. Using scientifically validated psychological assessments, Dr. Stein helps corporate organizations, military and government agencies, professional sports teams, and numerous reality television shows employ emotional intelligence to identify strong candidates, enhance operations, and build a more cohesive team.

Dr. Stein is a previous chair of the Psychology Foundation of Canada and has been president of the Ontario Psychological Association. He is a fellow of the Canadian Psychological Association, a former assistant professor of Psychiatry at the University of Toronto and was an adjunct professor in the Department of Psychology at York University. He currently teaches at The Directors College, a university-accredited corporate director education program in Canada.

He is married to his wife, Rodeen, and has two daughters and two lovely grandchildren. You can sometimes find him playing the saxophone in one of several bands he performs with.

Index